Helion & Company Limited
26 Willow Road
Solihull
West Midlands
B91 1UE
England
Tel. 0121 705 3393
Fax 0121 711 4075
email: info@helion.co.uk
website: www.helion.co.uk
Twitter: @helionbooks
Visit our blog http://blog.helion.co.uk

Published by Helion & Company 2016
Designed and typeset by Farr out Publications, Wokingham, Berkshire
Cover designed by Paul Hewitt, Battlefield Design (www.battlefield-design.co.uk)
Printed by Henry Ling Limited, Dorchester, Dorset

ISBN 978-1-910777-89-3

British Library Cataloguing-in-Publication Data
A catalogue record for this book is available from the British Library

CONTENTS

CHAPTER 1

A CASE OF BAD TIMING

The events taking place between May and July of 1954 in the Central American republic of Guatemala, which led to the overthrowing of the government of Lt. Colonel Jacobo Arbenz, still to this day stir passions in all sides of the political spectrum in that country, and to some extent, in the rest of Latin America.

For some, the clandestine operation to oust Arbenz, staged by the U.S. Central Intelligence Agency – CIA – thwarted the consolidation of democracy in a country that had suffered through a long line of dictatorships upon becoming a republic in 1847.[1] For others, however, that intervention saved Guatemala from becoming another satellite nation of the Soviet Union and a dangerous Communist beachhead, too close for comfort for the U.S. and its allies in the region, at a time when something like a Communist Cuba was unthinkable and still distant in the historical landscape.

Because of these diametrically opposed points of view, rivers of ink have flowed in to writing about the coup, its motivations, and its outcomes. Due to the unavoidable ideological baggage, however, most of the published works lack objectivity and impartiality, contributing to deepen a socio-political polarization that not only sparked a 33-year-long Civil War, but that also has kept the Guatemalan society bogged down in disagreements.

Not even the two major declassifications of the operation's documents, released by the CIA in 1996 and 2003, were able to dispel the myths and set the facts straight. In many cases, authors and analysts only grabbed the information that was consistent with their political views and ignored the rest.

Thus, for setting the stage for this study it is of utmost importance to establish, in an unbiased manner, the three main factors that triggered the U.S. intervention and describe the context under which it unfolded.

First, we must mention the convoluted political scene in Guatemala by the end of WWII, a time when its population finally began embracing the notions of freedom and democracy being spread across the world by none other than the U.S. and the Allied forces. As noted above, the country had had its share of dictatorships for most of the first half of the 20th Century, with power swinging from "Conservative" to "Liberal" caudillos, and revolts being the most expedient method for ousting the dictator in power.

The exception to this rule occurred by mid-1944, when a group of renowned citizens, intellectuals and political leaders, organized a series of massive demonstrations against the Liberal dictatorship of General Jorge Ubico, who at the time had been in power for 14 years, with the complete acquiescence of the Legislative Assembly.

To most everyone's surprise, and despite the demonstrators' violent repression at the hands of the police, Ubico resigned on July 4, 1944. Historians still debate the dictator's motives for his resignation, and some affirm that the presence of good friends of his among the malcontents depressed him to the point of leaving the presidency

Aerial view of Guatemala City's downtown and Central Park area. (Photo credit: Guatemalan Air Force.)

The Revolutionary Junta. From left to right: Capt. Jacobo Arbenz, Jorge Toriello and Maj. Francisco Javier Arana. (Photo credit: Revista Militar.)

in despair. For some others, it was a clever maneuver to deflect the society's pressure upon him and his administration.

Whatever the case might have been, instead of allowing the Legislative Assembly to decide who would succeed him in the presidency, as it was mandated by the Constitution, Ubico unilaterally designated General Federico Ponce as the head of a ruling junta, securing a transition to a government that would remain loyal to him.

It didn't take long for Ponce to send Army troops to besiege the Legislative Assembly building in order to force its members to approve and somewhat legalize the Junta's dissolution and appoint him as the new president. After three months, it was more than evident that Ponce's intentions were to stay in power indefinitely, even when the Legislative Assembly had called for general elections. As expected, the population took to the streets once again, and once again, the police mercilessly crushed the demonstrations.

This time however, a group of politicians and middle-class citizens, sensing that there was no other way to get rid of Ponce, staged a revolt during the evening of October 19, with the help of several young Army officers and their troops. University students and members of the very few labor unions that existed at the time also joined them.

General Ponce finally surrendered by midday October 20, but the heavy fighting that preceded his resignation left hundreds of civilian casualties and a widespread feeling that something similar should not happen ever again.

This "Revolution of 1944", much cherished and celebrated by Guatemalans even to this day, is considered by many as the beginning of the country's most important political and social period, during which democracy finally flourished, when important laws of social benefit were enacted, and where long needed institutions were established. However, in a typical case of "too much, too soon", the Revolution, and the freedom that it brought, also led to a debacle.

A three-member "Revolutionary Junta" was conformed within hours of Ponce's resignation, with civilian Jorge Toriello being the leader due to his experience in political matters. Major Francisco Arana, one of the rebellion's planners, and a retired Captain named Jacobo Arbenz Guzmán, who had left the Army in disgust right after Ponce became president, were the other two members.

The nascent "Revolutionary Junta" took upon itself the task of introducing as many reforms as necessary for transitioning the country into a true democracy, while staying in power for the shortest period. Accordingly, civil freedoms were reinstated and a new constitution drafting assembly was conformed to replace the Bill of Rights dating back to 1879. Additionally, a Congress replaced the Legislative Assembly, and the general elections that had been scheduled for December during Ponce's government were reconfirmed.

Beneath the surface however, the cohesive front that had managed to depose Ponce was now splintering into a myriad of interest groups that spared no effort in trying to influence the Revolutionary Junta's decisions. Among these groups, there were sympathizers of the deposed dictatorships who felt that, without an "iron hand" at the reins, the country would soon plunge into chaos. There was also a relatively small group of Communists, clandestinely organized since 1940, who began infiltrating left-wing political parties, labor unions, and university student societies with the aim of expanding their popular base. Some young Army officers were also introduced to this "new" ideology, including a restless Arbenz and his wife, Maria Vilanova, who had several Communist friends in Guatemala and in El Salvador. Last but not least, there were groups of businessmen, landowners, retired Army officers and bureaucrats who, worried about losing their privileges, were constantly trying to ingratiate themselves with the Junta, but didn't hesitate in plotting against it whenever their *status quo* was threatened by a new law or reform.

With all these forces trying to intervene, it was virtually impossible for any government to consolidate its authority and move forward. Inevitably, it didn't take long for the Junta to send troops to the highlands in order to quell minor revolts organized by dissident groups that used the local ethnic population as cannon fodder. These power struggles and the resulting polarization became even more evident during the presidency of Juan Jose Arevalo, the winner of the December 1944 elections.

Politically savvy and determined, Arevalo soon introduced a series of reforms that included a new labor code, a considerable increase to the minimum wage and the creation of a Social Security system. The government also facilitated the organization of new unions and was adamant in protecting them. This however, put President Arevalo on a collision course with businessmen and landowners, who were affected by what was considered an over-protective labor code and most of all, by the mandatory increase of the minimum wage. Right-

Wreckage of FAG-54, a North American AT-6D of the Guatemalan Air Force that crash-landed at La Aurora Airbase after sustaining damage while strafing the Guardia de Honor garrison during the July 19, 1949 failed revolt. Lieutenants René Valenzuela (pilot in command) and Carlos Samayoa (rear gunner) survived with minor injuries. (Photo credit: Guatemalan Air Force.)

wing political parties sided with them immediately, and several public demonstrations followed, demanding the end of "Communist practices" in the country.

Sensing that the situation could get out of hand, government officials and members of left-wing parties that supported President Arevalo, secretly organized brigades of high school and university students[2] and sent them to violently dissolve the protests. As it would be expected, the resulting clashes generated much discontent among the population and the political scene to such extent that, from then on, the government had to quell coup attempts nearly every month. It seemed like anyone with the means and the motivation was plotting against Arevalo.

The country's polarization soon reached the Army too, driven not only by the delicate situation, but because there were two categories of commissioned officers among its ranks. First, much of the "old guard" was comprised by "line" officers who had gone through their military lives without professional studies and had earned their ranks through hard work, lucky breaks or simply by being loyal to the dictator in turn. On the other hand, there were the "career" officers who had attended the "Escuela Politécnica" -the Guatemalan Army's Military Academy- and had started their careers as Second Lieutenants, achieving their ranks by rigorous promotions every four years.

Due to their academic background, the career officers tended to look down on the line officers, even if the latter held higher ranks, and were considered uncouth remnants of dictatorial times. The resulting division was more than evident in almost every activity held at the Army garrisons, but it was accentuated when the now Lt. Colonels Jacobo Arbenz and Francisco Arana, Arevalo's Defense Minister and the Chief of the Armed Forces respectively, hinted somewhat prematurely, that they wanted to participate in the presidential elections scheduled for November 1950. Such announcement, albeit still unofficial, sent shockwaves through the Army, since Arana was a line officer, while Arbenz had graduated, with the highest honors, from the Escuela Politécnica.

In a matter of a few days, the political scene rearranged itself, with a coalition of right-wing parties backing Arana, and the center left-wing "Partido de Accion Revolucionaria" – PAR – supporting Arbenz. It is worth noting here, that a handful of PAR leaders, and many of its members, was also part of the "Partido Guatemalteco del Trabajo" –PGT – that was originally a Communist organization.

As the situation in the country grew tense, President Arevalo had to draw on all his sagacity to convince Arbenz to wait and let Arana be the next "official" candidate. This so-called "gentlemen's agreement" did not sit well with the PAR leadership and soon they began pressuring Arbenz to renege on it. In the end, Arbenz agreed and resigned from his position as Minister of Defense in order to begin campaigning.

The pro-Arana coalition, seeing that even at such an early stage of the presidential run Arbenz's popularity was fast growing, decided to pressure Arana to stage a coup as soon as possible and then suspend the upcoming elections. However, after careful considerations, and even when he regarded Arbenz as a traitor for having broken their agreement, Arana refused.

With such decision, Lt. Colonel Arana became a major obstacle for the coalition, because their leaders still wanted to stage a coup and would have to face him if they decided to proceed. With no options left, they began to plot for his physical elimination. To make things even worse, the rumor about Arana staging a coup had spread like wild fire among government officials and the PAR members. It didn't take long for them to begin considering his assassination, too.

Lt. Colonel Arana was killed during an ambush in the outskirts of the town of Amatitlan, some 17 km Southwest of the Guatemalan capital, Guatemala City, on July 18, 1949. On that date, Arana had seized a large cache of arms that President Arevalo had been hiding

The Guardia de Honor garrison in all its glory can be seen in the background of this photo, while a Cessna 140 of the Guatemalan Air Force practices "on the spot" landings. (Photo credit: Guatemalan Air Force.)

from prying eyes after a failed invasion to the Dominican Republic, staged a month earlier by a group of exiles and mercenaries based in Guatemala, namely the "Caribbean Legion", that was being supported and sheltered by the President himself.

To this date, there are many conflicting versions of what really happened on that day or what were the motivations behind the assassination. The government, through a stark press release, only stated that the assassins seemed to be "*mysterious outlaws, friends of Arana*", who had killed him after having an argument.

However, many friends and acquaintances of the deceased Lt. Colonel soon learned that Arbenz's bodyguards, various PAR members and even a congressman, had been involved in the assassination. Some accounts even placed Arbenz in a hill nearby, watching the ambush unfold.

Fearing an unavoidable major revolt as soon as pro-Arana officers would get wind of the government involvement in the assassination, Arevalo called Arbenz out of retirement and appointed him Chief of the Armed Forces, so he could be in charge of the government's defense.

As Arevalo had anticipated, a large group of Army officers, supported by leaders of the pro-Arana coalition and sympathizers, staged a revolt at the Guardia de Honor garrison within hours of Arana's assassination. Arbenz, on the other hand, summoned labor union members and peasants with whom he organized civilian battalions that joined the few loyal Army troops in the defense of the government.[3] What followed was the largest and bloodiest rebellion that Arevalo's administration had to face during its period. It was put out after three days of heavy fighting, and many rebel officers were arrested or executed upon surrendering.

But the restlessness was already planted among the Army ranks and a year later, a group of officers led by Lt. Colonel Carlos Castillo Armas, who later would be appointed as the leader of the CIA's "Liberation Army", tried once again to topple Arévalo by seizing the "La Aurora" Military Base and spark a revolt from there, but troops loyal to the government crushed it almost immediately.

When the dust settled, Castillo Armas, badly wounded, was found among a pile of corpses inside the base, and was taken to the Military Hospital against the wishes of Arbenz, who wanted him dead. To Arbenz's chagrin, the quick intervention of the Defense Council's Chief, Lt. Colonel Carlos Paz, prevented his execution and a couple of days later, Castillo Armas was transferred to the National Penitentiary, from where he escaped to El Salvador and then to Honduras. In any case, the failed revolts of July 1949 and November 1950, established the foundations for the anti-Arbenz movement that four years later would assist the CIA into accomplishing the military intervention in Guatemala.

After these serious rebellion attempts, Arevalo's Government barely made it to the next elections. Many controversial laws that left-wing parties wanted enacted were shelved and never sent to Congress out of fear of even another coup attempt. One of those laws was the so-called "Tenancy Law" that would mandate the expropriation of idle private lands and their distribution among poor peasants and Indians.

To no one's surprise, Arbenz overwhelmingly won the elections of November 1950, even when there were several allegations of fraud at many polling centers.[4] However, that did not stop him from taking power on March 15, 1951.

Arbenz based his government plan almost entirely on the recommendations that a joint U.S. – Canadian commission had drafted after a thorough study of the country's social and economic problems during Arevalo's administration. Such recommendations included the construction of a road linking Guatemala City with the Caribbean Coast, a new seaport in that coast and the construction of at least one hydroelectric power generation plant. The commission's document also listed 24 additional recommendations, mainly related to agriculture, mining, education, labor, and social issues.

The Communists, now with considerable influence over the Congress through a majority of PAR congressional representatives and with individuals occupying key positions in the cabinet, made the Commission's recommendations their own and set out to implement them at any cost. They also brought back the infamous "Tenancy Law" proposal and transformed it into a full-fledged "Agrarian Reform", selling it to Arbenz as the panacea that would end poverty and inequality in the country. Such controversial law was enacted in June 1952, and from there, the government rushed to create the framework that would allow its implementation, setting itself in the process, on a collision course with the landowners.

The enactment of Decree No. 900, the Agrarian Reform law, marked the beginning of the anti-Communist resistance front, comprised mainly by businessmen, landowners and right-wing political parties, who considered such law a direct attack on private property. Despite being able to stage a series of demonstrations at the country's capital, the anti-Communist front was facing problems to consolidate itself, as they lacked a political figure, a caudillo of some sorts, who could lead them.

Here we must introduce the second main factor that prompted the U.S. intervention in Guatemala: The presence of the United Fruit Company –UFCO- and how Arbenz's Agrarian Reform directly affected it.

Taking advantage of the U.S. political influence over Central America since the late 1800s, the "Frutera", as the UFCO was known locally, had established enormous banana plantations in every country of the region, and had monopolized the transportation and communication services.

Obviously, the convulsed political scene in Central America posed a challenge for the UFCO's operations, but their local representatives soon learned that the only options for securing their company's well-being were to bribe the dictators or get them removed from power.

The situation in Guatemala was no different. The UFCO had entrenched itself in the country since 1901, when the dictator in turn, Manuel Estrada Cabrera, hired an UFCO subsidiary to build and operate a railroad connecting Guatemala City with the Caribbean Coast. It didn't take long for the Frutera to start purchasing, at ridiculously low prices, vast tracts of government lands for the establishment of banana plantations, ancillary facilities, and its own shipping ports. In fact, and with the blessing of Estrada Cabrera, the company soon monopolized not only the railroad, but also the shipping of cargo and passengers, as well as radio, telegraph, and international cable communications.

Up to the early 1950s, the UFCO had remained oblivious to the country's developments, having only had a minor head butting with Arevalo when the Congress introduced the new Labor Code back in 1945. However, with Arbenz's Agrarian Reform, the company became a natural target.

When the land expropriations began in January 1953, the UFCO tried to negotiate with the government in order to be left out of them, but soon realized that the old methods of bribing and manipulating its way out were now futile, such was the discipline, determination and ruthlessness of the Communists conducting the Agrarian Reform.

Back in Boston, where the UFCO had its headquarters, its Public Relationships office decided to launch an extensive discrediting campaign, publishing in renowned media outlets a series of articles that presented damning evidence –real and exaggerated- of a deep Communist penetration in Guatemala. The campaign went to such extents that a full-length film about the country's precarious situation was produced and then screened across the U.S. As expected, the notion of a Communist Guatemala spread rapidly around the world, convincing the public opinion that the Soviets had finally set foot in the Latin American continent.

However, the UFCO efforts didn't stop with this discrediting campaign. They soon began lobbying the U.S. Department of State, attempting to obtain a reaction from the Truman administration, which in turn, began taking timid steps towards fixing the situation. It was not until January 1953, when the Eisenhower administration was inaugurated that the idea of a covert military intervention gained enough traction. Some historians link this decision to the fact that the Secretary of State and the CIA Director, John Foster and Allen Dulles respectively, had been in the UFCO's board of directors and had done legal work for the company. But blaming the Dulles brothers would only neglect the third and perhaps the most important factor that contributed to the U.S. intervention in Guatemala: The so-called "Cold War."

What was perceived as an Arbenz's flirtation with Communism, and the ensuing threat to U.S. commercial interests in Guatemala, occurred during a very distressing period of time in which both Super-Powers –The U.S. and the Soviet Union- were engaged in increasing their political and economic influence around the world, while avoiding constantly a direct confrontation that could end in mutual nuclear annihilation.

Nations had to take sides, whether it was by their own will or by subjugation. In addition, there was such hypersensitivity in the air that any political action, even if well intentioned, could place a country under scrutiny or be considered a threat by any of the two super-powers.

Even when Arbenz seemed convinced that the reforms were necessary to introduce a fairer capitalist system in which poverty and inequality could be eradicated, the Communists in his administration didn't hide very well their ultimate goal of transforming the country into a fully Communist nation by any means. The Communists' intentions became even more evident when activists and labor union representatives in the countryside began promoting the illegal occupation of private lands. These uncontrolled expropriations became the proverbial straw that broke the camel's back, sending the country down a very dangerous path of political and social polarization, alarming not only the U.S. but also the neighboring countries.

CHAPTER 2
PBFORTUNE

Even before the enactment of the Agrarian Reform law in June 1952, political analysts in the U.S. Department of State had reached the conclusion that there was incontrovertible evidence of Communist influence in Arbenz's regime. The initial reaction of the Truman administration was to impose diplomatic and economical pressure upon the Guatemalan government, but they only strengthened Arbenz's image, encouraging him to continue with the reforms, amid an almost constant anti-imperialist rhetoric not only at the Congress but also on the streets.

In March, a CIA "National Intelligence Estimate" confirmed what everybody in Washington D.C. feared: The situation in Guatemala was condemned to a slow and inevitable deterioration. The country was well on its way to becoming the first Soviet satellite on the continent.

That same month, the then CIA Director, General Walter Bedell Smith, ordered the Agency's Western Hemisphere Division -WHD- to explore ways to assist the Guatemalan anti-Communist organizations in devising a plan for ousting Arbenz. Accordingly, the WHD's chief, Colonel Joseph Caldwell King, ordered a group of operatives, assigned to the CIA station in Mexico, to go to Honduras and El Salvador where the majority of anti-Communist activists where living in exile, and contact their leaders. A couple of operatives also went to Guatemala in order to establish links with the nascent anti-Communist movement there.

Within days, the CIA operatives arrived in Central America disguised as representatives of an "anonymous group", allegedly comprised by "persons dedicated to the cause of free men and opposed to the dangers of Communism", who were willing to fund a military venture to overthrow President Arbenz.

Initially, the representatives of "The Group" approached Miguel Ydígoras, an old general who had served loyally under the Estrada Cabrera and Ubico regimes, to see if his organization in El Salvador had the military capability to spark a rebellion in Guatemala. The next candidate to be contacted by the CIA operatives was Lt. Col. Carlos Castillo Armas, who had his own anti-Communist organization in Honduras.

During the meeting that took place in the Honduran Capital, Tegucigalpa, Castillo Armas assured them that he had the financial and logistical backing of the Nicaraguan and Dominican regimes, and that he was already working on a plan for starting a major uprising by the end of the year. Whether Castillo Armas' assertions were real or just an elaborated show remained to be seen, but at the time, the CIA operatives were delighted.

Both Ydígoras and Castillo Armas had established close relationships with the leaders of the anti-Communist movement in Guatemala, namely Roberto Barrios (a retired Army colonel), Carlos Simons and Juan Cordova Cerna. In the eyes of the CIA, this was something of utmost importance, since any rebellion should be initiated by this front from within the country, and then be supported by an "invading force" that would launch from Honduras or El Salvador.

The problem was that the anti-Communist front in Guatemala was far from being consolidated, as it was comprised of several contentious and tiny groups that were immersed in a constant power-struggle that prevented them from reaching any consensus. The CIA would have to help these groups to organize themselves in order to build upon them an effective resistance movement.

After the initial contact with the Guatemalan anti-Communist leaders, it became clear for King and the WHD's planners that the best option for ousting Arbenz would be to use Castillo Armas' organization as the required "invading force. Accordingly, in July, the CIA's Deputy Director of Plans, Allen Dulles, formally requested the U.S. State Department the approval for initiating a covert operation against the Arbenz's regime. It was going to be conducted by Castillo Armas with assistance from the Agency.

Codenamed "PBFortune", the project was placed under the command of Colonel King and comprised the shipment of several tons of arms and equipment for Castillo Armas' organization in Honduras. However, right from the beginning President Truman imposed a series of restrictions for maintaining plausible deniability, and these crippled the whole project even before the first shipment had left the U.S.

The most critical of these restrictions had to do with the use of cargo aircraft: President Truman did not want any U.S. plane, civilian or military, to be anywhere near Honduras, and the only approved flights were to the Coco Solo Naval Station in the Panama Canal Zone. From there, Col. King would have to come up with a method for transporting the arms and supplies to Honduras in a covertly manner. Not losing any time, King acquired an old and battered landing craft with which his operatives barely managed to make a couple of runs to the Honduran port of La Ceiba, before ending stranded on an island near Nicaragua due to a major engine malfunction.

From there, PBFortune evolved into a rather simplistic covert operation aimed mostly at funneling money and a few weapons to Castillo Armas' organization, usually through circuitous and complicated routes. The project's *coup de grâce* came by the end of 1952 when the Nicaraguan President Anastasio Somoza García -who was also involved in PBFortune- blew the project's cover by making some indiscreet comments during a summit in Panama. From there, it didn't take long for Arbenz to find out additional details about the covert operation and Castillo Armas' intentions. As it would be expected, King was ordered to put PBFortune on hold, immediately.

If Colonel King had any hopes about resuming the project at some point in the near future, his expectations came crashing down on March 28, 1953, when a group of Guatemalan anti-Communists staged a poorly planned revolt at the remote town of Salamá, which was promptly thwarted by the Guatemalan Army. After this failed uprising, the government unleashed a wave of repression during which many anti-Communist leaders were imprisoned or assassinated, effectively dismantling the already fragmented and weakened resistance movement. A couple of days later, project PBFortune was officially terminated.

The CIA's activities against Arbenz's regime entered in a hiatus for the next five months. However, King had convinced the CIA Director to keep Castillo Armas on The Group's payroll and to finance his organization while waiting for the right conditions to try a new attempt.

By mid-1953, winds of change began to blow through the U.S. Government, and especially in the CIA. The newly elected president, Dwight Eisenhower, had appointed Allen Dulles as the Director of Central Intelligence, and had the National Security Council –NSC- already exploring new ways for fighting the Cold War.

Among the new directives that emerged from these NSC's meetings,

Anti-Communist organizations demonstrating in Guatemala City's downtown. Although usually neglected by historians, social unrest was alive and well during Jacobo Arbenz' regime. (Photo credit: Guatemalan Ministry of Interior.)

Members of the Guardia Civil (Civil Guard) take cover at the Central Park during a clash with anti-Communist protesters. (Photo credit: Guatemalan Ministry of Interior.)

and from then on shaped the foreign policy of the Eisenhower administration, was the extensive use of covert actions in order to achieve political objectives in the international arena.

It didn't take long for the CIA to enforce the new directive: Early in August, Eisenhower approved Project TPAjax, aimed at overthrowing Iran's Prime Minister Mohammad Mosaddegh, and on August 12, the President green-lighted a proposal for a covert operation against Arbenz. On that same day, Dulles ordered Colonel King to put together a "General Plan" for this new attempt.

In the wake of the successful completion of project TPAjax, King decided to base the Guatemalan operation –now codenamed PBSuccess- entirely on the methodologies, tactics, and strategies that had been applied in Iran. Thus, PBSuccess would rely on the extensive use of propaganda and psychological warfare; the main difference with TPAjax however, would be the use of a small paramilitary force, funded, trained, and controlled by the CIA, which would launch an invasion as a measure of psychological pressure that, hopefully, would create within the country an "active opposition" against Arbenz.

When the final version of the "General Plan" was submitted for Dulles' approval in November, many in the Agency considered it a masterpiece. The main objective would be to gradually build tension among the population, and specifically among the Guatemalan Army officers, by means of creating chaos and uncertainty. For this, a propaganda sub-project would be created, and its central feature was to be a clandestine radio station for broadcasting calls to action, incendiary messages, and false rumors in detriment of Arbenz's government. Additionally, leaflets, newspapers, and other printed media would be produced and then clandestinely distributed in Guatemala. Besides the propaganda efforts, acts of passive sabotage would be initiated while a general discrediting campaign would be launched, both locally and internationally. At some point, an invasion would be announced, followed by acts of active sabotage that would target communications and governmental infrastructure.

Billboard on the road to Mixco, announcing Arbenz's agrarian reform. (Photo credit: *Life* Magazine.)

Once a critical point had been reached, a "Liberation Army" would invade from neighboring Honduras and El Salvador and seize the Guatemalan Army garrisons in the towns of Puerto Barrios, Zacapa, Chiquimula, Jalapa, Jutiapa, Cobán, and Quetzaltenango. Then the Liberation Army's leader – a charismatic caudillo – would establish a "constitutional government" and demand Arbenz's resignation. If by that time the Army hadn't toppled Arbenz, the Liberation Army would place Guatemala City under siege, parachute troops for seizing the National Palace, and capture the President.

Frank Wisner, the Deputy Director of Plans, approved Project PBSuccess' plan on November 16 and submitted it for the CIA Director's approval on that same day. Allen Dulles, on his part, took it to Eisenhower and the NSC for analysis and approval in the following

Lt. Colonel Carlos Castillo Armas. (Photo credit: Guatemalan Ministry of Defense.)

Allen Dulles, Director of Central Intelligence. (Photo credit: U.S. National Archives.)

Frank Wisner, the CIA's Director of Plans and the mastermind behind Project PBSuccess. (Photo credit: Wisner Family.)

week, and it was then when the plan encountered the first difficulties: Some NSC members and Eisenhower's military advisers had their reservations about such an extremely complex covert operation. Even the renowned CIA case officer, Kermit Roosevelt, who had been in command of TPAjax, wasted no time in warning King and Wisner that prior to launching PBSuccess they at least needed to make sure that the Guatemalan Army -and the population- wanted Arbenz and the Communists out, or they would fail miserably.

However, the relatively quick success achieved with Project TPAjax had unleashed an optimistic euphoria at the CIA, and it soon reached the higher spheres of the U.S. Government, prompting President Eisenhower to approve Project PBSuccess on December 9, 1953.

Dulles was instructed to obtain results fast as it was necessary to get rid of the Communist germ in the region before it would become contagious. Thus, to avoid any bureaucratic processes, the CIA Director decided to transfer the project from the WHD to the Directorate of Plans, relieving King and his men and replacing them by Frank Wisner and his team. From then on Wisner assumed exclusive control of PBSuccess, neither seeking nor receiving assistance from any other directorates, and answering only to Dulles. Not even Robert Amory, the Deputy Director of Intelligence, was briefed about the project, and the CIA stations involved in PBSuccess were ordered to avoid sending him any related reports.

As soon as King was relieved, he began causing trouble. Thus, for avoiding King's constant obstructions and other bureaucratic annoyances, Wisner requested authorization for the project to have its own and separate chain of command, communication facilities, logistics and infrastructure. Wisner even wanted to set up the project's headquarters as far from Washington D.C. as possible. Dulles immediately approved the requests.

CHAPTER 3
LINCOLN

PBSuccess' first phase called for a thorough assessment of the situation in Guatemala. It was necessary to determine if the anti-Communist resistance movement could be rebuilt and explore the possibilities of recruiting "assets" among government officials, pro-Communist groups, agricultural circles, and especially in the Army. Accordingly, operatives from the CIA station in Mexico travelled to Guatemala, this time posing as coffee-importing businessmen, and began approaching potential candidates.

After an initial survey, it was more than evident that Arbenz's government had been very effective in thwarting the anti-Communist front. The prevailing feeling among landowners, businessmen, and the few remaining right-wing activists was of total discouragement. In other words, it would be almost impossible for PBSuccess' operatives to build something useful around them. On the other hand, approaching Communist activists and government officials had proved difficult, as they were fanatically loyal to Arbenz.

Under those circumstances, PBSuccess' planners placed their bets on the Guatemalan Army as a suitable replacement of the resistance movement, as they considered it *"the only organized element in Guatemala capable of rapidly and decisively altering the political situation."* The problem was that the Agency didn't have a clear idea about what was the consensus among the officers and their troops towards Arbenz and Communism. Most of the intelligence available by then had been collected by the USAF attaché, Major Manuel Chavez, during much of 1952, but he had left the country later that same year.

In order to overcome this serious problem, Major Chavez was contacted by the CIA and offered to return to Guatemala City on a "personal trip" for visiting his friends in the Army and find out what their thoughts were. In the meantime, PBSuccess' operatives would have to create the much-needed assets from scratch, using whoever was left from the anti-Communist front and by approaching Army

General Anastasio Somoza García (center), the Nicaraguan dictator who played an important role during Project PBSuccess, seen here with the Argentine president Juan Domingo Perón (left.) (Photo credit: Revista Militar de Nicaragua.)

William "Rip" Robertson, PBSuccess' Field Commander, seen here during the ill-fated Bay of Pigs operation against Cuba in 1961. (Photo credit: CIA.)

officers, most of them acquaintances of Castillo Armas and Ydígoras, who could help the cause.

After a couple of days however, the picture that emerged was not encouraging. The majority of Army officers were simply fence-sitting, and even though they despised the government's Communist leanings, they hadn't found a good reason for opposing its reforms. They were being paid regularly and there were offerings to re-equip and train them in the short term. Obviously, there was a small group of officers extremely loyal to Arbenz, but they weren't able to exert any influence upon their fellow brothers in arms.

This indifference towards the government had its roots in the new Guatemalan Constitution that had transformed the Army into an autonomous entity ruled entirely by a Defense Council, integrated by officers elected democratically by the ranks, which only answered to the Congress. The lawmakers' intentions with this arrangement had been to prevent any future use of the armed forces for dubious purposes like establishing a new dictatorship or repress the population, as the President was no longer the "commander in chief."

What the Guatemalan lawmakers failed to realize however, was that such radical transformation broke the traditional chain of command, creating in the process a fourth independent and co-equal branch of the government. The Guatemalan Army was in such a comfortable position that, as long as its officers were kept well paid, well trained and appropriately equipped, it wouldn't interfere with any of Arbenz's actions, even if he aimed at transforming the country into a Communist dictatorship.

With this in mind, Wisner and his team decided that most of PBSuccess' propaganda campaign and psychological warfare would be designed as to induce the Army to stand up against Arbenz, mainly by terrorizing them and shoving down their throats the need to stage a coup.

PBSuccess' next phase required that the U.S. Department of State be taken on board for securing the cooperation of the governments of Honduras, El Salvador, and Nicaragua. The first step was to brief the U.S. Ambassadors to El Salvador and Nicaragua, Michael McDermott and Thomas Whelan respectively, about the project. Then, Withing Willauer, the legendary co-founder of the CIA's "Civil Air Transport" airline, was appointed as Ambassador to Honduras (Willauer would serve also as an advisor to the project's Air Support Unit.)

It didn't take long for the U.S. ambassadors to subscribe "cooperation agreements" with presidents Juan Manuel Gálvez from Honduras and Anastasio Somoza Garcia from Nicaragua, which allowed the CIA to establish secret paramilitary, communications and logistical facilities in their respective countries in exchange of overt economic assistance. The only president who hesitated was Lt. Colonel Oscar Osorio from El Salvador. At the time, he had a "non-interference pact" with Arbenz and feared that if the Guatemalan President learned about his involvement in the clandestine operation, there could be grave implications for his country. However, Ambassador McDermontt was ordered to keep trying to convince him.

Guatemala's economical vulnerability did not escape PBSuccess' attention either, and several firms –mainly in the coffee and cotton importing businesses- were prompted by the Department of State to severe ties with the country, cutting off an important source of revenue for the Government. Other businessmen in New York would covertly apply economic pressure by creating shortages of vital exports.

Perhaps the State Department's biggest contribution to the project was the appointment of John Emil Peurifoy as Ambassador to Guatemala. With vast experience in dealing with the Communists,

There is considerable evidence that Lt. Col. Vincent Pivall, the case officer in charge of paramilitary training during PBSuccess was, in fact, the CIA operative David Sanchez Morales, who years later got involved in the Bay of Pigs operation against Cuba. (Photo credit: CIA.)

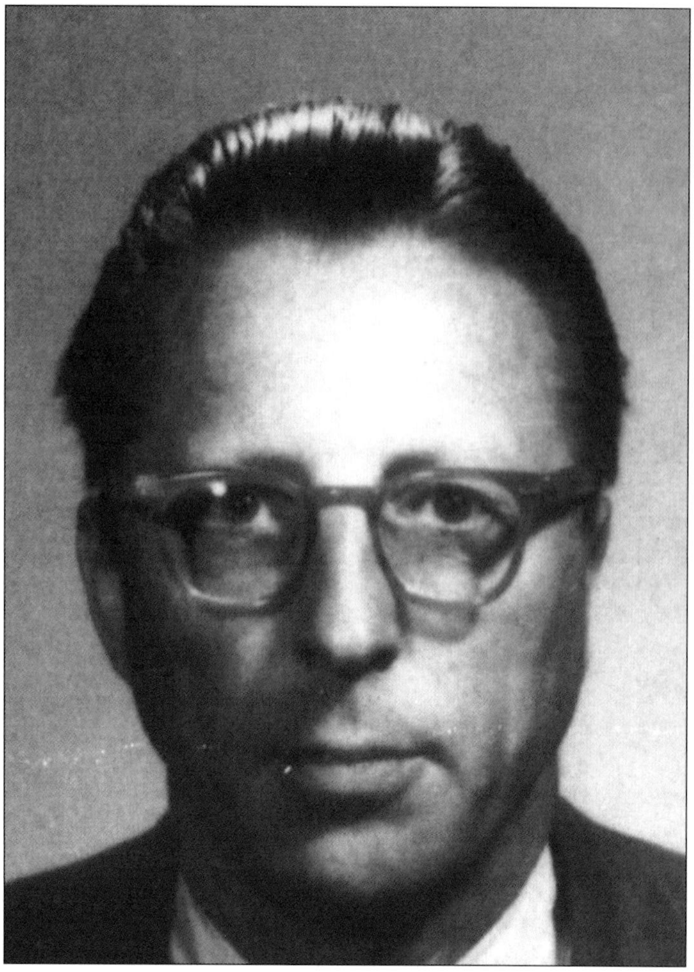

CIA operative Tracy Barnes was PBSuccess liaison officer and the project's second in command. (Photo credit: CIA.)

especially in Greece, where he had helped that country's government to get rid of them after the Civil War, the old diplomat would be in charge of exerting direct, up-and-close pressure on Arbenz, while orchestrating all diplomatic efforts required by the project in the region.

The U.S. Air Force and Navy were also brought into the project, mainly for providing logistical support and for staging "shows of force" whenever it would be required.

On December 23, project PBSuccess headquarters, codenamed "LINCOLN", went fully operational at a nearly abandoned naval air station located in the Opa-locka airport, some 19 km North of Miami. The CIA declassified documents mention that the initial PBSuccess' project manager was found lacking after a couple of weeks and was replaced by Colonel Albert R. Haney, the former chief of the CIA station in Seoul during the Korean War and vastly experienced in clandestine operations. Al Haney would answer only to Wisner, who in turn would be running the project from Washington D.C.

A Former member of the Office of Strategic Services –OSS- (the forerunner of the CIA) named Tracy Barnes, would serve as the liaisons officer between PBSuccess headquarters and Washington; he would also assist Al Haney in whatever he required for accomplishing the mission.

During the first week of January 1954, Wisner, Barnes and Haney set to work on putting together an important element of the project: The Liberation Army. For this, representatives of "The Group" (codenamed "SKIMMER" in the CIA declassified documents) got in contact with Castillo Armas in Honduras once again.

In contrast with what had happened during PBFortune, this time The Group offered to provide him with arms, equipment, and training for his organization, but also with logistical, tactical, and political support. In return, he would have to come up with enough troops, adhere strictly to orders emanating from The Group, and conform a "Junta" (which in time gained the codename "SYNCARP") that could take over Guatemala once Arbenz and the Communists were gone. As it would be expected, Castillo Armas quickly jumped at the opportunity.

By the end of January 1954, the negotiations between The Group and Castillo Armas had progressed fairly well, and an operational plan was already being devised. In fact, even though a "collaboration pact" with Castillo Armas hadn't been formalized yet, Wisner sent Barnes to Nicaragua for establishing training camps for the Liberation Army troops.

With the help of Nicaraguan officials, Barnes was able to find the perfect spots. The training camp for regular troops, sabotage teams and officers, codenamed "SARANAC", was to be established at the Momotombito Island, in the Managua Lake, while the training camp for radio-operators, codenamed "SCRANTON", would be set up at a remote farm near the town of Tamarindo, some 46 km North from the Nicaraguan capital, Managua.

President Somoza also provided a couple of houses where Barnes established the project's Field Command Post and a communications center equipped with a recording studio for producing the tapes to be aired by the clandestine radio station. Before departing Nicaragua, Barnes designated William "Rip" Robertson, another former OSS operative, as the project's Field Commander and an experienced U.S.

John Emil Peurifoy, the U.S. Ambassador to Guatemala and perhaps PBSuccess' most important "asset" in the field. (Photo credit: World Wide Photos.)

Army Lt. Colonel, going by the pseudonym of Vincent Pivall, as the case officer in charge of training the Liberation Army troops.

Back in Washington, Wisner designated David Atlee Phillips as the case officer in charge of the psychological warfare sub-program, codenamed "SHERWOOD." In such capacity, Phillips was sent to Guatemala City, so he could get a "feel" for the situation down there, and to collect material that could be used in the programs that the clandestine radio station would be airing.

It was by this time however, that PBSuccess ran into its first pitfall when Arbenz made public a large collection of documents that detailed, with stunning accuracy, the plans, and arrangements being made by Castillo Armas in order to oust him. Arbenz also claimed that some "northern government" and the Honduran and Nicaraguan regimes were involved in the nefarious plot.

Inevitably, the Guatemalan authorities rushed to unleash yet again the persecution of the few remaining anti-Communist activists, right-wing politicians, and the occasional by-standers. In the process, many of the assets that the PBSuccess' operatives had recruited during the last couple of weeks ended up detained or had to escape the country. Because of this, the Guatemalan government came to know even more details about the clandestine operation. Inevitably, the negotiations between Castillo Armas and The Group were put on hold while Wisner, Haney and the PBSuccess' planners assessed the damages.

In Washington D.C. everyone involved in the project, up to the CIA Director, were appalled. The possibility of cancelling PBSuccess was being seriously considered, favoring instead a more "direct" method for getting rid of Arbenz and the Communists. In fact, the CIA went so far as to establish a short-lived program[1] under which assassins were recruited and trained, while "hit lists" were drawn up.

On his part, Lt. Col. Pivall had to evacuate the troops' training site in a rush because the Nicaraguan newspapers, echoing Arbenz's press conference, had published its exact location and a swarm of journalists were already heading there. Pivall's aides and the few Castillo Armas' troops that had arrived a few days earlier, had to make a run for the Managua shore in the middle of the night, relocating to the radio-operators' training camp, while a new site could be secured.

Wisner started a thorough investigation[2] to determine how those documents had been leaked and by whom. It didn't take long for a name to surface: Jorge Isaac Delgado, a Panamanian businessman and diplomat, who served as a courier for Castillo Armas in Central America, had been providing sensitive documents to the Guatemalan government since mid-December, 1953. Now Arbenz had solid proofs of Castillo Armas' intentions, his negotiations with the "anonymous group" and his ties with the Nicaraguan and Honduran governments.

Determined to make the best out of a terrible situation, Wisner decided to build upon the notion that Castillo Armas' organization had some sort of "foreign support." The CIA planners were convinced that if the Guatemalan Army and the population in general were able to read between the lines, they would conclude that such "foreign support" was actually the U.S. government. And if so, they would change their minds towards Arbenz real soon, fearing a large military intervention that surely would include a significant number of U.S. Marines, at the least.

On January 29, and despite the turmoil caused by the leakage, Castillo Armas was smuggled into the U.S. for a meeting with The Group's most important representatives: Mr. Joshua Smith and his assistant Robert Ford, obviously Haney and Barnes under their respective pseudonyms. At an ample meeting room in the Opa-locka headquarters, the trio spent most of the next day going over an initial version of the project's plan, discussing meticulously every aspect involved. Later, Haney, Barnes, and Castillo Armas signed a three-page "agreement"[3] containing, in broad terms, the objectives, framework, funding, communication channels, and definitions of responsibility for the paramilitary operation. And with that, Castillo

Armas became formally the project's much-needed "caudillo."

Castillo Armas was smuggled back into Tegucigalpa on February 7, with orders to prepare a list of his men and their respective skills, as the project's planners needed a rough estimate of the force's composition and capabilities in order to prepare the training program.

The newly appointed Caudillo simply disappeared upon landing at Tegucigalpa, however, and PBSuccess' operatives in Honduras tried insistently to contact him during the following days, to no avail. It was not until two weeks later that Castillo Armas reappeared, bearing discouraging news: On a cable sent to The Group, he stated, or rather confessed, that his organization was lacking funds for paying the troops' salaries and the morale was low. Under no circumstances, his organization was prepared to conduct a military operation of any kind.

Haney rushed two of his operatives to Honduras in order to assess the situation and their report was even more somber: The force, if such a bunch of trembling and hesitant chaps could be called that, was comprised of less than 150 men, and the 15 officers in charge were having a hard time trying to stop the numerous desertions. The worrying part was that Castillo Armas had turned evasive when the operatives had asked him about the rest of his troops; the same happened when he was questioned about his "internal organization" in Guatemala, supposedly composed of more than 900 individuals.

During the negotiations at Opa-locka, Castillo Armas had asserted that he had no less than 300 troops and specialists "in the mountains of Honduras", and these were additional to the 150 he already had in Tegucigalpa. The truth was that no one, besides the Caudillo, knew with certainty the real strength of the Liberation Army.

With no other option but to press on, Wisner ordered that money, uniforms and infantry equipment be sent to Tegucigalpa immediately. The Group also informed Castillo Armas that the training program for his troops would be regularized in the next couple of weeks.

The morale boost that the new uniforms and the paychecks caused among the Liberation Army ranks quickly turned into a security problem when some of the troops began appearing at bars and restaurants in Tegucigalpa, fully combat-equipped, wearing the brand-new khaki fatigues and "Liberation Army" badges in their left arms. The local press took notice soon and inevitably, the news reached Guatemala after a couple of days.

Wasting no time, PBSuccess headquarters arranged the moving of the troops out of Tegucigalpa, and far from prying eyes, to the training camps in Nicaragua. It also meant that PBSuccess' planners had to start working on the next and very complex phase of the operation: Moving the remainder of PBFortune's arms and equipment out of New York's Free Zone and deliver them to the Liberation Army.

CHAPTER 4

FJHOPEFUL

Resupplying the Liberation Army's training camps turned out to be a complicated issue. The initial plan called for transporting the arms and supplies that Col. King had stored at the Coco Solo Naval Station during PBFortune, to Nicaragua. However, it depended from the sporadic flights of a Douglas C-118A transport that the USAF used to move supplies for the embassies in the region. As it should be expected, the first troops that arrived at the training camps soon found themselves living under extremely harsh conditions. There wasn't enough food or drinking water, and medicines were a scarce commodity. Inevitably, within a couple of days, dysentery and malaria set in.[1]

Under these circumstances, it was evident that some sort of air support was urgently needed for improving the troops' situation and speed up their training. The problem was that the "Air Support Plan" proposed for PBSuccess still was doing the rounds in Washington, where anyone who had access to the document was trying to limit its scope.

The first draft of what came to be PBSuccess' air support plan[2] was based on a document that J.C. King and his planners had produced for Project PBFortune, and that President Truman hadn't authorized at the time. That document proposed the extensive use of a small fleet of transport and utility aircraft for maintaining a coherent and expeditious logistical chain aimed at keeping the invading troops well supplied and communicated, both at the training sites and at the "staging points" from where the invasion was to be launched. The fleet would also conduct resupplying flights over the battlefield once the troops had crossed into Guatemala.

Frank Wisner had submitted the plan to the CIA Director early in January 1954, and with that began a tedious process for getting the approval from the members of the NSC and from the Department of State. As expected, the use of aircraft during the project was drawing much criticism because it could expose the involvement of the U.S. government. The general thought was that the presence of any type of aircraft in a clandestine operation, especially in a "third world scenario", would give away the much sought plausible deniability as there were no precedents in the region of revolting factions using aircraft for achieving their means. One only can but wonder how these "experts" had done their historical homework, as aircraft –including fighters- had been involved in two failed attempts to invade the Dominican Republic and during the revolution in Costa Rica five years earlier.

In any case, the air support plan that emerged from the approval process came with restrictions that posed serious challenges for PBSuccess' planners. First, the CIA Director strictly prohibited the use of any U.S. pilots; if there were going to be planes involved, Castillo Armas had to provide capable aircrews, recruited from the Guatemalan dissidents and the exiled community in Honduras and El Salvador. A livid Frank Wisner tried to get rid of such an absurd limitation, stating that it would be virtually impossible for the Caudillo to come up with enough aviators, if any, especially when he still was having serious problems recruiting men for a more or less credible ground force.

The next restriction had to do with the types and quantities of aircraft to be used. Originally, the plan made provisions for at least five transports and five liaison planes for the project; Castillo Armas, on his part, had submitted an impressive "wish list" that included an armada of 6 four-engine bombers, no less than 10 fighters, and an equal number of transports. Obviously, these proposals, considered ludicrous, were ignored and Dulles limited the aircraft types to those available in the civilian market, namely Douglas C-47s and small Cessnas, and they would not exceed two transports and two light planes. Again, Wisner protested at yet another absurdity, but Dulles was adamant.

Aerial view of the hangars and housing area of France Air Force Base, commonly known as "France Field." Here was located the PBSuccess' logistics center and was designated also as the project's "Regional Command Station." (Photo credit: Dan Hagedorn.)

Since struggling against these and other restrictions became a time-consuming process, Wisner decided to re-enlist his archenemy, Col. J.C. King, and place him in charge of procuring the approval for the air support plan. From then on Col. King was the one giving lengthy explanations to CIA top officials and NSC members, trying to get the document approved as he had originally conceived it. This also gave him the chance to pull off a stunt that almost cost him his head.

During the second week of January, the deplorable situation at the training camps in Nicaragua had reached critical levels and the troops' morale was now spiraling to the ground. Thus, Col. King requested authorization to fly them food and medicines with utmost urgency, but Dulles didn't approve it.

On January 14, King learned that a Douglas C-47 belonging to the CIA's "Civil Air Transport" airline –CAT- had arrived in the Washington D.C. area for an scheduled 1000-hour overhaul. Without thinking too much about it, the Colonel immediately loaded the plane with tropical rations, medicines, and small amount of paramilitary items from the lot that he had stored at the New York's Free Zone and dispatched it down to Managua. The C-47 hadn't landed yet when King was already taking heat for having authorized the flight. The CIA Director and Frank Wisner were furious, and PBSuccess' operatives in Managua almost had a heart attack when they learned that the C-47 had reached Nicaragua without authorization.[3] In an extensive report that King was ordered to submit, he stated that he had security and administrative concerns regarding the overall air support plan and that the flight had been a "proof of concept" for testing the project's capabilities to fly cargo and armament in an efficient and secretive manner to Central America.

In the end, the cargo was successfully transported to the training sites, but King's daring feat brought even more restrictions upon the air support plan. First, a very complicated authorization process was established for every flight to be conducted during PBSuccess. No plane was to leave the ground if Dulles or the CIA Deputy Director, General (USAF) Charles P. Cabell, hadn't been notified about it, without excuse. Additionally, the notification had to include the purpose of the flight, its destination, type of cargo, alternate landing airfield and the names of the crewmembers; and last but not least, each flight had to be announced 24 hours prior to takeoff, and the crew had to wait for the CIA Director's approval before proceeding.

Col. King soon realized that the whole process could take from six hours to two days, depending on the availability of Dulles or Cabell, affecting directly the speed with which the cargo could be flown to the different destinations. If that process was to be followed, the air support unit could very well end up flying planeloads for the next eight to ten months, delaying the launch of the invasion, which the project's general plan had set for late May or early June.

During the following days, King tried to get rid of the restrictions that undoubtedly would cripple PBSuccess' air operations. He even enlisted the help of General Cabell, who reviewed the plan and surprisingly, took it under his wing. Less than 24 hours later, the General delivered a new document with a bunch of the non-sense removed, which also included his own views about how the air support for PBSuccess should be conducted. An essential part of this proposal was precisely, the involvement of USAF's aircraft for expediting the transportation of the arms and equipment from the U.S. to the Canal Zone, where a logistical center should be established. CAT crews

General Charles P. Cabell, CIA's Deputy Director (Photo credit: USAF.):

would be in charge of flying such arms and equipment from the Canal Zone to where they were required in Central America.

Despite the overwhelming opposition, Cabell's version of the plan was finally approved on January 25. However, as it was the case with other aspects of PBSuccess, Dulles would have the prerogative of changing it at any time, and no stage of the plan was to be launched if it had not been thoroughly discussed with him first.

Five days later, when King was arranging the acquisition of the first couple of planes for the project, the security breach propitiated by Jorge Isaac Delgado took place and Lt. Col. Pivall had to evacuate the training camps in a rush.

Fortunately, President Somoza allowed Pivall to relocate both the troops and the radio operators training sites, to an isolated ranch near Puerto Cabezas, in the Caribbean Coast of Nicaragua. This however, posed a serious logistical and communications problems since more than 350 km of dense jungle now separated them from the Field Command Post in Managua.

Still with no aircraft at hand, the Field Command Post attempted to resupply the training sites by truck but it soon became impracticable due to the weather and the sorry state of the roads. Then, as it had happened during PBFortune, the CIA tried to resupply them by ship, from the Canal Zone. In the end, both methods were discarded leaving the training sites to their own devices, at least temporarily.

During the first week of February, Col. King finally set to implement the air support plan. It comprised three phases: Phase I called for the transportation of 250 tons of weapons and equipment from the U.S. to France Air Force Base, know locally still as simply "France Field", in the Canal Zone, where the USAF had facilitated two small hangars and administrative space for PBSuccess.

At France Field the CIA would establish a "logistical center", codenamed "FJHOPEFUL", where the arms and supplies that King had stored at the adjacent Coco Solo Naval Station, would be moved and consolidated with the planeloads that were to be brought in from the U.S. Once the weapons and supplies had been consolidated, they would be classified and repacked into infantry kits for distribution to the Castillo Armas' troops.

Phase II involved the transportation of the infantry kits from France Field to the training sites in Puerto Cabezas and supplies for the Field Command Post in Managua.

The third and last phase was comprised of two stages: Phase IIIA would be aimed at flying arms and equipment to Tegucigalpa and to the "staging points" in Honduras and El Salvador in preparation for the invasion. During Phase IIIB the aircraft would resupply the troops on the battlefield once the invasion was on its way, mainly by parachuting ammunition, food and additional weapons where needed. As part of this stage also, the aircraft would be required to fly on psychological warfare missions deep inside Guatemala.

All three phases would have to be accomplished by only two Douglas C-47 transports, since neither Cabell nor King had been able to convince Dulles about lifting the restriction on the number of aircraft to be used during the project.

On February 12, Frank Wisner designated a retired USAF Lt. Colonel, going by the pseudonym of Malcolm H. Brodfrost, as PBSuccess' Chief of Air Support. On that same day, Brodfrost was thoroughly briefed and less than 24 hours later, he departed Opa-locka for France Field, where he began coordinating the efforts to bring in the first cargo flight from the U.S. As Brodfrost assistant, Wisner appointed a young captain going by the *nom-de-guerre* Wallace C. Cowden, who was "on loan" from the USAF.

Meanwhile, PBSuccess' disinformation machinery set to work: On February 19 a load of Soviet weapons was "discovered" by fishermen in the Nicaraguan Pacific coast; President Somoza rushed to affirm that such arms were part of a larger shipment that Guatemalan Communists were trying to smuggle into the country for an internal resistance movement. From there the U.S. media picked the news and embroidered it with other notes, deliberately planted by the CIA, which spoke of Soviet submarines docked at Guatemalan ports and assassination squads being funded and trained by Arbenz for killing President Somoza.

The whole thing was part of a PBSuccess' sub-project codenamed "WASHTUB", aimed precisely at casting negative light upon the Guatemalan government, especially during the general meeting of the OAS that was to take place in Caracas, Venezuela, during the first half of March. The debut of this sub-project was so successful that the OAS voted 17 to 1 in favor of condemning Communism in Guatemala. It also encouraged PBSuccess' propaganda operatives to further expand the sub-project, and from then on, loads of Soviet weapons began appearing deep inside Nicaragua whenever the Guatemalan government tried to deflect international pressure.

Regarding the air support plan, Phase I's first flight took place on February 22, conducted by one of the three Douglas C-124C transports that the USAF had assigned exclusively for PBSuccess use. It departed Andrews AFB, in Washington D.C., for France Field, carrying 60 tons of communication equipment, weapons and food. In the following weeks, the three planes completed no less than four additional flights without a glitch, and the only incident reported was the failure of the belly cargo platform in one of them, which forced the USAF ground crews to unload the plane by hand. For the record, the C-124s involved were 51-5191, 52-0990, and 52-1008, the three attached to the 1600th Transport Group, 20th Air Transport Squadron, based at the Westover Air Force Base, in Massachusetts.

As the planeloads continued arriving at France Field, the situation kept worsening at the training camps in Puerto Cabezas, and some of the trainees had attempted to mutiny on several occasions while some others had deserted. In order to boost his troops' morale, Castillo

The USAF assigned three Douglas C-124C transports exclusively for PBSuccess use. These massive airplanes were attached to the 1600th Transport Group, 20th Air Transport Squadron, based at Westover Air Force Base, in Massachusetts. (Photo credit: B. Balogh, via Dan Hagedorn.):

Armas had insistently requested permission to visit them but Somoza hadn't allowed it, worried that his presence could compromise the already damaged project. Lt. Col. Pivall was also trying to improve the camps' conditions by getting them supplied regularly by any possible means, including packs of mules. He went as far as to request PBSuccess headquarters for permission to use Jorge Delgado's Cessna 180, at the time abandoned at the Las Mercedes airport in Managua. However, the reply was blunt: Delgado's Cessna was off-limits. PBSuccess headquarters didn't want anything to do with that plane, mainly because it was now openly linked to the Castillo Armas' organization.

The presence of the little Cessna was deemed so sensitive that on March 1 PBSuccess' Field Command Post decided to get rid of it by giving it to Castillo Armas[4], so he could have some sort of air mobility in Honduras. With that, Delgado's Cessna became the very first acquisition of the nascent "Liberation Air Force."

The Cessna was flown to Tegucigalpa by Castillo Armas' personal pilot, a Colombian named Alfredo Silva Romero, and its original Panamanian registration "HP-195" was dropped in favor of the spurious Colombian registration "HK-592", which was then painted on its wings and vertical stabilizer. For those interested, the airplane manufacturer's serial number –MSN- was 30114, and had been originally registered as N2914A in the U.S.; later on it was flown to Costa Rica where it gained the civil registration TI-224, and then relocated to Panama as HP-195 around 1953.

By March 3, Col. King and his men had spotted two Douglas C-47s available for leasing in the Washington D.C. area and had done the paperwork for obtaining them on behalf of Castillo Armas' organization. Both planes were then flown to Andrews AFB for a complete "sterilization", that is, the removal of all data-plates and markings that could reveal their origins, including their legitimate registrations.

The CIA went to great lengths in trying to conceal these transports' identities. In declassified documents the aircraft are referred to as "3708" and "3520", which would correspond to a pair of former USAAF C-47s with the serials 42-23708 and 42-23520 respectively. In both cases, the real planes had crashed between May 1944 and March 1945, and the third candidate, serial number 42-93708, was assigned to the Rhein-Main AFB in Frankfurt, Germany, at that time.

With the C-47s already secured and being readied at Andrews, King and his team set out to look for suitable aircrews. For this, CIA operatives assisted by the U.S. Ambassador to Honduras, Whiting Willauer, selected a group of twelve CAT pilots who didn't have "nefarious" pasts or hadn't been involved in previous covert operations in Latin America. Among them were Bill Welk, Harold Wells, and Doc Johnson, the three with well-established reputations amongst their peers in the CIA's *façade* airline. As these pilots couldn't be hired directly from CAT, they were asked to go on leave and then apply for the jobs offered by Castillo Armas' organization. By March 5, the CIA had conformed four aircrews of three men each, and was ready to fly them from Taiwan to the Hawaiian Islands.

Upon arriving to the islands, and in order to maintain secrecy, the men were split in pairs and ordered to board commercial flights to Miami where they had to get rooms in the Miami Beach area, and then call PBSuccess headquarters for obtaining the time and place of their first briefing and for further instructions.

Lt. Col. Brodfrost and two USAF advisors briefed the CAT pilots on Monday March 8. During the meeting, the crews were told about the nature of their mission, their aircraft, and the characteristics of the area where they would be operating. Then, one of the USAF officers went through a series of aerial reconnaissance photos and navigational maps of Central America, detailing air routes, alternate airfields, and no-fly zones. Before finishing, Brodfrost gave the pilots the "cover story" they had to memorize and tell in case they were asked about their activities while in the field.

On that same day, the aircrews boarded commercial flights bound to Havana, Cuba, where they met a representative of The Group who, on Castillo Armas' behalf, presented them with their contracts. Then, the pilots were checked in at the "Nacional" Hotel, where they were told to sit tight and wait for further orders. From then on, and with nothing better to do, the men set out to enjoy the beaches and nightlife of the Cuban Capital.

The next issue that Col. King had to tackle in order to establish the project's air support unit was recruiting load masters (also called "load kickers" in the CIA declassified documents) for loading and unloading the planes and perform the parachute drops of the cargo

This battered Douglas RB-18B, formerly operated by the infamous "Caribbean Legion", spent a considerable time at La Aurora Air Base and, despite its sorry state, at some point it was considered a threat for project PBSuccess and the neighboring countries that supported it. (Photo credit: Emil Tkachick via Dan Hagedorn.)

over enemy territory. Hiring and moving the CAT crews had been proved expensive, so using CAT kickers was out of the question. Instead, Col. King tried a different approach: A handful of USAF Airmen already assigned to France Field were offered the jobs and Brodfrost began training them shortly after.

During the third week of March, when Phase I was nearing its completion, the CIA Director ordered a thorough revision of the air support plan, with emphasis on phases II and III, since the presidents of Nicaragua and Honduras had mixed feelings about authorizing the "black flights" –as the resupplying missions were called- into their respective countries. Additionally, some U.S. presidential advisors and members of the NSC still had doubts about using the CAT aircrews for these flights, especially if they were to be conducted under combat conditions.

In an effort to calm everybody down, Dulles ordered Col. King to come up with an alternate plan in case the flights were not authorized by the Central American presidents; then, he gave Lt. Col. Brodfrost two days for establishing a sound contingency plan for emergencies, crashes, diversions to alternate airfields and even capture of the crews. He also wanted the Canal Zone's Air Defense and Air Traffic Control Service involved in the air support plan, as to make sure that the aircraft would depart and arrive safely from France Field.

By March 20, King had produced the alternate plan that Dulles wanted and that comprised the use of trucks and small ships for moving the arms and equipment from Nicaragua to the staging points in Honduras and El Salvador. Brodfrost also had come up with a contingency plan and had contacted the Canal Zone's Air Defense and Air Traffic Control Service to coordinate with them the complicated process for launching and recovering the flights safely and secretively. Only then, did Dulles give the green light for Phase II and Phase IIIA, which were to be conducted almost simultaneously.

Two days later the project's C-47s at Andrews were flown –by USAF crews- to France Field via West Palm Beach, Florida, arriving during the small hours on March 23. The same day the CAT crews at Havana were ordered to board a commercial flight bound to Albrook Air Force Base, in the Canal Zone. Once there, CIA operatives picked them up in pairs and, following devious routes, drove them to the city of Colón, in the Panamanian Caribbean Coast, where they were checked in at the "Washington" Hotel, conveniently located a couple of miles Northwest of France Field.

The CAT crews spent the next couple of days checking their aircraft and making sure that the sterilization conducted at Andrews hadn't left any traces of the planes' identities; Lt. Col. Brodfrost also ordered them to begin practicing cargo drops at night and takeoffs and landings on unprepared airstrips, using for that purpose the runway at the neighboring Fort Sherman.

The pilots were also introduced to the procedures for launching, conducting and recovering the black flights, following the complicated set of rules mandated by the air support plan. First, the two C-47s would be operating out of France Field without filing any flight plans and in almost complete radio silence. PBSuccess' Air Support Unit –by then codenamed "PBCABOOSE"- would initiate each flight by phoning the senior air traffic controller at the Canal Zone Air Traffic Control Center –ATC- in Albrook AFB, giving him details of the plane involved, the time of departure and the duration of the flight. Only when this exchange had taken place the plane was allowed to take off.

The crews were authorized to break radio silence and contact Albrook ATC only in case of an emergency. Incredibly, Albrook ATC wouldn't be allowed to launch a search and rescue party in the case they received a distress call. Instead, the senior air traffic controller was to notify PBSuccess' Air Operations Officer or Lt. Col. Brodfrost directly, who in turn would coordinate their recovery with the USAF's Air Rescue Service.

The other occasion when the crews were allowed to break radio silence was upon nearing the Canal Zone's airspace during their return leg. For this, the pilots would contact Albrook ATC and announce their intentions. Once Albrook had cleared the plane, it would be directed towards France Field for landing. In the event of being unable to contact the ATC, the crews were instructed to call any USAF facility in the area, so anyone there could alert Albrook about the incoming plane. This procedure was of utmost importance because if any crew failed to alert the ATC, it was more than likely that a couple of fighter jets would be scrambled as soon as the C-47 appeared on the ground radar screens.

PBSuccess' planes were to fly at the published minimum safe altitude along the Central American air routes, since Albrook ATC had reserved it specifically for them. That granted the crews a pre-assigned altitude if they needed to switch to IFR conditions, while minimizing the chances of mid-air collisions along the way.

For administrative and internal communication purposes, each C-47 was assigned a number and a radio call sign; accordingly, plane No.1 became "Fireball" and No.2 "Skyrocket." As for the flights, each one was assigned a four-digit number, with the first digit related to the plane's number and the last two to the day of the month on which the flight was to take place, e.g.: Flight "1005" involved plane No.1 and was scheduled for the fifth day of the month. In the case of plane No.2 the last two digits were reversed, that is, if the flight were going to take place on the fifth day of the month, the flight number would be "2050." If for some reason the flight was still en route by 12:01 AM, the last two digits were changed to reflect the new day.[5]

On March 24, the last flight of Phase I brought a load of hand grenades, Madsen sub-machineguns, and all the broadcasting equipment needed for setting up the clandestine radio station. Also on that day, the USAF officially placed France Field's facilities, equipment, and personnel under PBSuccess' control. Lt. Col. Brodfrost thus became the air base's commander, and from then on, the air base was re-designated as the project's "Regional Command Station."

Meanwhile, back at the training camps, Lt. Col. Pivall had managed to graduate 37 sabotage trainees and the first field officers of the Liberation Army. However, the harsh conditions in which these men had been training caused a riot that broke out on March 23, led by a young captain named Fernando Romero.[6] Pivall had to draw on all his commanding skills to quell the mutiny and calm down the troops. In the end, Romero was detained and taken to El Salvador's capital, San Salvador, where CIA operatives took him into custody for the remainder of the project.

By March 27, and to help ease the delicate situation at the troops' training site, Opa-locka headquarters obtained authorization from the Nicaraguan government to conduct a flight for resupplying them. Accordingly, one of the C-47s at France Field was loaded with tropical rations, ammunition, and medicines. Additionally, the broadcasting equipment for the clandestine radio station was also loaded into the plane. The C-47 landed first at Managua for unloading the radio station's equipment and then continued to Puerto Cabezas. As it would become customary, the flight was conducted at night, and great care was taken in coordinating the landings and takeoffs with the Nicaraguan Air Force.

Castillo Armas also played his part in order to boost his men's morale, as he arrived in the training sites the next day, after having convinced Somoza that the visit was critical. On a report submitted by Castillo Armas to The Group a couple of days later, he stated rather enthusiastically that he had found his men in high spirits and anxious about going into battle. Obviously, no one at PBSuccess headquarters bought it, and Pivall was ordered to finish the training program as soon as possible, close down the camps, and move to Honduras for preparing the invasion.

Up to that time the U.S. ambassadors to Honduras and El Salvador still were trying to get the authorization for the black flights to those countries[7], so the staging points could be defined and resupplied. On one hand, Honduran President Juan Manuel Galvez didn't want the CIA planes landing at Toncontin for security reasons. Instead, he was proposing that the planes landed at an isolated airfield located 57 km Northwest of Tegucigalpa[8], which was being used for training by the Honduran Air Force (Years later this airfield would become the Palmerola / Soto Cano Air Base.) He also offered unrestricted use of a short unpaved airstrip near the town of Las Flores, some 18 km Southwest of Santa Rosa de Copan, as an alternative.

On his part, the Salvadoran President Oscar Osorio still was hesitant about allowing any clandestine activity in his country. It took a great deal of maneuvering for Ambassador McDermott to convince him about allowing the use of the Ilopango Airport for bringing in the weapons and equipment. After days of negotiations, Osorio approved the flights, on the condition that there would be no more than two or three of them, and that they were to be conducted late at night, providing there wasn't any air traffic at the airport.

Even though President Somoza had already authorized the black flights into Nicaragua, he still had some reservations. His concerns were about the project's security and secrecy, as it was more than evident that neither the CIA nor Castillo Armas were handling them very well. In fact, during an informal meeting with Ambassador Whelan, Somoza told him that his intelligence agents in Guatemala had reported that one of Castillo Armas' operatives, named Carlos Lorenzana, had been detained at La Aurora Airport while carrying correspondence for the Caudillo. In the process, the Guatemalan authorities had seized important documents that detailed plans for smuggling arms into that country, the location of stockpiling sites, and the names of many members of Castillo Armas' internal organization.

Additionally, Somoza had got wind of a group of Nicaraguan exiles, funded, and supported by Arbenz, who were about to launch an air raid aimed at bombing his house and the presidential palace. For this, they had secured the use of a "bomber" that had been acquired by the Caribbean Legion five years earlier. This bombing mission was to be flown by an "U.S. pilot" who had arrived recently to Guatemala City.

Under those circumstances, Somoza was worried that the black flights into Nicaragua, if discovered, could give Arbenz an excellent excuse for encouraging the exiles to act against him.

The Agency rushed to determine if the information that Somoza had was accurate. In the end, the CIA station in Guatemala reported that indeed, a very battered Douglas RB-18B (ex Costa Rican registration TI-205) and a Lockheed Model 14, both registered to former President Juan Jose Arevalo, were kept at La Aurora Air Base, but there weren't any pilots qualified to fly them among the Air Force's crews. Besides, no U.S. pilot had been seen anywhere near La Aurora in months.

When Somoza was informed about this, he reluctantly allowed the black flights but restricted them to the nighttime, placing much emphasis in that they should be conducted in complete secrecy.

The first flight of Phase II took place on Saturday April 3, when one of Brodfrost's C-47 departed France Field for Puerto Cabezas carrying paramilitary equipment for the training camps and a load of RS-1 "Spy Radios" for the radio-operator trainees. The C-47 hadn't made it back to the Canal Zone when PBSuccess headquarters suspended the air support operations due to a rather serious reason: There had been a coup attempt against Somoza and the whole country was in chaos. It all had started when a group of civilians and a handful of former military had tried to assassinate the President. However, by sheer luck, he had changed his plans and instead of going to a ranch in the outskirts of Managua, had decided to stay in the Capital, avoiding an ambush that the rebels had set up on the Pan-American Highway. Even though the Nicaraguan National Guard managed to capture most of the rebels, there were groups of armed men causing trouble in nearby towns. It would take the government almost three weeks to pacify the country.

Images of Douglas C-47s operated by the CIA front airline "Civil Air Transport" are hard to come by. This one shows "B-811" at Saigon, French Indochina, sometime in 1950. (Photo credit: University of Texas – Dallas.)

Four days later, and with the air operation still suspended, Brodfrost requested an additional C-47 and its crew. The delay imposed by the situation in Nicaragua was narrowing the chances of getting the training camps resupplied on time, and to meet the project's schedule, the airlift capabilities would have to be augmented. Col. King also tried to convince the CIA Director about acquiring not one, but two C-47s and their crews for the same reason. In both cases, Dulles refused on the basis that increasing the number of planes would denote an U.S. involvement. Unabated, Brodfrost kept requesting the additional transports during the following two days, and he even went to Opa-locka to plead for them in person, but the answer was the same: No more planes would be allowed.[9]

On April 10, Frank Wisner was ordered to brief Henry Holland, the Assistant Secretary of State, about the project. During the meeting, Holland was informed about Delgado's information leakage in January and other security breaches that had plagued the project during the last couple of months. Shocked, Holland ordered a top-level review of the whole operation, which would include not only the Secretary of State but also the President himself. Meanwhile, PBSuccess and all its sub-projects were suspended.

The order to hold all activities was wired to PBSuccess' stations in Central America during the morning on that same day. In the case of Castillo Armas, The Group informed him that the flights for resupplying his troops would be delayed a couple of days "as a test for reaction." As expected, the news did not suit well with the Caudillo.

Although there is only fragmentary evidence in the CIA declassified papers, it seems that, by Castillo Armas' request, Brodfrost managed to arrange an unauthorized flight to Tegucigalpa, obviously with the help of Ambassador Willauer. Castillo Armas even convinced President Galvez about letting them use the Toncontin airport from then on, in order to hasten the preparations for the invasion.

This obscure episode[10] began on the same day that PBSuccess had been suspended, with a call that the Air Support Assistant Officer, Capt. Cowden, received at 1:00 PM from Brodfrost, ordering him to disregard Washington's directive prohibiting the planes from leaving France Field and to dispatch a C-47 loaded with 4000 lb. of sabotage equipment to Tegucigalpa. A bemused Cowden asked if the CIA Director or anyone at the Opa-locka headquarters had approved the flight, to what Brodfrost replied that Col. King had authorized it and that he would take full responsibility. 20 minutes later C-47 "Fireball" departed France Field.

Half an hour had passed since the plane's departure when Capt. Cowden received a call from Jake Esterline, the CIA's Task Force Chief, telling him that no aircraft was to leave the Canal Zone under any circumstances, and that those were orders from Col. King. Cowden, now really confused, informed Esterline that, following Brodfrost orders, he had just dispatched a C-47 to Honduras. Furious, the Task Force Chief told him to order the plane back at once.

Upon hanging up, Cowden contacted the Canal Zone's ATC and asked them to call "Fireball" and tell the pilot to return to France Field as soon as possible. However, the air traffic controller, despite trying different frequencies for more than an hour, wasn't able to contact the plane.

Even though Cowden had informed PBSuccess' operatives at Tegucigalpa about the C-47's imminent arrival, the flight caught everybody off guard,[11] as they were unable to implement all the required security measures at the airport.

The C-47 was being unloaded at the military side of the airport when Castillo Armas and his entourage arrived to supervise the process. Ambassador Willauer also arrived, mainly to evaluate if the project's secrecy had been compromised. To save face however, the Honduran Air Force's personnel had already spread the word that the plane was theirs and had been conducting "*a nocturnal training mission.*" An hour later, "Fireball" finally took off and headed back to Panama.

Brodfrost was severely reprimanded for having pulled off the stunt as well as Willauer, who was recalled to Washington for questioning. Nevertheless, this wouldn't be the last time that Brodfrost or Willauer had got in trouble for going beyond authorized operational procedures.

A couple of hours after the C-47's departure, Castillo Armas began lobbying The Group in order to get their approval for additional flights to Toncontin, since he needed to equip the first troops that were arriving to Honduras from training. Ambassador Willauer also recommended that two or three additional flights were allowed before the air operations were definitively suspended. In the end, Opa-locka authorized two more flights, both of them taking place on April 18.

On that day also, the top-level revision committee ordered the CIA headquarters to dispatch security officers to Opa-locka, France Field, Managua and the rest of the Agency's stations involved in PBSuccess, for auditing their security measures. What they found would blow everybody's mind in Washington.

CHAPTER 5

A MAJOR "FLAP"

By the third week of April, the auditing of the overall security measures implemented in all PBSuccess' facilities was in full swing, and the initial findings were horrifying. Microphones, seemingly of Soviet manufacture, had been discovered at the residence of Ambassador Willauer in Tegucigalpa and at the U.S. embassies in Managua and Guatemala City. It was never determined who planted them, but their existence was a good indication of the carelessness with which the project was being conducted so far.

In the same week, more security issues continued to pour in: PBSuccess' operatives in Managua reported that a Nicaraguan immigration officer, who had assisted them to coordinate the black flights into the country, had sought asylum in the Guatemalan embassy, taking with him invaluable details about the project. The CIA station in Guatemala also reported that on April 17, Jorge Isaac Delgado had arrived in Guatemala City for a meeting with Arbenz's officials, during which additional details about Castillo Armas' plot were revealed.

The internal security of the project had been compromised also, since in two separate occasions CIA's classified correspondence had been handed over by mistake to Castillo Armas, effectively breaking the project's compartmentalization, and giving the Caudillo a good indication that the Agency was funding and equipping his organization. In another occasion, a PBSuccess operative forgot a pouch, containing sensitive information related to the troops' training program, at his hotel room in Managua; it took two full days for Lt. Col. Pivall's aides to retrieve it and now PBSuccess' operatives were trying to determine if the documents had been exposed. Something similar happened to a box full of audio tapes, containing pre-recorded radio programs that were to be broadcasted across Guatemala, which went missing for a couple of days at France Field while waiting to be flown to Nicaragua.

The security issues were deemed so serious that in a report to the CIA Director, Jake Esterline stated, "The Guatemalan Government is well into the details of PBSUCCESS and they have decided to let the operation proceed undisturbed until they have prepared and documented a brief for presentation to the OAS."[1]

However, the CIA's security officers didn't stop after discovering the many internal failures. They soon went after Castillo Armas' organization, and as it would be expected, they were in for a treat. Posing as security experts hired by The Group, they initiated background checks of top and mid-level members of the Liberation Army, spotting rather quickly a handful of informants and double agents infiltrated by the Guatemalan government. Not satisfied with the background checks, they brought in a polygraph team to examine not only the top members of the Liberation Army, but the Caudillo himself. Obviously, the polygraph tests were taken badly by Castillo Armas and his officers, and the situation soon developed into a serious problem since the Caudillo refused to sever ties with those who had failed the tests or were involved in suspicious activities. It took a great deal of maneuvering and a couple of trips to Honduras on the part of Tracy Barnes, to convince him to let go of those who were deemed a risk.

Back in Washington D.C. the top-level review committee also found out that, organizationally, PBSuccess was a mess. The main problem that surfaced was with the paramilitary program, as it became evident that the few trainees supplied by Castillo Armas did not have the required qualifications for being field officers. In fact, upon a thorough inspection by Rip Robertson, the project's Field Commander, he had come to the conclusion that the few recruits at the training sites were "tenth-grade" and in a report submitted to the CIA Director he went as far as to state, rather sarcastically, that in the U.S. Army, Castillo Armas wouldn't have made it past sergeant. To make things worse, the troops' numbers didn't add up: So far, Lt. Col. Pivall had graduated only 37 sabotage leaders, 6 shock troop officers, 16 organizers, 4 staff personnel and had rejected 19 recruits as they had been found incompetent. In total, only 63 men had received combat training at Puerto Cabezas.

Up to then, the project's planners had based the paramilitary program, and the invasion plan for that matter, on the belief that the Liberation Army had between 260 and 300 men for use as "shock troops" and specialists, apart from the 63 that had been training in Puerto Cabezas. They were also considering the existence of a "fifth column" comprised of resistance groups that, if required, could attack and seize their assigned targets without any external help. However, the harsh reality was that no one in the project had been able to determine for real how many men Castillo Armas had. Since the signing of the agreement with the Caudillo in January, both PBSuccess headquarters and the Field Command Post, had tried repeatedly to obtain an accurate report about his force's composition and strength, but he always turned evasive or gave only a very rough estimate that varied from one questioning to the other.[2]

When the committee's attention focused on the tactical radio-operators' training program, a similar grim situation emerged. The two PBSuccess' officers in charge were having a very rough time trying to graduate the only 13 trainees that Castillo Armas had supplied. The main problem was that the majority of these men couldn't read or write well, much less operate the intricate RS-1 radios that they would have to carry into combat. Additionally, it was expected that the men would learn to encrypt and decrypt messages, read maps and above all, communicate clearly. It was for this reason that the invasion's D-Day had been pushed back twice in the last couple of weeks, and at that time, PBSuccess headquarters was considering pushing it back a third time.

Intelligence collection was also found lacking. The operatives assigned to the CIA station in Guatemala had been unable to rebuild the net of contacts after the last wave of arrests launched by the government, and so far, they were working with only two informants that Castillo Armas had provided. Another aspect of their mission, which was to encourage defections of top-officials among the Army

The infamous Oerlikon anti-aircraft 20 mm cannons of the Guatemalan Army, seen here emplaced at the North end of La Aurora Airport, in Guatemala City, during training exercises carried out in March 1954. (Photo credit: Guatemalan Air Force.)

and the government, had also failed miserably. The performance of the CIA station in Guatemala was deemed so unacceptable that its chief was promptly replaced while the two informants, referenced in CIA papers as ESODIC and ESODIC-1, were taken clandestinely to Honduras for a polygraph test and a thorough evaluation.

The organizational mess had also reached the CIA headquarters itself. Frictions between Frank Wisner and Col. King had escalated into a "civil war" that threatened to endanger not only PBSuccess but also other covert operations that the agency was conducting at the time.

There were rumors that Col. King was closely allied with the United Fruit Company, and Wisner believed that, given the chance, he could steer the project to meet the UFCO's agenda. The situation almost got out of hand when Thomas Gardiner Corcoran, the UFCO's chief lobbyist, appeared unannounced at PBSuccess headquarters, demanding to see Albert Haney and be briefed about the status of the project. Wisner, not losing any time, accused King of having revealed the base's secret location.

In retaliation, the Colonel began criticizing every decision made by the PBSuccess' Project Manager, and accused him of trying to start "*another Korean war*" by taking excessive risks. In fact, for King, the many security failures that the reviewing committee had uncovered were all Haney's fault.

The war was put to rest when the CIA Director, who right from the start had sided with Wisner, sent to Opa-locka his special assistant, Richard Bissell, to calm things down. Wisner also sent Tracy Barnes but with the mission of keeping Col. King out the way at any cost.

Inevitably, PBSuccess was now facing a growing opposition from the State Department and the NSC, especially after learning about the committee's findings. Henry Holland went as far as to declare, "The project as presently conceived is a dishonorable way of accomplishing our aims and objectives in Guatemala." For him, the many security failures and the clumsiness with which the operation had been conducted so far had clearly "identified the project with the official United States Government."[3]

Even Frank Wisner, the Agency's saint patron of all lost causes, was seriously considering ditching the project and move on towards less complicated scenarios elsewhere in the third world for fighting the Cold War. Allen Dulles shared Wisner's feelings, and with the meeting for deciding the future of PBSuccess scheduled for April 20, he began considering –once again- alternate ways for getting rid of the Communists in Guatemala.

Then, all of a sudden, the tide began to turn. During a conversation between the Salvadoran President and Ambassador McDermontt, the former confided that a large shipment of arms was on its way to Guatemala, and that he was worried about Arbenz's intentions. Days later, the CIA stations in Europe confirmed what President Osorio had said and they even had zeroed in on a ship that could be the one transporting those arms: The M.S. *Wulfsbrook*. Immediately, PBSuccess headquarters went into "crisis mode" and assigned a dedicated team for tracking that ship and two additional ones, the M.S. *Haarlem* and the M.S. *Werratal*, both headed also for the Caribbean. Back at Washington, CIA intelligence operatives began reviewing and analyzing reports generated during the last couple of months, looking for additional clues about the surprising arms purchase. The story that began emerging was, to say the least, intriguing.

In January 1954, CIA stations in Europe had reported very unusual activities of Arbenz's minister without portfolio and leading Communist in the cabinet, Jose Manuel Fortuny. He had toured Czechoslovakia, the Soviet Union, and other countries behind the "Iron Curtain" for at least fifteen days. The CIA operatives hadn't been able to determine the objective of Fortuny's trip, and the reports were soon shelved.

A couple of days after Fortuny's return to Guatemala, the CIA station there reported that President Arbenz and the Chief of the National Agrarian Department, Major Alfonso Martínez Estevez, had a heated argument during dinner at the Pan American Hotel's restaurant. Less than 48 hours later, it transpired that Martínez Estevez had left the country. The Guatemalan government in a short press release published on January 23 confirmed this situation.

Coincidentally, six day later, on January 29, the Czech Ambassador presented his credentials to the Guatemalan government, establishing formal diplomatic relations between the two countries. The same day, it was reported that Major Martinez Estevez had reappeared in Prague and was sustaining meetings with Czech government officials.

During the first week of March, CIA operatives monitoring the Guatemalan government's bank accounts in New York and New Orleans noticed that an unusual and complicated financial transaction, which comprised US$4,467,000, was in progress. The funds were being transferred, by means of several separate steps, to the account that the Czechoslovakian National Bank had with the *Banque de Suisse* in Switzerland. Then, on March 29, the Czech government withdrew that same amount of money by cashing two checks, thus, completing the transaction.

Once the CIA analysts were able to put together all this information, it became easy for them to connect the dots: Fortuny, during his trip to Eastern Europe and the Soviet Union, had made the necessary contacts. Then, Major Martinez Estevez had simulated having an argument with Arbenz in order to have an excuse for leaving the country, supposedly for exile. Once in Prague, he inspected the weapons and arranged their shipment to Guatemala.

The disturbing part was that the amount of money spent on this single arms purchase exceeded the Guatemalan defense budget of the two previous years, and the CIA hadn't the slightest idea what type of armament had been acquired.

Educated guesses suggested that Arbenz had purchased infantry weapons and related equipment, as well ammunition for the Army's 20mm *Oerlikon* anti-aircraft cannons that had been acquired a couple of years earlier. However, some analysts suspected that the acquisition included fighter aircraft as well as tanks and heavy artillery.

PBSuccess' analysts then reviewed the arms purchase history of the Guatemalan government to determine what armament the Army already had, and what could be the current requirements; this would give them a rough estimate of the type and quantity of weapons and ammunition acquired in Czechoslovakia.

Guatemala's arms purchase history was, to say the least, complicated. Due to an U.S. arms embargo, imposed since 1949, the government had turned to Colonel Hubert Fauntleroy Julian, the infamous "Black Eagle of Harlem", for obtaining arms and equipment for the Army. In fact, Col. Julian had been designated Guatemala's "official arms procurer."[4] This advantageous position allowed him to pull off incredible frauds on three separate occasions in which he supplied the Army with obsolete weapons, equipment, and military vehicles at exorbitant prices. A good example were the 20mm Oerlikon cannons mentioned earlier, as Julian had to supply a large amount of live ammunition with them. Instead, the crooked Colonel delivered crate upon crate of only practice rounds. In the end, he was dismissed for boasting publicly about his profits from the Guatemalan sales, something that had made Arbenz furious.

In any case, the analysts weren't able to determine what type of armament comprised the shipment. The only thing they knew for sure was that the recent purchase was a complete departure of what have been the military acquisitions of the last five years.

When the *dossier* about the Guatemalan arms purchase that the analysts had prepared landed on Frank Wisner's desk, he came up with the idea of blowing it out of proportion in order to justify the need of resuming Project PBSuccess. The CIA Director had a similar idea, but on a greater scale: It could be presented internationally as evidence of an imminent military strengthening in Guatemala, which could end with the expansion of Communism in the region.

The top-level review committee's final meeting on April 20 was presided over by the Undersecretary of State, General Walter Bedell Smith. The CIA Director and Frank Wisner arrived carrying a "position paper"[5] that contained a thorough break-down of the objectives reached so far by the project in terms of intelligence, paramilitary, logistical and psychological warfare, and a very general report on the situation of Castillo Armas' organization, which didn't mention a thing about his force's strength and composition.

Wisner brought also the dossier about the Guatemalan arms purchase[6], now adorned with several hypothetical scenarios that included an imminent re-equipment of the Guatemalan Army or even the creation of militias, which could pose a serious threat for the Central American region. To back up Wisner's statements, the CIA Director presented a report, prepared by the Board of National Estimates, which concluded more or less the same as the arms purchase dossier: The situation in Guatemala could transcend borders, spilling Communism not only in Central America but also in the Caribbean.

After the initial round of negotiations, General Smith had acknowledged that getting rid of the Guatemalan Communists was necessary. However, the Department of State wanted the paramilitary program terminated, since it was considered the source of all the problems that had plagued the project so far. Instead, their bets were placed in having a well-orchestrated propaganda campaign coupled with diplomatic pressure, for forcing the Guatemalan Army to revolt.

In the end, Wisner was able to convince General Smith about not terminating the paramilitary program, because without it, they wouldn't be able to exert any control upon the new Guatemalan government once Arbenz had been toppled. If someone besides Castillo Armas or any other individual outside the CIA's control took power, Guatemala could soon resume the path to Communism. This scenario would put under great risk the relationships with the neighboring countries, as they were expecting the U.S. to make sure that the Guatemalan Communists would not seek revenge against those nations who were supporting Castillo Armas.

Even though PBSuccess was allowed to continue, it did not reemerge unscathed. The top-level committee wanted the security aspects of the project revised, improved, and increased. In addition, Wisner was ordered to implement "new ways and means of improving cover and deception" for the project in order to maintain what was left of any plausible deniability.

The paramilitary program, although not terminated, was scaled down and its objectives changed. The committee ditched the full-fledged invasion and ordered Wisner to come up with a new plan limited to a short incursion followed by a series of hit and run operations for wearing down the Guatemalan Army, simulating the presence of a major invading force. The idea behind this was to create

Colonel Hubert Fauntleroy Julian, the "Black Eagle of Harlem", was Guatemala's "official arms procurer" during the Arbenz regime. (Photo credit: Wide World Photos.)

the appropriate environment for a long-term armed resistance activity that would build pressure up against Arbenz's regime and, through cumulative effect, force the Guatemalan Army to depose him. Castillo Armas however, was to be kept as the front man, since it was expected that he would negotiate his way towards the presidency with the Guatemalan Army.

Regarding the propaganda and psychological warfare programs, the committee had it its way: Wisner was ordered to improve their effectiveness and increase their coverage, placing emphasis on the clandestine radio station that should have to be ready no later than May 1st.

On its part, the air support unit would have to begin leaflet-dropping flights by the second week of June, whether Phases II and IIIA had been completed o not, as it was necessary to show the Guatemalan population and the Army that an active opposition against Arbenz existed and was willing to act in the short term. Finally, yet importantly, the production of printed media was ditched as it had been considered ineffective and too difficult to maintain. By the end of the meeting, Gen. Smith ordered Wisner to submit daily reports about the project's progress, not only to him, but also to the Head of Middle American Affairs' Office, Raymond Leddy.

The resumption of PBSuccess operations was notified to all stations on April 28. In a cable, sent by Wisner that day, it was stated that the project now had the "full green light" from the CIA Director and the Department of State. All PBSuccess' sub-programs were now authorized to continue, and he warned his men that there could be "operational considerations" requiring the project to "shift forward from the current phase", and that they should be able to introduce certain degree of flexibility in their respective approaches towards reaching their particular objectives. Curiously, no mention was made about the need of improving the security measures.

Back at France Field, Lt. Col. Brodfrost received the news with mixed feelings. After almost two weeks of inactivity, he was sure that his crews wouldn't be able to fly all the arms and equipment required for the paramilitary program on time, whether it had been scaled down or not. The interesting part was that PBSuccess headquarters, citing the "flexibility" bit mentioned in Wisner's cable, was pressuring him to step up his efforts. Brodfrost's immediate reaction was to renew his pleas for obtaining a third C-47 and an additional crew, but once again, a very annoyed Dulles turned him down.

Still stored at France Field's hangars, there were 89 tons of arms equipment and supplies. This cargo had been arranged into three types of bundles: 43 tons had been packed into waterproof containers that were going to be smuggled into Guatemala and then cached near the objectives that the Liberation Army troops intended to attack. These supplies were needed to arm and equip the several internal groups that Castillo Armas allegedly had within the country, and for resupplying the invading troops. Fifteen tons of ammunition, hand-grenades, and tropical rations had been packed into parachute-rigged bundles, which were to be air dropped over the battlefield once the invasion had started. The remaining 31 tons of basic infantry and field communications kits for the shock troops had been packed into regular bundles and would be taken to Honduras for distribution to the troops.

According to the project's general plan, the priority was now to fly the waterproofed bundles and the 31 tons of equipment destined for the shock troops; this had been arranged in that way because the invasion's staging points were about to be defined and Castillo Armas was planning to start smuggling arms and equipment across the border within days. It also meant that Phase IIIA of the air support plan had to be initiated.

The black flights resumed the same day that the project was green-lighted. During the morning, and shortly after having received Wisner's cable, Brodfrost was ordered to send a C-47 loaded with 5000 lb. of communication equipment and assorted supplies for the Field Command Post in Managua. During the afternoon, both C-47s were dispatched to Tegucigalpa carrying 5100 lb. of cargo each.

As it has been mentioned, the flights to Honduras and Nicaragua had to be conducted at the minimum published altitude; this meant that the planes had to fly low and slow, and be subjected to turbulence and inclement weather along the route. It posed no problem during most of the flight, since the crews were ordered to fly over the sea as long as possible in order to conceal their aircraft's presence. However, when nearing their destination, whether it was Managua, Tegucigalpa or any other airfield in Honduras, the crews had to fly over terrain while maintaining the same altitude. Thus, the pilots had to switch to "contact flying" while detouring around the many obstacles scattered along the approach route. Under normal circumstances, a flight to

A PBSuccess C-47 takes off from the Nueva Ocotepeque airfield after having delivered ammo and supplies to the Liberation staging point nearby, as part of Phase IIIA of the Air Support Plan. (Photo credit: *Life* Magazine.)

Honduras would take from 90 minutes to two hours to reach its intended destination, but under the air support plan's restrictions, it became a nightmarish odyssey of four hours. A round trip between France Field and Tegucigalpa, for example, would take seven to eight hours, plus an hour that the plane had to spend on the ground being unloaded and refueled.

To further complicate this scenario, the Honduran authorities had allowed the black flights into their country only during the nighttime[7], even when its airfields, including Tegucigalpa's airport, Toncontin, were not suitable for nocturnal operations. This forced PBSuccess' operatives to improvise a lighting system by means of torches placed at the edges of the runways and car headlights at both ends. Last but not least, Toncontin was -and still is- considered one of the most dangerous airports to land in the world, due to the many mountains and hills along its final approach corridors and for its short runway. That the CAT crews were able to land there at night surely is a testimony of their professionalism, or their disdain for common wisdom!

Under those restrictions, Brodfrost was able to launch only two flights to Honduras on a daily basis, much to the chagrin of the project planners who wanted the frequency increased to four or five a day. In contrast, flying to Nicaragua was a more relaxed experience, since President Somoza, after the coup attempt of April 3, had lifted all restrictions for the black flights. Now the crews were authorized to land at Las Mercedes and at Puerto Cabezas day or night, but as the air support plan's Phase II neared its completion, these flights were spread far in-between.

Regarding the cargo loads flown to Tegucigalpa and other points in Honduras, most of the infantry kits destined for the shock troops were being stored at the Liberation Army's headquarters and at several safe houses that Castillo Armas had established throughout the country. The waterproofed bundles in contrast, were being trucked across the border to a couple of ranches located in the Southeastern region of Guatemala, where they were picked up by aircraft belonging to a seldom-documented clandestine cell, called "Special Group A"[8] in the CIA declassified documents. This group was composed of a handful of businessmen and landowners who had volunteered their planes, mostly small Cessnas, for supporting Castillo Armas' organization.

Flying out of unpaved airstrips scattered around the many ranches and towns in Puerto Barrios, Zacapa and Chiquimula, these pilots not only carried the waterproofed bundles to the stockpiling sites within Guatemala, but also conducted missions for infiltrating and exfiltrating Castillo Armas' operatives, and performed low-level reconnaissance flights over military facilities. Surprisingly, all these missions were being flown virtually unchallenged, since the Guatemalan government did not have any radars and the Air Force launched patrol flights only occasionally.

The Commanding Officer of this small air component was Doctor Carlos Sosa Barillas, a wealthy private pilot and former Health Minister who had escaped Guatemala for joining Castillo Armas shortly after the failed Salamá uprising of 1953.

The second and third in the group's command were Manfredo Lippman and Escolastico Ortega Peña, both renowned and wealthy landowners who lived in Guatemala City and usually operated out of La Aurora airport. Other members of the group were Enrique Arimany, Jose Maria Valdez, Héctor Pivaral, Alfredo Delgado, Pedro Ciani, Ricardo Novales, Roger Altenbach, Salvador Oliva, and Carlos Lima. Additionally two Americans who lived in Guatemala City had also volunteered: One was the former Deputy Chief of the U.S. Air Mission in Guatemala, Major (R) Ferdinand Schoup, and the other was Jerry Fred Delarm, the owner of a car dealership and a small air service, but also an intelligence operative working for President Somoza in Guatemala.

As part of air support plan's Phase IIIA, Lt. Col. Brodfrost had considered sending at least a daily flight to the Salvadoran capital in order to resupply one of Castillo Armas' columns that was based there. When he notified Opa-locka about his intentions, however, PBSuccess headquarters ordered him to hold the flights to El Salvador, because President Osorio had backpedalled from authorizing them, fearing that the C-47s' presence could draw unwanted attention. Instead, all the arms and supplies for these troops should be taken to Nueva Ocotepeque, in Honduras, where Castillo Armas' trucks would pick them up and carry them to their final destination in San Salvador. In the meantime, the flights to Honduras had top priority.

By then, Lt. Col. Pivall had managed to finish the troops' training and had moved to Tegucigalpa, where he began assisting Castillo Armas in modifying the invasion plan so it could meet the new directives. In order to do this, he needed to know the exact composition of the Liberation Army, but once again, the old problem of Castillo Armas' evasiveness surfaced.

After a couple of days, Pivall decided to personally visit the camps where Castillo Armas' troops were awaiting orders, and it was then when he finally realized why the Caudillo had been evasive about his order of battle all this time: His main force was comprised of only 165 men.[9] Pivall also determined that the fearsome "fifth column" that Castillo Armas claimed to have within Guatemala was much smaller, as only 100 individuals had been recruited so far; by then his operatives were desperately scouting the country for more candidates.

When PBSuccess headquarters got wind of this, Al Haney ordered Pivall to recruit as many Nicaraguans, Hondurans, Costa Ricans as he could[10], including "*any other interested parties*" who would want to join the Liberation Army. In addition, fifty saboteurs and agitators, who had been training in Honduras and were ready to be infiltrated into Guatemala, were incorporated into the main force.

With the passing of days, Pivall became increasingly invested into delineating a sound invasion plan, now under the premise of only harassing the Army garrisons in the Southeastern region of Guatemala. Accordingly, the targets were reduced from the original seven to only four, these being Puerto Barrios, Jutiapa, Zacapa, and Chiquimula. The small village of Esquipulas located near the border with Honduras, and with no significant Guatemalan military presence, was to be the only target that the Castillo Armas' forces would be occupying, since their Advanced Command Post would be established there.

The other problem that Pivall had to tackle while coming up with the new plan was to change the mentality of Castillo Armas and his officers. Since the beginning, their idea was to act like an occupation force once they were in Guatemala; now Pivall wanted them to embrace and apply the concepts and tactics of guerrilla warfare in order to wear down the Guatemalan Army and, above all, avoid being decimated.

Additionally, if by sheer luck the Liberation Army troops ended in a winning position after a clash, under no circumstances were to demand an unconditional surrender from the Guatemalan Army officers. Instead, they would invite them to join the Liberation Army and together demand Arbenz's resignation.

Switching to guerrilla tactics was taken badly, not only by the Caudillo but also by his officers. All of them had graduated from the Escuela Politécnica where the virtues of conventional warfare were considered paramount and had been ingrained in their minds. They simply couldn't process the idea of acting like bandits, hitting their targets first and then running away. In the end, they agreed to it, but somehow, Pivall knew that out in the battlefield and without any supervision, these people would put up the fight in a conventional manner, even though they didn't have enough troops. The winning hand, Pivall reasoned, would have to be supplied by another PBSuccess sub-project, perhaps the propaganda, or the psychological warfare programs. Or could it be some form of air power?

CHAPTER 6

WSBURNT

During the last week of April, Project PBSuccess saw a considerable increase in its activities. Lt. Col. Pivall had finished the tactical plan and Castillo Armas had agreed on it, thus allowing the Field Command Post to establish the five staging points from where the invasion would launch. Four of these were located in Honduras, no less than 20-30 kilometers from the border with Guatemala, near the towns of Macuelizo, Los Tarros, Copán Ruinas and Nueva Ocotepeque, while the fifth was at the town of Santa Ana, in El Salvador, close to the Guatemalan border also. By then PBSuccess headquarters was already considering June 15 as the invasion's D-Day, but it would depend on how fast the troops could be assembled and resupplied at the staging points with the remainder of the arms and equipment still stored at France Field.

As soon as the camps were activated and properly secured, trucks loaded with troops and weapons began arriving from Tegucigalpa and elsewhere in Honduras. However, the task of transporting them soon turned into a nightmare because the battered vehicles provided by Castillo Armas couldn't cope with the terrible conditions of the Honduran roads. The situation worsened when the first rainstorms of the "rainy season", which went from May to November, made those roads virtually impassable.

When the project's Field Command Post realized that the weather and the condition of the roads would compromise the plan's schedule, Rip Robertson decided to call in Brodfrost and his pilots for transporting the troops and resupplying the staging points directly by air. It meant that Phase IIIB of the air support plan had to be initiated. As expected, the Chief of Air Support was livid; Phase IIIA hadn't been completed yet and his pilots still were flying around the clock, conducting daily cargo runs to Tegucigalpa and Managua. It would be virtually impossible for them to resupply the staging points with the aircraft at hand.

As it had happened in other occasions, Brodfrost flew all the way up to Opa-locka to request personally at least an additional C-47. This time surprisingly, instead of turning him down, both Frank Wisner and Al Haney promised trying to obtain the approval from Dulles as soon as possible. In the meantime, however, he would have to initiate

Maj. Víctor Manuel Figueroa, an exceptional Guatemalan aviator, conducted several covert missions into Honduras on behalf of the Arbenz regime before the invasion. (Photo credit: Guatemalan Air Force.)

A pair of North American AT-6s and a solitary Beechcraft AT-11 of the Guatemalan Air Force, being readied for patrol missions at La Aurora Air Base. (Photo credit: Guatemalan Air Force.)

Phase IIIB.

The first flight to one of the staging points took place during the late hours of April 28. One of Brodfrost's C-47s, carrying a load of food, machineguns, ammunition and sabotage equipment, departed France Field for an unpaved airstrip near Copán Ruinas. Later, the second C-47 landed at a ranch near Nueva Ocotepeque, where the load would be picked up by a handful of Castillo Armas' trucks and then taken across the border to the staging point in Santa Ana, in El Salvador.

In the following days, the constant coming and going of the aircraft, the considerable traffic of trucks and the heavily armed men guarding the staging points, made it practically impossible to conceal their existence.[1] It took little effort for Guatemalan intelligence agents to discover that something "really big" was brewing along the Honduras-Guatemala border, much to the dismay of the Honduran Police and Castillo Armas' operatives who did their best in trying to detain the spies wandering around the staging points.

President Arbenz soon got wind of what was happening and decided to stop Castillo Armas immediately. His plan was to force the Honduran government to cut-off its support to the Liberation Army by causing a severe destabilization in that country and then kidnap or even assassinate the Caudillo.[2]

Left-leaning historians who usually tend to paint Arbenz as the helpless victim of a CIA-led conspiracy have seldom documented the aggressive measures that the Guatemalan President implemented against Castillo Armas and the Honduran government.[3] As it couldn't have been otherwise, Arbenz enlisted labor union workers and members of the PGT for infiltrating the UFCO's banana plantations

The entire "Bomber Squadron" of the Guatemalan Air Force seen here at La Aurora Air Base's northern apron in May 1954. (Photo credit: Guatemalan Air Force.)

Despite its obsolescence, the Boeing P-26A "Peashooter" was considered by the Guatemalan Air Force as a "front-line fighter." The two surviving aircraft in the FAG's inventory flew several missions before and during the invasion. (Photo credit: Guatemalan Air Force.)

By May 1954, the Guatemalan Air Force had only two C-47s in its Transport Squadron, besides a single Beechcraft C-45. In this photo, both airplanes can be seen at the La Aurora Air Base's Northern sector. (Photo credit: Guatemalan Air Force.)

Seldom photographed, the Guatemalan Air Force's Cessna JRC-1 (UC-78) "Bobcat" was assigned to the Agriculture Ministry during the Arbenz administration. (Photo credit: Peter C. Boisseau via Gary Kuhn.)

By May 1954, the Guatemalan Air Force had in its inventory at least two Vultee BT-15s, and both were assigned to the Escuela Militar de Aviación (Military Aviation School.) This photo, taken in 1946, shows one of the planes still bearing the "old" two-digit serial. (Photo credit: Peter C. Boisseau via Gary Kuhn.)

The Guatemalan Air Force's Escuela Militar de Aviación (Military Aviation School) was established at the Los Cipresales Air Base. In this photo, taken in December 1953, the three surviving Ryan STMs and the recently acquired Fairchild PT-19A can bee seen. (Photo credit: Guatemalan Air Force.)

across Honduras and induce a general strike. Then, agitators were sent to Tegucigalpa and San Pedro Sula where they organized riots that effectively paralyzed the country and forced the government to send the Police to quell them.

By the last day of April, the situation was so serious that PBSuccess headquarters advised Castillo Armas and his staff to be ready to depart the country at the first sign of events getting out of hand. Additionally, Lt. Col. Brodfrost was ordered to prepare an emergency plan[4] for airlifting the Liberation Army out of Honduras, just in case President Gálvez was ousted.

Trying to counterbalance Arbenz's aggressiveness, but also as part of the propaganda campaign to be initiated prior to the invasion, PBSuccess headquarters launched the clandestine radio station, now christened "Radio Liberación" (Liberation Radio), with the mission of taking over Guatemala City, albeit not militarily, but by psychological means.

It may never be clear how many Guatemalans listened to Radio Liberación's first broadcasting on May 1st, as it occurred on a Saturday, but those who tuned in were treated with the Guatemalan National Anthem followed by this statement: "Guatemala! Dear country! Guatemalan Brothers! We have begun the work of this clandestine radio!" Then the male announcer continued: "Radio Liberación, broadcasting from a secret place within the Republic, will be on the air twice a day, from 7:00 to 8:00 AM and from 21:00 to 22:00 during the first weeks. Later, and when technical circumstances permit, we will increase our broadcasting hours."[5]

From then on, the broadcastings consisted mainly of "segments" during which the announcers openly attacked Arbenz and ridiculed

The crew of a Guatemalan Air Force North American AT-6D posing in front of their mount during a deployment at the Puerto de San José Air Base, on the Pacific Coast, in May 1954. (Photo credit: Guatemalan Air Force.)

A Guatemalan Air Force North American AT-6 during a low-level reconnaissance flight near the Salvadoran border in May 1954. (Photo credit: Guatemalan Air Force.)

government officials through jokes or exaggerated news. The many ties that the government allegedly had with international Communism were continually exposed and false or real acts of corruption were pointed out. All of this was accompanied by popular music and "field reports" about the "fearsome Liberation Army" that was preparing for the upcoming invasion.

Radio Liberación targeted every sector of the Guatemalan society by airing especially designed segments at women, workers, intellectuals, businessmen, and landowners. However, great emphasis was placed on the Guatemalan Army officers, as the announcers recited repeatedly a "Military Decalogue", a statement of military values aimed to persuade them to take action against the Communists. To top it up, the announcers also stressed constantly that Arbenz was building up and arming a militia to take over the country, something that, over time, ceased to be an exaggeration and almost became a reality.

Inevitably, with each broadcasting the audience began to grow. People gathered at homes of friends and relatives to listen and discuss every segment aired by the enthusiastic Radio Liberación. The real possibility of an invasion began to take shape in the collective mind, and there was no other subject the Guatemalans talked about.

The audience grew even more when the Government's radio station, TGW, went off the air for a couple of weeks due to a fortuitous malfunction. Radio Liberación quickly seized the opportunity and began broadcasting using TGW's own frequency. David Atlee Phillips, the mastermind behind Radio Liberación, couldn't believe his luck. Within days, it seemed that everybody in the country was listening.

The operation of the clandestine radio posed a logistical problem however, since all the broadcastings were made from audiotapes produced at Opa-locka, while the transmitter was located near the

Colonel Luis Antonio Girón Cartagena, the Guatemalan Air Force's Commander during the difficult period of the invasion. (Photo credit: Guatemalan Air Force.)

Guatemalan border in Nueva Ocotepeque, Honduras.[6] These tapes had to follow a rather long journey before being aired; first an U.S. Marines' B-25 bomber, assigned to PBSuccess for courier duties, flew them on a daily basis to France Field; there, they were dispatched to Nueva Ocotepeque in one of Brodfrost's C-47s, whether it was in a regular cargo run or in a flight launched specifically to carry them.[7] In Nueva Ocotepeque, Castillo Armas' operatives received the tapes and delivered them by car to site where the radio transmitter was installed.

The original plan had been to set up the Radio Liberación's transmitter at Managua, but it simply did not have the broadcasting power to reach Guatemala City, and during the initial tests, PBSuccess' operatives had confirmed that most of the time, the station was barely audible. Then, Phillips proposed to set the transmitter on a barge anchored near the Guatemalan Caribbean Coast, but PBSuccess headquarters deemed it to risky and complicated.

Obviously, the flights for taking the tapes to Nueva Ocotepeque came to embroil even more the juggling act that Brodfrost and his pilots were carrying out. Sometimes, a completely empty C-47 had to be dispatched for delivering the next day's broadcasting, while the other had to be overloaded in order to comply with the airlift schedule. The "damn tapes" had to be flown to their destination despite bad weather or any other adverse condition. And to make things worse, the CIA Director was taking his time for analyzing the possibility of acquiring a third transport for the project.

Meanwhile, in Guatemala City, it didn't take too long for the government's reaction to materialize. The *Policía Judicial* (Judiciary Police) and the *Guardia Civil* (Civil Guard) set to look for the clandestine radio station in houses, buildings and even catholic churches, effectively starting a very obscure and nefarious period of the Arbenz' administration during which hundreds of Guatemalans were tortured or assassinated. By May 3, the search had moved to the banana plantations, towns and villages down the Motagua Basin, a region bordering with Honduras, as it was suspected that the transmitter was hidden somewhere in that area. Two days later, Guardia Civil troops began arriving to the towns of Zacapa, Chiquimula, and Puerto Barrios, for conducting searches in those towns and in the neighboring villages and plantations. On May 7, the government finally realized that the transmitter wasn't located in the country, and the search efforts were discontinued.

Frustrated by the lack of results, Arbenz ordered the conformation of a special group of Policía Judicial agents who would infiltrate into Honduras with the mission of kidnapping or assassinating Castillo Armas and the rest of the Liberation Army leadership. The group began infiltrating into Honduras on May 8, and the silent confrontation that unfolded in Tegucigalpa between the Guatemalan agents and Castillo Armas' operatives deserve an entire book.[8] Suffice it to say that the Caudillo managed to escape unharmed from a couple of ambushes. Some Guatemalan agents, in contrast, sought the easy way out and surrendered to Castillo Armas as soon as they reached the Honduran Capital.

Although the plan to neutralize Castillo Armas seemed to be falling apart, President Arbenz was undeterred and kept sending infiltrators into Honduras. Even the Guatemalan Air Force Attaché for Central America, Major Víctor Manuel Figueroa, an exceptional aviator, began conducting limited incursions in his own Cessna 140, carrying undercover Policía Judicial agents as well as supplies and money for the strike organizers and agitators operating in San Pedro Sula and the Honduran Capital.

Amid the turmoil and other forms of social unrest across the country, the Honduran intelligence learned that Arbenz was about to send saboteurs for blowing up military garrisons and critical infrastructure, all in preparation for a large military operation that surely would include a limited invasion of Honduran territories.

The situation grew even tenser when news of the unauthorized landing of a cargo plane in San Pedro Sula reached Tegucigalpa.[9] For a couple of hours many government officials thought that the mysterious plane was the first sign of the much-anticipated Guatemalan military escalade, and that an invasion was on its way. However, everybody sighed in relief when it was announced that the plane, a Curtiss C-46F operated by "Aerovías Sud Americana", U.S. civil registration N4871V, had got lost over the Caribbean and ended landing at San Pedro Sula after having entered inadvertently into Honduran airspace.

For president Gálvez, this incident was the proverbial straw that broke the camel's back, whether it was related to Arbenz's nefarious intentions or not. Without losing any time, he asked the U.S. to send Navy warships, packed with Marines, to the Honduran Caribbean Coast as a preemptive measure.

In Guatemala, the incident with the C-46 acquired heroic proportions as it was rumored that a pair of Guatemalan Air Force fighters had intercepted and strafed a Castillo Armas' cargo plane, forcing it to escape -badly damaged- to Honduras, where it had crash-landed. So widespread was the false rumor that a couple of foreign correspondents reported it as factual to their respective newspapers.

On May 9, President Arbenz finally ordered the Fuerza Aérea Guatemalteca (the Guatemalan Air Force) –FAG- to start patrolling the Motagua Basin and the Bay of Amatique as part of a defense plan against what was now considered an unavoidable invasion.

At least on paper, and for Central American standards, the FAG was an impressive air arm.[10] Seven North American AT-6C/D *Texan* armed trainers, three Boeing P-26A *Peashooter* fighters, three Beechcraft AT-11 *Kansan* bomber-trainers, two Douglas C-47

Lieutenant Juan Adolfo Castillo Ralda, getting his North American AT-6 ready for take off on a patrol mission in May 1954. (Photo credit: Guatemalan Air Force.)

transports, a Beechcraft C-45 light transport, and a Cessna UC-78 utility plane comprised its inventory. All these aircraft were based at "La Aurora" Air Base, located within the Capital's international airport. The FAG's flight training was conducted at the "Los Cipresales" air base, in the Northern part of the City, where there were a Vultee BT-15, a Boeing PT-17, 15 Fairchild PT-19As, two Waco VPF-7s and five Ryan STM-2s, the latter capable of bear a machine-gun over each wing..

The FAG was in tatters, however, since The U.S. arms embargo had affected the service directly, and there weren't enough spare parts for keeping its fleet airworthy. According to an U.S. Air Force intelligence report dated on April 30, 1954, the FAG kept only a few of its planes operative, and not all of them were combat-capable, as there weren't reflector nor Norden sights available for the fighters and bombers. And worst of all, fuel, ammunition and bombs were considered a luxury due to budgetary cuts and restrictions imposed by the Guatemalan Army's high-command, who saw the air arm as an abomination to the prevailing infantry-centered doctrine.

The FAG had other problems too, since Arbenz didn't trust the majority of its personnel. As a direct result of PBSuccess' psychological warfare, the number of disgruntled officers that opposed the government had increased during the last couple of weeks. The FAG hadn't been an exception, and of its 51 officers and 183 NCOs, only a handful was considered politically reliable. For this reason, only a few trusted pilots and mechanics were allowed near the planes, while the Policía Judicial kept the rest under constant scrutiny.

It was under those difficult circumstances that the FAG Commander, Col. Luis Antonio Girón Cartagena, was ordered to deploy two AT-6s to the military airfields in Puerto Barrios and Zacapa and begin flying low-level reconnaissance missions, photographing every mile of tropical jungle, banana plantation, and arid plain along the border with Honduras and El Salvador. For the job, Col. Girón designated two of Arbenz's most trusted officers: Major Pedro Granados and Captain Julio Ernesto Gálvez, both considered excellent pilots. In their rear cockpits there would be NCOs armed with *Leica* hand-held cameras, snapping photos away.

Neither the type of mission nor the terrain were strange to Granados and Gálvez, since they had flown several times over the region, precisely conducting photo reconnaissance work as part of an Army's combat exercise held in August 1953. In fact, Col. Girón expected to compare the images obtained back then with those that Granados and Gálvez would produce during their sorties in order to determine if there were suspicious movements that could reveal any preparations for the invasion.

Major Víctor Figueroa was also ordered to conduct his own reconnaissance missions but clandestinely, inside Honduras, focusing mainly on the Liberation Army's staging points and the UFCO's banana plantations scattered near the border. The objective was to determine the Liberation Army's composition, strength, and equipment, and if possible, to anticipate their initial movements once the invasion had been launched.

Figueroa began this highly secret mission on May 9 also, conducting what could be considered the most dangerous and complicated flights that the FAG personnel had to carry out at that time. Initially he limited himself to fly low and slow over the assigned targets, avoiding being seen and shot at; however, as he gained confidence, the Major occasionally landed his Cessna near suspicious installations and conducted limited searches on foot near the Liberation Army's staging points. Ironically, the daredevil pilot was detained while conducting a completely different type of mission, and very far from his intended targets.

On May 11, Figueroa took off from La Aurora Airport in a FAG AT-11 (serial 0874, C/N 3362, ex USAAF 42-36982)[11] for a covert mission to San Pedro Sula and the port of La Ceiba, both in Honduras. He was carrying money and supplies for labor workers of the Tela Railroad who were about to start their own strikes in those towns.

After a couple of hours, he was able to land at San Pedro Sula without any problems as he informed the airport authorities that he

Besides the North American AT-6s, the Guatemalan Air Force also launched its Beechcraft AT-11s on patrol missions before and during the invasion. In this photo, taken in June 1954, the crew checks for any suspicious movements in the southern sector of the Capital. (Photo credit: Guatemalan Air Force.)

Despite being described as bombers, none of the Beechcraft AT-11s of the Guatemalan Air Force carried any bombs due to the ever-present armament shortages caused by budgetary cuts. (Photo credit: Guatemalan Air Force.)

was "*on a routine mission to Tegucigalpa*" and acting in the capacity of the Guatemalan Air Force Attaché for Central America. Then, he continued the flight to La Ceiba, but upon landing there, the Police seized his plane and detained him. It turned out that, all of a sudden, the Honduran government no longer recognized him as the Guatemala Air Force Attaché, and his flight was considered an illegal incursion. The fact that his plane was a "bomber", although an unarmed bomber-trainer, only made the situation worse.

As soon as Ambassador Willauer got wind of this incident, he promptly informed PBSuccess headquarters about it. In his report, he stated that several tactical navigation charts, on which numbers in pencil marked the various UFCO plantations along the Honduran Caribbean Coast, were found in Figueroa's plane. Strangely, the Liberation Army's staging points didn't appear marked on such maps.

In Opa-locka, everybody was shocked. The presence of FAG's aircraft over the Guatemala-Honduras border and the illegal crossing of Major Figueroa in a "bomber" could be considered strong indications that President Arbenz was onto something, and it all had the appearance of being preparations for a major military move. The large shipment of Czech weapons acquired by Arbenz in March, which the CIA had been unable to locate so far, reinforced this hypothesis. Additionally, there were unconfirmed reports, received by CIA stations in Europe, about the purchase of a handful of Avia S-199 (reported in the CIA declassified documents as Messerschmitt Me 109s) and Supermarine *Spitfire* fighters by the Guatemalan Government in Czechoslovakia and Sweden[12] respectively.

Wisner got so worried about the imminent rearming of the Guatemalan Army and the possibility of an invasion to Honduras, that he requested the CIA Director for permission to sink any ship heading to Puerto Barrios, whether it was by torpedoing them or by ramming them with boats loaded with explosives, as soon as they entered the Bay of Amatique.[13] Fortunately, Allen Dulles did not approve the plan due to the diplomatic implications that it could have. Instead, he told Wisner to pressure Castillo Armas in order to obtain reliable information about Arbenz's intentions and the arms shipment, through the few remaining contacts that the Caudillo had within the Guatemalan Army.

The problem was that not even the Guatemalan Army officers knew the whereabouts of the arms shipment or what were Arbenz's intentions. The only ones who had all the details were the President's Communist advisors, who were already organizing civil defense brigades, comprised of labor union workers and peasants, which would replace the Guatemalan Army. All they were waiting for was precisely the arrival of the Czech weapons.

Meanwhile, Dulles ordered a new revision of PBSuccess' air support plan, focusing especially on Phase IIIB which, as it had been mentioned, comprised the aerial resupply of the Liberation Army troops in the battlefield once the invasion had been launched, and conducting psychological warfare missions over Guatemala.

With the proposed D-Day less than a month away, everybody in Opa-locka thought that the CIA Director would loosen his grip a bit, and would authorize additional planes for the project. Instead, due to some reservations that NSC's members and Department of State officials had, Dulles imposed new restrictions upon the plan. First, he didn't want the CAT pilots flying over enemy territory. As expected, both Wisner and Brodfrost protested at such a non-sense, but the CIA Director weighed in and it was decided that the CAT pilots wouldn't be authorized to fly into Guatemala under any circumstances. Even the USAF cargo kickers already at hand would have to be replaced. For this, the Chief of Air Support would have to recruit "unwitting" personnel as to conform four four-men crews. These new aircrews, once they had been found, would be hired by Castillo Armas' organization, for 60 days, and would be based at Las Mercedes Airport in Managua, Nicaragua, from where all Phase IIIB's flights would originate.

The new requirement put Brodfrost in hot water almost immediately, as it was virtually impossible for him to come up with enough qualified individuals in time. Initially, he attempted to hire Latino pilots flying for Pan American Airways and Braniff, but the majority declined when they were told that most of the flights would be conducted over "unfriendly" territory and that it would involve "some shooting." Then, he scouted the Miami area and even went to the USAF aviation school at Bartow AFB, looking for any foreign flight instructors with combat experience, but again, his search was fruitless. In the end, Tracy Barnes offered to see what he could do about it.

During Dulles' revision of the plan, he finally made a decision about acquiring a third plane for the project. Thus, a very battered Douglas C-47A was acquired in the Washington D.C. market. Instead of only leasing it just like the previous ones, this transport was purchased on behalf of Castillo Armas. The idea behind this was that, if the plane was shot down or had to make an emergency landing in Guatemala, its origins could only be traced back to Castillo Armas' organization that, essentially, was the "legal" operator and owner.

The newly acquired C-47A was quickly incorporated into Phase IIIA's flight schedule, which by then was nearing its completion. For operating it, Brodfrost had been authorized to conform a temporary two-men aircrew by hiring a pilot in the U.S. West Coast and a Flight Engineer -already available at France Field- who would fly as co-pilot. By May 14, this C-47A was already flying cargo missions to Managua and Tegucigalpa, giving a much-needed break to the over-worked CAT pilots. From then on, the three aircraft were flown simultaneously, dramatically improving the transportation of the last bundles with arms and supplies to their respective destinations.

On May 14 also, Castillo Armas' informants noticed that the FAG's two C-47s were airlifting, from Guatemala City to Puerto Barrios, what seemed to be a full company of troops from the Guardia de Honor garrison. Several platoons were also being hastily transported by truck to the Caribbean port.

Amid the already tense situation between Guatemala and Honduras, this new development shocked everybody at PBSuccess headquarters. The unusual military movement could very well be the beginning of the much-hypothesized invasion to Honduran territories. During the small hours on May 15, however, the situation got even stranger when the recently arrived troops stormed the UFCO port and established a security perimeter around the dock and the ancillary installations, preventing anyone from entering or leaving, and allowing only the stevedores to remain in place.

A couple of hours later, one of the FAG's transports brought the Defense Minister, Col. Angel Sanchez, and the Guardia de Honor Commanding Officer, Col. José Barzanallana, who then took control of the port. The arrival of these senior officers drew the attention of Castillo Armas' informants, as it denoted that something very important was about to happen. Finally, yet importantly, the Chief of the National Agrarian Department, Major Alfonso Martínez Estevez, also arrived in Puerto Barrios by mid morning.

It was not until the next day that PBSuccess headquarters learned what had happened. In a cable[14] sent from Puerto Barrios at 3:16 PM on May 16, a Castillo Armas' operative reported that the M.S. *Alfhem*, a Swedish ship, had docked around 10:00 AM at Puerto Barrios the day before, carrying what seemed to be a large shipment of arms and military equipment. The crates however, were marked as "optical equipment." Colonels Sanchez and Barzanallana had personally supervised the unloading of the ship, something that had taken almost 18 hours to complete due to a severe rainstorm.[15]

Upon receiving the cable, PBSuccess' exploded in feverish activity. First, Cpt. William Kirten Jr., the U.S. Navy attaché for Honduras, was asked to fly as soon as possible to Puerto Barrios and inspect the cargo. Then, Castillo Armas was ordered to send three sabotage teams to San Pedro Sula, and have them ready to infiltrate into Guatemala for blowing up the railroad tracks leaving Puerto Barrios. Lastly, PBSuccess' operatives contacted the officials of the railroad company, which was an UFCO's subsidiary, and asked them to delay the transportation of the crates to Guatemala City for as long as possible.

On May 17, the U.S. Ambassador to Guatemala confirmed that, far from being the start of an invasion, the military movement had been aimed at seizing the large shipment of arms and equipment that Arbenz had purchased in Czechoslovakia in March. By then, seven flat cars, carrying the first crates, were en route to Guatemala City, much to the dismay of the railroad officials, who had tried to stop them under a myriad of bureaucratic subterfuges.

Not losing any time, PBSuccess headquarters set to determine the types of arms and equipment that comprised the shipment, and for this the U.S. Navy Attaché for Honduras arrived on the scene on May 19, but was prevented from getting near the cargo.[16] Something

The arrival of the M.S. *Alfhem* to Puerto Barrios in May 1954, carrying an important load of arms and ammunition, surely pressed the CIA to hasten the invasion's execution. (Photo credit: Life Magazine.)

similar happened to members of the U.S. Army Mission in Guatemala City, when they visited the *Gerona* railroad warehouses, where the crates were being stored. Castillo Armas' agents also joined the efforts and set to monitor the unloading of the cars. However, their first reports were rather confusing, as they speculated that at least a handful of disassembled MiG-15 jet fighters[17] had been brought in, along with soviet-made tanks and armored personnel carriers, while others reported that the crates contained only machineguns, rifles and mortar tubes.

As the conflicting reports were piling up in Opa-locka, an intelligence advisory meeting, which took place in Washington, determined that the arms shipment on the *Alfhem* posed a threat to the Panama Canal and urged the NSC to take urgent actions. The U.S. Department of State did its part also and denounced publicly the "*important arms shipment*" acquired by the Guatemalan government from Communist sources. Even President Somoza joined the outrage and ordered his Ambassador for Guatemala out of the country, together with all the embassy's personnel, effectively breaking diplomatic relations with Arbenz's government. Honduran President Gálvez also recalled his Ambassador, but decided not to break diplomatic relations with Guatemala, at least for the time being.

Not wanting to risk the possibility of any "sophisticated" armament reaching Guatemala City, PBSuccess headquarters ordered Castillo Armas to deploy the sabotage teams awaiting orders at San Pedro Sula.[18] These men crossed into Guatemala on May 20, and proceeded to set two explosive charges in a bridge near the town of Castañeda, some 26 km from Puerto Barrios. When a train pulling eight cars reached that bridge, the saboteurs detonated the charges, but only one exploded. As the train stopped, the saboteurs began to fire their machineguns at the soldiers who were guarding the cargo. A heavy firefight ensued in which two saboteurs were killed. Guatemalan Army Sgt. Fidel Aldana, the leader of the squad guarding the cargo, was also killed.[19] To the saboteurs' dismay, the train was able to proceed unharmed towards Guatemala City in less than an hour. Three days later, on May 23, there was a second attempt to blow up a train, but again, the charges failed to explode and the Guatemalan troops managed to keep the attackers at bay. A third and last attempt took place on May 25, and as before, it failed miserably.

CHAPTER 7
SOMERSET

The arrival of the arms shipment at Puerto Barrios inevitably changed the scenario in which Project PBSuccess was unfolding. In Washington, the fact that the Alfhem had reached Guatemala undetected was chalked up as a major blunder of Frank Wisner's Directorate of Plans, and the CIA as a whole, as it denoted that the Agency needed a serious reengineering in order to fulfill its mission statement.

In contrast, the U.S. Department of State went ahead with its plan and blew the incident out of proportion by means of a very effective propaganda campaign aimed at exerting international pressure upon Arbenz, which forced the Guatemalan President to deny insistently that the arms purchase was proof of his ties with international Communism. In several news items published in the local newspapers, he defended the country's right to arm itself and said that due to the U.S. arms embargo, the government's only choice had been to acquire the weapons in Czechoslovakia. His claims however, were simply overwhelmed by the innumerable news notes around the world, saying that Guatemala was now a beachhead of the Soviet Union in Latin America.

The arrival of the arms on the other hand, strained even more the already tense relationship between Arbenz and the military. When news of the Alfhem's imminent arrival transpired, many senior Army officers, up to the Minister of Defense, were livid and took it upon themselves to seize the arms shipment.[1] By doing this, they would prevent the conformation of the civil defense brigades –something that was unconstitutional, since only the Army was allowed to have combat equipment in the country- and would show the President that the Army had had enough.

When Arbenz learned that the Army officers were about to seize the shipment, he rushed Major Martínez Estevez, the man in charge of organizing the civil defense brigades and Chief of the National Agrarian Department, so he could take over the port and protect the crates. However, he arrived just a little too late.

Arbenz then sent to Puerto Barrios a group of poorly organized "agraristas" with the mission of retrieving the arms. Given the large number of soldiers guarding the trains, nevertheless, they only managed to organize some strikes and several riots in the UFCO plantations and at the railroad company, hoping that the turmoil could stall the departure of the cargo, but to no avail. This happened shortly before the failed attempts of Castillo Armas' saboteurs to stop the trains.

Back in Opa-locka, PBSuccess' analysts were trying to make the best of a very confusing situation. Besides the uncertainty about the type and quantity of the armament acquired[2] by Arbenz and the unconfirmed reports about several high-performance fighter aircraft being assembled at La Aurora airbase, now there were rumors about Soviet or East European pilots arriving in the country, allegedly for training the FAG aircrews.

PBSuccess headquarters soon arranged a series of low-level reconnaissance flights to be conducted by the pilots of Castillo Armas' "A Group" over the San José Airbase on the Pacific Coast and other military locations where it was suspected that the fighters were hidden. The USAF was also called in, and under the cover of revising the very few navigational aids in Northern Central America, a couple of its airplanes conducted high-altitude photo reconnaissance flights across the country. However, those attempts weren't enough to dispel any doubts about what was really happening. Not even Castillo Armas' operatives in charge of monitoring the two air bases in the Capital were able to confirm the presence of either the fighters or the pilots.

In contrast, CIA operatives on the U.S. West Coast were luckier than their PBSuccess' counterparts, as they had been able to pinpoint a series of financial transactions that the Guatemalan government was conducting in order to acquire fighter aircraft. It turned out that the FAG Commander, Col. Girón, had contacted Hubert Fauntleroy Julian yet again, this time for purchasing through him whatever fighters he could get in the surplus market. It only took a couple of days for Julian to spot 22 North American P-51D *Mustangs*, formerly operated by the *Armée de l'Air*, and 25 ex-Rhodesian North American *Harvards* (the British Commonwealth version of the legendary AT-6 *Texan*) that were available for sale. Not losing any time, Julian arranged the shipment of the Harvards from Rhodesia to Costa Rica, where the planes would be assembled and then flown to Guatemala; then he travelled to Paris in order to do the same with the Mustangs. However, this time the U.S. Department of State reacted quickly and asked the French Police to detain the crooked Colonel as soon as he stepped down from the train, and to take him to the U.S. Embassy. Once there, Julian signed a sworn statement indicating that he was not procuring arms for the Guatemalan Government. Days later, when he arrived back in New York, the FBI seized his passport and forced him to end his arms trade business.[3] As for the Harvards, the airplanes didn't make it beyond Miami, as they were seized and impounded as soon as the ship carrying them arrived to port for a technical

This is perhaps the only known photo of the Nicaraguan Air Force Douglas A-20G "Havoc" while still in service with that air arm. At some point, the PBSuccess' Air Support Unit was interested in acquiring this attack plane for leaflet dropping missions, but President Somoza declined to sell it. (Photo credit: Revista Militar de Nicaragua, via René Sanchez.)

Even though the USAF's good-will flight to Nicaragua with its Convair B-36 bombers wasn't picked up by the Guatemalan press, the psychological impact on the military was considerable, and forced them to begin looking for ways to get rid of Arbenz. (Photo credit: USAF.)

stopover. Days later, the U.S. Department of State was able to thwart yet another Guatemalan government's attempt to procure a handful of ex-Australian P-51D *Mustangs* and an ammunition shipment that was seized in Hamburg.

After a thorough analysis of the available information, PBSuccess headquarters concluded that the only real danger for the project's air operations was the anti-aircraft artillery that the Guatemalan Army already had at hand. With this in mind, the project's analysts urged Frank Wisner to change the air support plan by including fighters for escorting the C-47s on their flights into Guatemala once the invasion had been launched, and eventually for providing close air support to the Liberation forces. For this it was suggested that a handful of Douglas A-26 *Invader* attack planes or North American F-51D *Mustang* fighters be acquired from the USAF.

However, when the CIA asked the USAF about the possibility of obtaining such aircraft, the Air Force quickly turned them down, alleging that the types requested were considered "front-line" aircraft and were not available for sale. Instead, incredibly, the USAF offered 10 Lockheed F-80C *Shooting Star* jet fighter-bombers that were about to be retired[4], but the CIA declined the offer due to their excessive price and high maintenance costs. Besides, the presence of jet fighters in the Guatemalan skies would compromise the U.S. plausible deniability. In the end, the CIA requested " ... any propeller-driven aircraft type" that could fly from Managua to Guatemala and back, had considerable firepower and that would be capable of sustaining heavy damage.

Under these criteria, the obvious choice was the Republic F-47N *Thunderbolt*, which still was operated in small numbers by the units of the U.S. Air National Guard. The problem was that the USAF was reluctant to sell some of these aircraft to the CIA, arguing that they were a maintenance nightmare and that there were not enough spare parts to keep them operational under combat conditions. Additionally, the USAF was worried about how these fighters would be transferred to Castillo Armas and who was going to fly them. Inevitably, the issue was taken to the highest level in Washington, and it would take a couple of weeks for all those involved to agree on how and when these airplanes could be made available to the Caudillo.

Meanwhile, PBSuccess headquarters deemed that a "show of force" was necessary to further convince the Guatemalan Army that it was time to rise against Arbenz. First, on May 20, the U.S. Navy was asked to begin an air and sea blockade along the Guatemalan coasts in order to prevent the arrival of more arms shipments. This operation, officially known as "Hardrock Baker", also included the assembly of an evacuation force equipped with helicopters and amphibious assault ships that would rescue the Liberation Army troops in case they were defeated and forced to escape. Finally, yet importantly, some of the cruisers assigned to this operation would provide security to the Honduran ports, just as President Gálvez had requested.

In addition, Lt. Col. Brodfrost was ordered to launch a leaflet dropping flight over Guatemala City. Not wanting to compromise Phase IIIA's flight schedule by taking away one of the C-47s, he cast around seeking an additional aircraft to fly it. The first candidate considered was a Douglas A-20G *Havoc* attack aircraft[5] parked in the military area of Las Mercedes airport that he had observed during one of the flights to Managua. The plane was the only survivor of two acquired by President Somoza in July 1949. Brodfrost thought that this plane was ideal for the leaflet drop, as it had enough range, could be armed and would already be "sterile."

Not losing any time, Brodfrost talked to Somoza about making the attack plane available for Castillo Armas' use, either on a rental basis or by selling it to him. However, at the last minute Somoza refused, saying that the A-20 was the only one of its type in the region and everyone knew it belonged to his Air Force.

With no other options in sight, Brodfrost resigned himself to use one of his C-47s for the mission. Now the problem was to find a couple of "unwitting" pilots and a cargo kicker who could conduct the flight safely, since the aircrews for Phase IIIB hadn't been recruited yet and the CIA Director had expressly forbidden the CAT crews from flying

Col. Rodolfo "Fito" Mendoza who, later on, was appointed as Chief of the Liberation Air Force. (Photo credit: El Imparcial Newspaper.)

over Guatemala. Fortunately, this time Castillo Armas was able to provide at least one competent pilot. His name was Jerry Fred Delarm.

Usually dressed in black and carrying a .45 automatic pistol on his belt at all times, Delarm was the archetype of the gunslinger whose only language was money. The Chief of the USAF Mission in Guatemala, Col. Richard Hutchinson, considered him a psychopathic killer. However, not one of those who knew the pilot had the same opinion about him. For some he was a loyal friend; for others, he was a treacherous pathological liar.

Delarm was born in San Francisco, California, in 1923. He was the son of Isabelle Amador and Edward Orville De Larm, an Arapahoe who became the first Native American pilot to get involved in commercial aviation in the U.S.

Little Jerry learned to fly sitting on his father's lap while smuggling distilled alcohol out of Mexico, and soloed when he was only nine years old. He went to Central America for the first time in 1939, following his father who had been hired by Lowell Yerex's airline Transportes Aéreos Centroamericanos –TACA- that was based in Honduras. Delarm became his father's copilot there, and within a couple of months, he was flying TACA's Ford Tri-Motors as a Captain too.

The adventures of Delarm in Central America could fill a thick volume. Suffice it to say that during his Central American adventures, he became involved with the renowned flyer Jimmy Angel, established a couple of air services in Costa Rica which failed, and was appointed Colonel in the short-lived "*Fuerza Aérea Costarricense*" (the Costa Rican Air Force) during that country's Revolution of 1948. Then, he moved to Nicaragua where President Somoza took him under his wing, appointing him as Colonel of the *Fuerza Aérea de la Guardia Nacional* (National Guard's Air Force) also known by its Spanish acronym as the FAN.

When Delarm joined the FAN, Somoza was taking steps to secure his country in any possible way, since he feared an invasion by Nicaraguan exiles supported by the Guatemalan government. For this he acquired a pair of Lockheed P-38L *Lightnings*, considered the most advanced fighters in Central America at the time. Those P-38s were constantly flown on patrol missions along the country's Pacific Coast, intercepting suspicious aircraft and ships. It was during those missions that Delarm developed his fighter pilot skills. All of a sudden getting near Nicaraguan territorial waters became a risky proposition since Somoza's pilots, and especially Delarm, decided unilaterally when a ship or plane was inside the country's territorial limits, and acted accordingly, usually with tragic results.

On the ground, Delarm loved to brag about his combat flying during the late stages of WWII over the Pacific. Only very few people knew that his "*there I was...*" tales were only fabrications, since he never joined the U.S. Army Air Forces nor the Navy, and had spent the whole conflict flying in Central America.

In 1949, President Somoza sent Delarm to Guatemala with the mission of becoming his eyes and ears there. The Nicaraguan President wanted to closely monitor the upcoming presidential elections and, if possible, turn the results against Arbenz. As a cover for his secret activities, Delarm established a car dealership and a small aviation service. Then, when the presidential campaign began, he offered his services to Arbenz's partisans for skywriting and aerial broadcasting. That gave him the excuse to tour the country, observing the people's behavior, the candidate's attitudes, and the elections' trends.

Late in 1953, Delarm finally got involved with Castillo Armas' organization as a contact between Somoza and the Caudillo's operatives in Guatemala. When Castillo Armas organized the "A Group" of civilian pilots, Delarm was one of the first to be called, obviously on Somoza's recommendation. As part of the "A Group" Delarm conducted daring flights carrying sabotage equipment and arms from Honduras to Guatemala. However, he had to escape to El Salvador when the Policía Judicial seized a handful of payment receipts that linked him clearly to Castillo Armas' organization. By the time when Brodfrost needed a pilot for the leaflet-dropping mission, Delarm had already telegraphed the Caudillo, asking for instructions and money. Two days later, on May 23, Delarm was ordered to proceed to Managua and contact Brodfrost. He had gotten the job.

Even though Brodfrost already had a pilot for the leaflet-dropping mission, he still needed to find a copilot and a cargo kicker as soon as possible. By then Tracy Barnes had scouted desperately the Opa-locka and Miami areas without any results. However, when Frank Wisner learned that the mission was in jeopardy, he decided to call his friend Gilbert Greenway, whose brother-in-law owned a flying school in Florida and knew many pilots with the required devil-may-care attitude. Surprisingly, in less than 48 hours, Greenway's relative was able to provide not only the sorely needed copilot, but also the four crews required for Phase IIIB. As for the cargo kicker, an individual was picked from among the Liberation Army troops and trained in a rush at Las Mercedes airport in Managua.

On May 25, Delarm and his newly formed crew reviewed the flight plan with Brodfrost and determined that it wasn't advisable to conduct the mission at night as PBSuccess headquarters had suggested. The pilot knew Guatemala City like the back of his hand and was aware that there were many peaks and towers that could pose a great risk while flying at low altitude and at night. Instead, Delarm suggested changing the mission timing, so they would arrive over the Capital

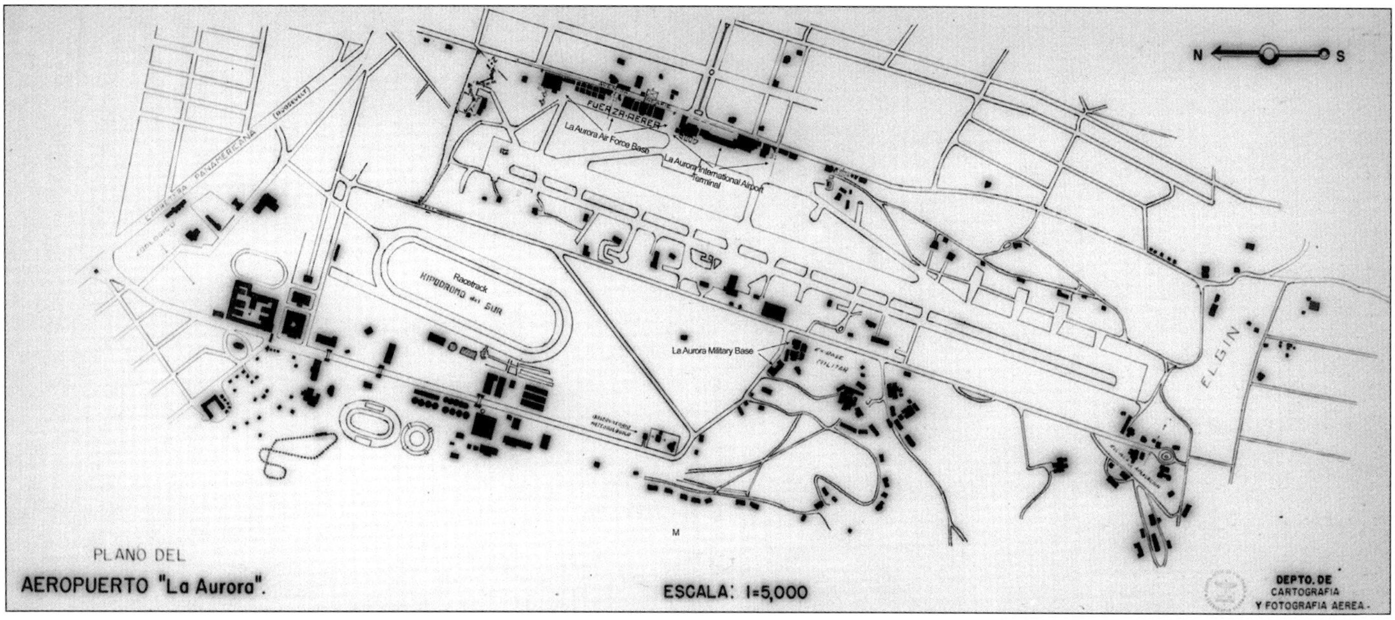

Map of La Aurora International Airport, including the location of the La Aurora Air Base and the military garrison in charge of its security. (Photo credit: Guatemalan Air Force.)

at dusk and take advantage of the last minutes of daylight for making the drops. That would have the added benefit of preventing the FAG AT-6s from being scrambled to try to intercept them, since these (and their crews) were not well suited for night flying.

A CAT crew flew the C-47A that PBSuccess had acquired two weeks earlier, from France Field to Las Mercedes airport during the night of May 25. As soon as the plane was tied down at the military ramp, the CAT pilots were ordered to return to their base, avoiding any contact with Delarm and his crew. This was necessary to maintain compartmentalization and secrecy. Early the next day, Delarm and his men arrived at the airport and checked the plane, making a couple of flights during the morning, so the cargo kicker could practice the leaflet drops.

It was around 4:00 PM when the C-47A took off from Las Mercedes airport in order to conduct the daring mission. According to the flight plan[6], and to conceal the airplane's real route, Delarm had to climb to 8,500ft as fast as he could, while flying to the Northeast, that is, in the opposite direction from Guatemala. Then, upon reaching a ranch codenamed "Punta Case", located near the town of Tomatoyita, in Matagalpa, some 50 km from the Nicaraguan Capital, he had to change course and head to the next waypoint, situated 770 km away, near the Acajutla port, on the Salvadoran Pacific Coast. After passing Acajutla, Delarm had to climb to 10,500 ft and turn to the Northwest, heading directly to Guatemala City.

By the time when the C-47A began its approach to the Guatemalan Capital, things got complicated because low clouds covered the city and it was starting to rain. Even when Delarm had the prerogative of calling off the flight, he decided to trust his instincts and continued the plane's descent until reaching 500ft over the terrain.

On his way into the city, and adding insult to injury, Delarm made a low pass over La Aurora airport's runway, where FAG personnel watched helplessly as the plane went by. The load kicker began to drop the leaflets as soon as the plane reached the city's outskirts, managing to cover most of the streets and plazas in the commercial area. At the Central Park located in front of the National Palace, it gave the impression that time had suddenly stopped. People, Civil Guards and government employees looking skywards, seemed mesmerized by the low flying airplane and the thousands of little leaflets falling upon them.

During the second pass, made from the North, Delarm ordered the load kicker to drop a whole package of leaflets over the National Palace's roof; thinking that the falling package was a bomb, many people in the park hit the ground immediately, while others ran for their lives. As expected, the Palace began to be evacuated in a rush, while the President was taken to the tunnel that connected that building to the neighboring "Casa Presidencial" (the presidential residence.) A second package was dropped over the Guardia Civil's headquarters scaring many people in the streets nearby. In the third pass, made from the West, another package was dropped over the Congress, but it ended up falling over the "El Imparcial" newspaper's building, which was evacuated in no time.

The load kicker ran out of leaflets just as Delarm was turning for a fourth pass from the East. Undeterred, the pilot decided to have some fun before calling off the mission and buzzed the city repeatedly, focusing on the Guardia de Honor garrison and the La Aurora airport. Surprisingly, there wasn't any reaction from the FAG, not even after an extremely low pass that Delarm made over the airbase on his way out.[7]

At 6:25 PM, less than 20 minutes after his arrival over the City, Delarm climbed to 9,500 ft while heading for the town of Escuintla in the Guatemalan Pacific Coast. From there the "escape route" would take them to Las Salinas, in El Salvador, then to the port of Corinto, in Nicaragua, and finally to Las Mercedes airport in Managua, where the C-47A landed at 9:00 PM.

Radio Liberacion's announcers went on the air that night, praising the brave pilots who had conducted the flight and reading an extended version of the text contained in the leaflets that had been dropped over Guatemala City. During the night, Brodfrost sent a detailed report of the mission to PBSuccess headquarters in which he praised Delarm for having displayed considerable courage while flying under terrible weather conditions. Even when Delarm's contract stipulated that he was being hired to conduct just a couple of flights, Brodfrost suggested that he should be hired for the rest of the project, as he was also a competent fighter pilot who would come in handy if the requested Thunderbolts were approved in the coming days.

During the morning of May 27, the consequences of Delarm's flight began to be felt in Guatemala. First, it was reported that the Honduran airline TACA had been prohibited from landing at La Aurora, and the aircraft of AVIATECA, the Guatemalan government's airline,

Aerial view of the Los Cipresales Air Base, located in the Northern sector of Guatemala City. (Photo credit: Guatemalan Air Force.)

had been grounded. A later report from Pan American Airways also indicated that they had been banned from the Guatemalan airspace. In Tegucigalpa, the Honduran Civil Aeronautics Directorate received an official notice from the Guatemalan government saying that from that day on the Motagua Basin and the regions bordering with Honduras were closed to all aircraft. The notice added also that any aircraft entering the no-fly zone would be shot down.[8]

For its part, the Guatemalan Army implemented defensive measures, although reluctantly. Arbenz had to exert his authority upon the officers in order to get them moving. By the end of the day only a handful of anti-aircraft batteries have been emplaced around the National Palace, along the perimeter of the La Aurora airport and at the Los Cipresales airbase, while at FAG's headquarters, the pilots were ordered to launch periodic patrol flights over the City and its surrounding areas. Additionally, they were authorized to shoot down any suspicious aircraft that failed to properly identify itself. Last but not least, civilian and commercial pilots were ordered to file their flight plans directly with the FAG and during flight they had to contact La Aurora's ATC every five minutes, to report their altitude and heading.

The USAF performed the third and final act of the show of force on the same day as Delarm's flight. Publicized as a "Non-stop goodwill flight"[9] three Convair B-36 nuclear bombers of the 7th Bombardment Wing (Heavy), departed Carswell AFB, in Forth Worth, Texas, for Nicaragua to take part in that country's "Army Day Celebration." Led by Brigadier General John D. Ryan, the 19th Air Division Commander, and Colonel Clarence A. Neely, the 7th Bombardment Wing Vice Commander, the three gigantic airplanes overflew the Nicaraguan Capital and the towns nearby at low altitude, putting up a very impressive display. Then, they headed back to Carswell where they landed on May 27, completing a 6,000 km flight without incidents.

The flight of the B-36s over Nicaragua did not make it to the headlines in Guatemala, since Delarm's flight had the newspapers' attention completely. However, the Guatemalan Army's Intelligence picked up the news the next day and passed the information not only to the Ministry of Defense but also to the commanding officers of all the major Army bases in the country. From then on, many of them were convinced that not only the Honduran and the Nicaraguan regimes were backing Castillo Armas, but also a much more powerful nation that would not hesitate in doing something radical if Arbenz insisted on not changing his ways.

Two days later, Colonel Rubén González Siguí, the commanding officer of the Army's General Headquarters, called for an urgent meeting[10] with the senior officers, during which they analyzed the country's grave situation, and as it would be expected, many of them suggested starting a major uprising to get rid of Arbenz and the Communists as soon as possible. Once this had been accomplished, they would look for a détente with the U.S. for preventing Castillo Armas' invasion.

Cooler heads prevailed, however, and it was agreed that the best approach would be to maintain the constitutional order while trying to convince Arbenz to steer away from the Communists. For this, they scheduled a meeting with the President, which would be held no later than the first week of June.

Inevitably, the unrest spread among the Army's lower ranks and many young officers were eager to revolt, while some others were seriously considering joining Castillo Armas. It took little time for the CIA station in Guatemala to find out about these disgruntled officers, and accordingly, the defection sub-project, which had been discontinued weeks earlier, was reactivated.[11] By May 30, CIA operatives had contacted no less than twelve potential candidates, eight of them being FAG pilots.

When PBSuccess headquarters was informed about this, the case officer in charge of propaganda, E. Howard Hunt, suggested that these pilots should defect in a spectacular manner by stealing a couple of FAG airplanes. Not losing any time, Opa-locka issued a set of instructions[12], to be handed to the defecting pilots by the CIA station, which they would have to follow as soon as they had defected. In addition, PBSuccess' personnel at the airports in Managua, El Salvador and Tegucigalpa were instructed on how to receive them.

Arbenz's Policía Judicial was close behind, however, and four of the FAG's aviators were detained in no time. The rest of them developed a case of cold feet and told the CIA station that they were going to wait for a "more appropriate time" for their defection. However, the arrest of these pilots was only the beginning. By May 31 the Policía Judicial had rounded up the majority of the core members of Castillo Armas' organization in Guatemala[13], including the CIA station's most important informants, referred as SECANT and SEMANTIC in the Agency's declassified papers. These two individuals had been providing critical intelligence about the Guatemalan Army, as they both were retired officers.

During this major crackdown, Arbenz came into possession of a considerable amount of documents that detailed almost in its entirety, the latest tactical plans for the invasion.

Back in Washington, Frank Wisner ordered a quick damage assessment in order to determine a course of action. When the Department of State and the NSC got wind of this new leakage, many suggested canceling the paramilitary program and look for alternative ways to accomplish the mission. Some others, especially Henry Holland, wanted the whole project terminated. And as it had happened before, thorough analyses were submitted and endless meetings were held, all in order to convince the naysayers that at this point there was no going back. If they couldn't get rid of Arbenz now, the situation soon would escape their control. In the end, the persuasiveness of Wisner and his team saved the project once again, and they were authorized to continue.

To dispel any doubts that PBSuccess had entered into combat mode, the Regional Command Station and the Air Support Unit –both of which had been based at France Field up until then- were ordered to relocate to Las Mercedes airport, in Managua, on June 2. Accordingly, Lt. Col. Brodfrost's C-47s began to fly the remaining cargo intended for the Liberation Army troops in Honduras and all the equipment and supplies needed to get the Command Station up and running at Managua as soon as possible. At Las Mercedes, Somoza granted them the use of a 13 by 60 mt building located in the East end of the airport, within the Nicaraguan Air Force's ramp. Most of that building's space was used for storage while only a small area was destined for administrative purposes. By June 4, the new Command Station became operational, receiving from then on the codename "SOMERSET."

On that day, and as part of PBSuccess' propaganda program, the "defection" of Col. (R) Rodolfo "Fito" Mendoza took place. He had been Chief of the Guatemalan "Cuerpo de Aeronáutica Militar" (Military Aeronautical Corps, the predecessor of the Guatemalan Air Force) from November 1944 to September 1947, and during the last couple of months he and his two brothers, also retired officers, had been helping Castillo Armas' internal organization.

According to the local press, Fito Mendoza took off from La Aurora airport[14] for a check flight in a Cessna 170A, civil registration TG-BIK[15] (C/N 19573), but never returned. It wasn't until two days later that the Government revealed that Fito, accompanied by his brother Col. (R) Miguel Mendoza and the former Deputy Chief of the U.S. Air Mission in Guatemala, Major (R) Ferdinand Schoup, who was also part of Castillo Armas' "A Group", had landed at the Ilopango airport, in El Salvador. They didn't remain there for too long, however, since the U.S. Embassy got them on a plane bound to Honduras, where they joined the Liberation Army.

As for TG-BIK, it was returned to its owner, Mr. Edgardo Calderón, by the Salvadoran authorities two days later (this Cessna was destroyed less than three months later, after taking-off, overloaded with coffee sacks, from the Cobán airfield. Mr. Calderón and a passenger walked away unharmed.)

On June 7, a second leaflet-dropping flight over Guatemala City was launched. The C-47A departed Las Mercedes at 6:10 AM and followed the same route that Delarm had flown during the mission of May 26. However, the pilot called off the flight after wandering around the Guatemalan Pacific Coast for more than two hours, as he couldn't find a passage through a heavy rainstorm. The plane landed back at Las Mercedes near 12:45 PM.

Undeterred, Brodfrost ordered another attempt during the afternoon and the C-47 took off again at 3:00 PM, arriving over Guatemala City less than two hours later, where it achieved a successful drop over the downtown area. However, this time the anti-aircraft defenses were waiting for the "avión fantasma" (the ghost plane) and the sky was quickly filled with tracers. Even when the pilot managed to dodge the heavy fire during the egress from the City, he soon realized that two FAG AT-6s had taken off from La Aurora and were now after him.

The battered Texans, flown by 1st Lieutenants Adolfo Castillo Ralda and Carlos Samayoa Paz, tried desperately to get the C-47 within shooting range, but to no avail. The transport was simply too fast for them, and as soon as the C-47 pilot had noticed them on his tail, he initiated a steep climb to "*... get the hell out of there*" immediately. The FAG's flight leader, Lt. Castillo Ralda, called off the chase when the C-47 crossed into El Salvador, and headed back to his base.

It took a couple of minutes for Lt. Castillo Ralda to realize that his wingman was not following him. Fearing that Lt. Samayoa Paz had made an emergency landing or had crashed, he descended as fast as he could and began searching for any wreckage in the ground. After an hour, he had to give up the search since the nightfall was setting in and his plane was running out of fuel. It was not until the next day that Castillo Ralda, and the rest of the FAG pilots, learned that Lt. Samayoa Paz[16] had landed at the Ilopango airport, in El Salvador. Even though it had been unplanned, the CIA had achieved another defection.

CHAPTER 8
THE LIBERATION AIR FORCE

Early in June, the CIA Director finally approved the use of tactical aircraft in PBSuccess even though the project didn't have any fighters yet. The USAF was still reluctant to release three of its Thunderbolts, and not even a series of "strong cables" -sent by the Department of State- had been able to break the bottleneck open. This serious limitation notwithstanding, Phase IV was added to the Air Support Plan[1] and Brodfrost was ordered to start looking for fighter pilots.

The Chief of Air Support had already hired Jerry Fred Delarm and Ferdinand Schoup, who had escaped Guatemala with Fito Mendoza on June 7, but the he still needed at least two more pilots and inevitably, CIA operatives ended up scouting the Miami area once again in what seemed to be a never-ending search for aircrews.

Anticipating that the delay of the Thunderbolts could become a problem, Brodfrost suggested that the project should acquire at least one fighter from "external sources." Thus, headquarters authorized him to approach President Somoza offering to purchase the FAN's surviving Lockheed P-38L *Lightning*. The deal was concluded two days later, with the sale "price" being one of the Thunderbolts that PBSuccess was about to receive, plus the Cessna 180 assigned to Castillo Armas. Both aircraft would be delivered once the project no longer needed them.

At the time, the U.S. Air Mission in Nicaragua, acting in the capacity of a "Military Assistance Advisory Group", was overhauling the Lightning and Somoza's decision to sell it to "mercenaries" didn't suit its personnel very well. In fact, they began interfering with the activities of the project's air support unit at Las Mercedes and blocked Brodfrost's mechanics from continuing the repairs on the Lightning. The situation got so bad that the Department of State had to intervene through its Embassy in Nicaragua to effect an "attitude adjustment" in the mind of the Chief of the Air Mission, Lt. Col. Woods W. Rogers, Jr.

However, repairing the battered fighter proved to be a difficult task because Brodfrost's mechanics discovered that – at some point in the past – its outboard wing fuel tanks had been disconnected. Without them, the fighter simply could not reach Guatemala. Hence, the wing panels had to be removed to take out the tanks, clean them and then reinstall them and have them properly connected. This task would take between 8 to 10 days at the least.

Meanwhile, PBSuccess headquarters decided to deliver another psychological blow to the Guatemalan government: At dawn on June 8, Brodfrost launched two of his C-47s for a leaflet dropping mission over the three most populated Guatemalan towns, namely Santa Cruz del Quiché, Mazatenango and Quetzaltenango, the latter being President Arbenz's birthplace. Jerry Delarm was flying one of the transports while an FAN crew, which had been provided by President Somoza just for the occasion, was flying the other. This mission, while riddled with difficulties due to bad weather and the Nicaraguan crew's unfamiliarity with the terrain, caused a commotion among the population to the point that the local press called it "a bad omen for Arbenz."

By midday, the Minister of the Interior, Col. Augusto Charnaud McDonald, announced that the Guatemalan Government had crushed "...the best organized plot in the history of the country", detaining 40 individuals linked to Castillo Armas' organization. Hours later, however, all constitutional liberties were suspended[2] and a strict press censorship was imposed. Then, "a reign of terror" was unleashed upon the population and hundreds were detained, tortured and even executed in a wave of repression without precedent, led by Col. Rogelio Cruz Wer and Major Jaime Rossenberg, Chiefs of the Guardia Civil and the Policía Judicial respectively.

During the evening, Arbenz finally met with the Army's leadership at the "Casino Militar" (the military officer's club.) Col. Rubén González Siguí was in charge of giving him the ultimatum: The Guatemalan Army would no longer tolerate the Communists in the cabinet, much less the organizing of militias. Seeking to avoid any confrontation, Arbenz asked them for some time to analyze their demands. He would give them a definitive answer on June 15. However, after the meeting, he pulled Col. González Siguí and the Army's Chief of Staff, Col. Enrique Parinello aside and ordered them to resign their positions at once. Both officers defiantly refused, saying that he was risking a major revolt if the cabinet wasn't purged as soon as possible. Arbenz left, furious. From then on, the Policía Judicial kept the members of the Defense Council and the Army's General Staff under close watch, but it was Col. González Siguí who took the brunt, as he had to go into hiding when Maj. Rosenberg's men tried to assassinate him.

The next day, June 9, Arbenz created a "parallel General Staff" headed by the Communist leader Leonardo Castillo Flores, assisted by Maj. Alfonso Martínez Estevez, who would supervise the Army's defense plans. Not expectedly, the military considered this decision a grave humiliation. But that was not all, since Castillo Flores, who Arbenz had appointed as Chief of the *Reserva de la Guardia Civil* (Civil Guard's Reserves) – the official name for the militias- called for the mobilization of all the agrarian and labor union members for joining the "Reservas." When only 400 individuals showed up at the recruiting center, the leftist political parties and university student organizations also began calling on their members, to no avail. For the military, however, it was the thought that counted.

Back in Opa-locka, PBSuccess headquarters was trying to overcome the damage caused by the recent capture of key Castillo Armas operatives. The most serious problem was that the arms smuggling plan had been compromised, and the Guardia Civil had raided the majority of the storage facilities. Without supplies already placed on the field, the Liberation Army would have to rely heavily on airlift during the invasion. Then, all of a sudden, CIA operatives scouting the region that was about to become the theater of operations began reporting that at least a handful of resistance cells had remained intact. Based on this information, PBSuccess headquarters ordered Castillo Armas to select special couriers that would infiltrate into Guatemala and establish contact with these cells and train them for receiving the parachuted cargo at the different drop zones that would be established prior to the invasion. In the following days, besides contacting the resistance cells scattered over the Northwestern and Southeastern regions of the country, the couriers reached two large groups, one at Tiquisate, in the Guatemalan Pacific Coast, and the other in Barberena, some 56 km Southwest from Guatemala City.

Not wanting to lose any time, PBSuccess headquarters ordered the pilots of Castillo Armas' "A Group" to airlift supplies and armament from the staging point in Nueva Ocotepeque to the different locations where the resistance cells had been found. However, by the third round of flights, the airlift had to be suspended since the staging point had run out of arms and ammunition. To make things worse, the rest

The Lockheed P-38L of the Nicaraguan Air Force sporting the service's colors and insignia. (Photo credit: Revista Militar de Nicaragua, via René Sanchez.)

of it was still stored in Tegucigalpa, more than 200 km away.

Rip Robertson, PBSuccess' Field Commander, ordered Brodfrost to send his C-47s to the Honduran Capital to pick up the rest of supplies and fly them to Nueva Ocotepeque immediately. However, the Chief of Air Support flatly refused. As per headquarters' orders, the two C-47s in Managua were assigned exclusively to leaflet-dropping missions, while the third transport was committed to flying the last supplies from France Field to Managua and Tegucigalpa.

In an unexpected turn of events, Withing Willauer, the U.S. Ambassador for Honduras, convinced Lt. Col. Hernán Acosta Mejía, the commander of the Fuerza Aérea Hondureña (the Honduran Air Force) – FAH – to lend one of the air arm's three C-47s for flying the supplies to Nueva Ocotepeque. In fact, the FAH C-47 accomplished no less than three flights on that day, allowing the "A Group" pilots to resume their resupplying flights into Guatemala.

Only then did the Field Command Post focus on the group in Tiquisate: It was the farthest location from Nueva Ocotepeque and to avoid detection, the flights had to be conducted mostly over water. For this mission, Castillo Armas designated Carlos Cheesman Mollinedo, a dual U.S. / Guatemalan citizen who had joined the Liberation Army recently and was considered to be an excellent pilot. Cheesman was able to complete two missions to Tiquisate in less than 24 hours, carrying 20 submachine guns, 5,000 rounds of ammunition, a case of hand-grenades and sabotage equipment in the first flight and two saboteurs and a resistance organizer in the second.

On June 10, the Field Command Post finally made the decision of infiltrating all the saboteurs, resident radio operators –RROs- and drop zone coordinators into Guatemala. The "A Group" pilots flew many of them to their respective destinations, while others were taken across the border in trucks and even on mules. Simultaneously, the recently graduated tactical radio operators – TROs – were assigned to their respective Liberation Army columns. That day also, Lt. Col. Acosta Mejía was asked to assign a second FAH C-47 for carrying the remaining bundles of arms and supplies stored in Tegucigalpa to the staging points in Macuelizo, Los Tarros and Copan Ruinas. In the following days, the two Honduran transports flew more than

The infamous Jerry Fred Delarm, seen here in December 1960. At the time Delarm was running an air service in Guatemala named "Servicio Interamericano de Aviación" or SIDA, providing services to the oil companies that were exploring the northern region of the country. (Photo credit: Charles Clausen.)

Aerial view of the La Aurora Airport and the City's racetrack, which some obscure Guatemalan Army officer wanted the CIA to bomb in order to spark a revolt to topple Arbenz. (Photo credit: Guatemalan Air Force.)

Douglas C-47 of the Honduran Air Force. At least two of these transports got involved in PBSuccess, mainly to fly Castillo Armas' troops and supplies to their respective staging points before the invasion. (Photo: Honduran Air Force via Honduras Air Museum.)

five tons of equipment before being grounded by what was termed acts of sabotage, since batteries and other critical components began disappearing from the planes.

Back in Guatemala City, the Army high command concluded that there was nothing left to do but start drawing defense plans for facing the imminent invasion. Castillo Flores and Martínez Estevez, Arbenz's "parallel General Staff", showed up -uninvited- at the Army's headquarters for the first planning meeting, and Col. Parinello had the humiliating task of explaining to them the troop movements that were being devised. At some point during the presentation, Col. Agustín Donnis Kestler, the Deputy Chief of Staff, grabbed Col. Parinello by the lapels yelling at him desperately to "do something to stop this!" while pointing at a very surprised Castillo Flores. After the meeting, Col. Donnis Kestler had to seek asylum at the Salvadoran Embassy.

Regarding the Army's defense plans, the main idea was to form a protective barrier along the border with Honduras and El Salvador, with troops from the Puerto Barrios, Zacapa, Chiquimula and Jalapa garrisons, reinforced by companies from the 1st and 2nd Infantry Regiments from the Guardia de Honor and the "La Aurora" garrisons respectively. This force took up the name of Ejército de Operaciones (Operations' Army) and was led by colonels Víctor M. León as Commanding Officer, Gustavo Solares as the G-1 officer (Personnel), Enrique Ruiz García as the G-2 (Intelligence), Eduardo Llerena Müller as G-3 (Operations) and Juan Martínez as the officer in charge of Logistics or G-4.

Guatemalan Army troops taking a break near Gualán, Zacapa, during the invasion. (Photo credit: Col. César Augusto Silva Girón.)

Guatemalan Army troops on patrol near the town of Los Amates, in Izabal, two days after the beginning of the invasion. (Photo credit: Col. César Augusto Silva Girón.):

Guatemalan Army troops patrolling the road between Chiquimula and Santa Barbara during the invasion. (Photo credit: Col. César Augusto Silva Girón.)

A Guatemalan Air Force North American AT-6 on a bombing run over Liberationist positions near Morales, Izabal. (Photo credit. Guatemalan Air Force.)

Following a suggestion made by the Minister of Foreign Affairs Guillermo Toriello, the protective barrier was to be set 20 km inland, creating a "buffer zone" between the border and the troops' positions. This was aimed at avoiding any international incident with the neighboring countries. That meant that all the troops and Guardia Civil agents guarding the border points had to retreat to the towns of Chiquimula, Zacapa, Jalapa, and Puerto Barrios.

Due to their strategic locations, the garrison at Zacapa became the headquarters for the Ejército de Operaciones, while the one at Chiquimula was selected as an Advanced Command Post. Incredibly, the remote and vulnerable airbase at Puerto Barrios became the logistical center for the campaign.

On June 11, the first troops from the 1st and 2nd Infantry Regiments departed Guatemala City in trains and trucks, carrying with them at least twenty-five 81 mm and 60 mm mortar tubes, a couple of 105 mm Howitzers, no less than ten 75 mm and 42 mm artillery batteries, and a handful of Browning .50 and .30 caliber machineguns. Each soldier was equipped with a Mendoza machinegun or a 7.8 mm VZ-

Three North American AT-6s of the Guatemalan Air Force scrambling out of Los Cipresales Air Base during the invasion. (Photo credit: Guatemalan Air Force.)

A North American AT-6 of the Guatemalan Air Force returning from a patrol mission in June 1954. (Photo credit: Guatemalan Air Force.)

Despite having only two Douglas C-47 transports, the Guatemalan Air Force established an efficient airlift to Puerto Barrios, where the Ejército de Operaciones had its logistics center during the campaign. (Photo credit: Guatemalan Air Force.)

24/33 Czech rifle, plus 100 rounds of ammunition. However, a few platoons were carrying old Mauser Model 1898 rifles. The officers were carrying each a .45 caliber sub machinegun and a .45 caliber Colt Automatic Pistol.

Even though the Guatemalan Army had six M3A1 Stuart and four Marmon Herrington light tanks, none of them were deployed initially, due to the terrain characteristics along the theater of operations. Nevertheless, four M3 Scout Cars were assigned to the Zacapa headquarters.

The FAG was also called in to help in the movement of the Ejército de Operaciones troops to the front. Accordingly, its two C-47s began airlifting men, equipment, and supplies to Puerto Barrios and Zacapa. Additionally, the air arm's three Beech AT-11s were launched on patrol missions over the border with El Salvador and Honduras. Simultaneously, two AT-6s were deployed, with their support personnel, to the airfields at Puerto San José in the Pacific Coast and Puerto Barrios, where they would start patrol flights aimed at intercepting the Liberation planes that, until then, had been entering Guatemalan airspace virtually unchallenged. Last but not least, the FAG was ordered to keep -at all times- an AT-6 or a Boeing P-26A circling over the Capital[3] at high altitude, for preventing any "ghost plane" from dropping leaflets or buzzing the City.

However, by the end of the first day of air operations, one of the AT-11s had failed to return to La Aurora from a flight over the Salvadoran border and the single AT-6 deployed to Puerto San José had been declared missing during the afternoon.[4] It was not until 10:00 PM that the Salvadoran Embassy informed President Arbenz that both planes were in the Salvadoran Capital, where the crews had requested asylum.

As a direct result, all FAG aircraft were grounded immediately and agents of the Policía Judicial subjected every pilot to long interrogations. In the end, four aviators were promptly arrested as it was suspected that they were involved in anti-government activities. From then on, no FAG plane could take off without first being expressly authorized by the President.

That night, the Defense Council convened an informal meeting to review the latest events. The ongoing defections were wearing down the Army's position and soon they wouldn't be able to exert any pressure upon Arbenz. On the other hand, the Communists' arrogance and their brazen attempts to seize control of the country had many young officers clamoring for a radical solution. It was more than evident that the Army was running out of options and soon they would have to do something to defuse the grave situation. That night, however, it was decided to maintain the constitutional order at least until Castillo Armas had been defeated. They would deal with Arbenz and the Communists later. In the meantime, it was paramount to contain the defections, especially within the FAG.

Ironically, two days later, on June 13, an AT-6 that had been flying one of the very few and heavily monitored patrol missions over the City, left the area unexpectedly and headed to the Southeast at full power, evading the Oerlikon anti-aircraft batteries emplaced around

One of the battered Boeing P-26s of the Guatemalan Air Force being readied for a patrol mission over the Capital. (Photo credit: Guatemalan Air Force.):

Nice air-to-air photo of a Beechcraft AT-11 while on a patrol mission near the Salvadoran border in June 1954. (Photo credit: Guatemalan Air Force.)

The six Republic F-47N "Thunderbolts" that the CIA acquired for the Liberation Army came from the Puerto Rico Air National Guard –PRANG- where they were about to be phased out due to maintenance problems. In this image, a trio of PRANG F-47Ns sporting the Puerto Rican distinctive shield in their fuselages. (Photo credit: USAF / Department of Defense.):

the Capital. Hours later it transpired that the AT-6 had to make an emergency landing at Santa Ana, 50 km Northwest of the Salvadoran Capital, after running out of fuel.[5] When President Arbenz was informed about the incident, the Salvadoran authorities had already taken the plane to the Ilopango airport, and its pilot had requested asylum.

Back in Opa-locka, Albert Haney was notified that –finally- the USAF had agreed to release three of its Thunderbolts for the project. In order to conceal their transfer to Castillo Armas, the fighters would be delivered to the Nicaraguan Air Force under the U.S. *Reimbursable Aid Program* (RAP, one of the variations of MDAP) at a price of $14,620 each, provided that the Nicaraguan government made a 15% down payment in cash first.[6] Behind the scenes, the process of getting the planes released had been a bureaucratic nightmare, both in the U.S. and in Nicaragua.

Initially, the CIA had to convince President Somoza to request the fighters through official channels. Seeing a great opportunity to reequip his air arm for free, the Nicaraguan President placed an order for eight Thunderbolts plus spares. Obviously, the USAF flatly refused and PBSuccess headquarters had to talk him out of it when he got furious. Then, Somoza requested only three fighters, but he wanted them "on loan" due to the "temporary emergency" his country was going through. Again, the USAF refused.

Ambassador Whelan had to draw on all his ability to convince Somoza to purchase the three fighters, assuring him that The Group supporting Castillo Armas would pay for them as soon as the clandestine operation had been completed. Besides, one of those planes was already his, in exchange for the Lightning. In the end, Somoza agreed.

However, after a couple of days, the Nicaraguan Ambassador for the U.S., Guillermo Sevilla Sacasa, began making excuses for not making the down payment required by the USAF.[7] At Opa-locka, everybody was holding their breath and a very worried Albert Haney informed the CIA headquarters that if the fighters were not in Managua for the beginning of the invasion, the project would be seriously compromised.

What happened next was described by Frank Wisner as "the best job of red tape cutting I have seen in years."[8] It turns out that William D. Pawley, the co-founder of the renowned American Volunteer Group (AVG) also known as the "Flying Tigers", now acting in the capacity of Special Assistant to the U.S. President, learned about the project's predicament during a meeting with Eisenhower. Sensing that Somoza was developing a case of cold feet, he phoned an officer of the Riggs Bank, where he had an account, and arranged to have $150,000 in cash ready when he arrived. Then, accompanied by Ambassador Sevilla Sacasa, they drove to the bank, stuffed the money in a briefcase he had brought and headed for the Pentagon where he made the down payment on behalf of the Nicaraguan Government.[9]

The three Thunderbolts selected came from the Puerto Rican Air National Guard (PRANG). Their USAF serials haven't been conclusively established so far, but there are four candidates according to the available documentation, their identities being: 44-89131, 44-89259, 44-89265, and 44-89400. Some USAF reports mention that the four planes were delivered to the FAN, but several CIA declassified documents contradict this, noting that only three arrived in Managua.[10]

In any case, The USAF offered to deliver the fighters no later than June 17, but the spares that were part of the deal were still being collected from airbases all around the U.S. and would have to be delivered on a later date. The USAF also offered three crew chiefs –to be added to the Air Mission in Nicaragua- for maintaining the aircraft. Obviously, PBSuccess headquarters declined the offer due to plausible deniability reasons, and only requested that the fighters be delivered in "combat-ready" condition, since the intention was to fly at least two of them as soon as they arrived.

During the afternoon on June 14, two Douglas C-124C transports (USAF serials 51-5191 and 52-0990) carrying ordnance for the Thunderbolts arrived in Managua. According to the cargo manifest, aboard the planes came forty 500 lb. M105 leaflet bombs, 240 cases of .50 caliber ammunition, 267 cases of armor-piercing / tracer .50 caliber ammunition, twenty 275 lb. M57 demolition bombs, twenty 555 lb. M64 demolition bombs, and their respective fins. Further loads would be delivered directly to France Field, since Brodfrost's plan was to have only a limited amount of ordnance in Managua, just in case the Air Support Unit had to get out of the country in a rush.

Meanwhile, PBSuccess headquarters decided to begin placing arms and equipment for the Liberation troops along the routes that they would follow during the invasion. For this, Lt. Col. Brodfrost was ordered to launch the two C-47s on a supply-dropping mission over Chiquimula. These two flights, that would be the first to be conducted by Phase IIIB's crews, were designated "C-1" and "C-2" following the new mission numbering system, with the "C" meaning that they were "cargo" flights.

The first C-47 took off at 6:00 PM, while the second left Managua 30 minutes later. Both planes arrived over their assigned drop zones in less than three hours. The C-47 flying mission C-1 had no problems finding the light pattern marking its target, and even when it was 5 km West of the prearranged location, the crew decided to make the drop. In contrast, the second C-47 had to make a couple of passes over the prearranged site since no light patterns could be seen. After a couple of minutes the crew decided to return to Managua with the cargo and both C-47s landed back at Las Mercedes around 1:00AM.

Less than two hours later, at 2:35 AM on June 15, the two C-47s departed Managua once again for another mission over Chiquimula. As it had happened in the previous mission, the receiving parties were nowhere to be found. Both C-47s circled the area for a while before returning to Managua with the cargo. These flights, recorded as C-3 and C-4 respectively, alerted the members of the agrarian unions in the region and by dawn, numerous checkpoints had been placed along the roads near Chiquimula and Zacapa, with the mission of seizing whatever the "ghost planes" were dropping.

Near 6:00 AM, the government's radio station went on the air, repeating every five minutes an official statement saying that the Guatemalan Army was more loyal than ever to President Arbenz, and that "no defections had taken place." However, during the morning a high-ranking Army officer -whose name remains unknown to this day- approached the CIA station in Guatemala, claiming that he could stage a coup as soon as the City's racetrack was bombed. This request left many scratching their heads at PBSuccess headquarters, and obviously, Al Haney refused to comply.[11] Instead, the CIA operatives offered to bomb any military installation he chose, but to no avail, the officer was adamant that the target be the racetrack! In the end, the CIA agents decided to pass on the opportunity and the officer wasn't contacted again.

Meanwhile, the pilots of the "A Group" were having difficulties in resupplying the resistance cells, since the government had seized all private and public airfields in the country and all civilian planes were prohibited from flying; not even the crop-dusters that swarmed over the cotton plantations in the Pacific Coast were allowed to take off.[12] Thus, PBSuccess headquarters decided to send the two C-47s on cargo-dropping missions to Tiquisate and other sites, deep inside Guatemala, where supplies were needed. However, as it had happened in Chiquimula, the receiving parties failed to show up and the transports had to return to Managua with their cargoes still onboard.

Near midnight, Castillo Armas' agents monitoring the La Aurora Airbase reported that there were unusual activities taking place. Cars assigned to the Presidency had arrived at the airfield, carrying bags and cases that were being loaded into a FAG C-47. Then, at 10:45 PM, the transport had taken off, escorted by two AT-6s, heading to the Southeast. Less than an hour later, both Texans returned to La Aurora[13], thus completing a highly dangerous mission, since the planes were not equipped for instruments flying and the crews were not current on such type of flights.

It was not until the next day that Castillo Armas' agents learned that the C-47 had taken Arbenz's mother, Octavia Guzmán, to El Salvador as a precautionary measure. In fact, during the rest of the week, many government officials would send their families out of the country, too.

At dawn on June 16, Brodfrost launched his two C-47s on a cargo-dropping mission over Barberena, near Guatemala City, for resupplying the resistance cell there. Flights C-7 and C-8 arrived on time but, as it was becoming customary, the receiving parties didn't show up. Suspecting that the problem was with his pilots, he sat down with the crews and reviewed every detail of the flights conducted to date. After a few hours, the Chief of Air Support had concluded that his pilots were following instructions to the letter, arriving at the prearranged locations accurately and on time. It was the receiving parties who were failing to show up.

Later on, Brodfrost questioned Castillo Armas about it, and the Caudillo replied that his receiving teams were doing their best to evade the Guatemalan authorities, which seemed to be everywhere, and that there wasn't anything he could do about it.

This image, showing a Republic F-47N "Thunderbolt" of the Puerto Rico Air National Guard is interesting because the "lightning bolt" insignia of the 198th Fighter Squadron can be seen in the main landing gear doors. The insignia survived even into the Nicaraguan Air Force service as the solitary identifying markings tying the aircraft to their PRANG origins. (Photo credit: Jorge J. Suárez via Luis Santos.)

By midmorning, Rip Robertson informed PBSuccess headquarters that "maximum readiness had been achieved" and that the Liberation Army was prepared for an "all-out effort." Accordingly, Frank Wisner set the invasion's D-Day for June 18 and the H-Hour to 8:20 PM.[14] However, when Castillo Armas was notified about this, he got furious. He wanted to launch the invasion in less than 24 hours, whether The Group allowed it or not. Rip Robertson had to be dispatched urgently to Tegucigalpa for convincing Castillo Armas to wait, telling him that The Group had a broader picture[15] of the situation and that the most propitious time to strike was June 18. Besides, his forces still were lacking tactical air support, since the Thunderbolts hadn't arrived in Managua yet.

In the end, Castillo Armas agreed on waiting for two more days, but he was so anxious that he failed to keep his mouth shut: During an interview with some foreign journalists he revealed the exact date for the beginning of the invasion. Deeply shocked, Frank Wisner ordered that the two CIA operatives "assisting him" in Tegucigalpa be replaced with officers who could handle the Caudillo's apparent "*lack of competence.*"[16]

The news travelled fast and during the afternoon, the Guatemalan Unions Confederation and the agrarian organizations called for a mass rally in support of Arbenz, to be held precisely on June 18 at 5:00 PM in the "Justo Rufino Barrios" plaza, near the City's train station.

That night, Radio Liberación warned the Guatemalans to stay away from this meeting, as it could turn into another "*Bogotazo*" (the massive riots that followed the assassination in Bogotá, Colombia, of leftist leader and presidential candidate Jorge Eliécer Gaitán on 9 April 1948.) Radio Liberación also warned the organizers that there would be serious trouble if they insisted in carrying out the rally.

At 8:15 PM Brodfrost launched flights C-9 and C-10 for dropping supplies for the Barberena resistance cell; minutes later he received a call from Castillo Armas saying that he wanted a dramatic appearance of "his" Liberation Air Force over Guatemala City, coinciding precisely with the mass rally that the Communists were organizing. The Caudillo wanted the two C-47s and the three Thunderbolts overflying the Capital in a tight V-formation.

Brodfrost tried to talk him out of such a crazy idea, but Castillo Armas insisted. With no options left, the Chief of Air Support informed PBSuccess headquarters about the flight that Castillo Armas was proposing. At first, Al Haney flatly refused to approve the flight. However, and in order to avoid any confrontation with the Caudillo, it was decided that two Thunderbolts would be sent to buzz the City in order to dissolve the mass rally and, if available, the Lightning could be sent for dropping leaflets.

Near midnight, the two C-47s that had been sent to Barberena, landed back at Managua with the cargo still onboard. Once again, the receiving committees had failed to show up at the drop zones. Exhausted, Brodfrost decided to call off all air operations until the next day.

At 9:20 AM on June 17, the project's Thunderbolts finally landed at Las Mercedes Airport, accompanied by a Lockheed C-121C that the USAF had provided for navigation during the ferry flight from Puerto Rico. As requested, the fighters arrived combat-ready, that is, with their eight .50 caliber machineguns working and fully loaded. But first, the USAF mechanics had to remove the long-range drop-tanks and make sure that the planes were completely sterile before officially handing them to Brodfrost. However, President Somoza did not even wait for the mechanics to finish their work and ordered one of the fighters to be taken to the FAN's main hangar. Then, the Nicaraguan President made it clear that "his" Thunderbolt was off-limits to Brodfrost and his pilots.

With somewhat of an air force now at hand, PBSuccess headquarters needed to come up with a cover story for it. In less than 24 hours, the Thunderbolts would be flying all over Guatemala and the press would be expecting a sound explanation concerning their origins and who was flying them. Accordingly, Castillo Armas was instructed to announce that he had acquired, with great sacrifice, a handful of "old" fighters, albeit much more powerful than those of the FAG.

The next step was finding a face for the "Liberation Air Force." For the job, Castillo Armas suggested Col. Rodolfo "Fito" Mendoza Azurdia, who had escaped Guatemala on June 7 and had been helping with the planning of the "A Group" air operations since then.

A PBSuccess C-47 dropping supplies over the Esquipulas air field in June 1954. (Photo credit: *Life* Magazine.)

PBSuccess headquarters approved the proposal immediately, and from then on Fito became the "Chief of the Liberation Air Force."

Obviously, Fito would only be a "front man" and PBSuccess headquarters made it clear to all involved that, under no circumstances, would Lt. Col. Brodfrost relinquish operational control over the project's aircraft and missions. Eventually, Fito could go on some of the cargo flights and serve as an advisor, but that would be all.[17]

PBSuccess' propaganda team wanted Fito's first public appearance to be via a Radio Liberación's broadcast, and for this, he was taken to Managua to record a message in which he would introduce himself as the Chief of the Liberation Air Force and encourage the non-Communist FAG pilots to defect with their aircraft and join him. The message would end with Fito announcing that he and his pilots would be flying over Guatemala soon, "leading the way to freedom."

The problem was, however, that Fito didn't want to record the speech. He feared that the Policía Judicial would harm his wife and children, still in Guatemala, as soon as Arbenz found out that he

An M3A1 Scout Car of the Guatemalan Army patrolling the City streets before the invasion, in June 1954. (Photo credit: *Vision* Magazine.)

was the one behind the "ghost planes" overflying the country. Many authors, including David Atlee Phillips, have stated that Fito made the recording after the Radio Liberación announcers got him drunk. However, according to CIA declassified papers, it was Brodfrost who persuaded him to make the recording, after promising him that The Group would make sure that his family was fine.[18] In the end, Fito's speech was aired during the evening broadcast on June 17.

That night, in preparation for the invasion, Brodfrost was ordered to launch the two C-47s on a cargo-dropping mission over the town of Quezaltepeque, some 20 km Southwest of Chiquimula. It was imperative that the armament and supplies were dropped on target, since the Liberation Army's Advanced Command Post would be established there. The two transports departed Las Mercedes at 7:30 PM, arriving over their assigned drop zones two and half hours later. As usual, the reception committees failed to reach the prearranged area, even when PBSuccess' Field Commander had stressed on the importance of the supplies. The pilots decided to circle the area for more than 20 minutes, while Brodfrost tried desperately to contact Castillo Armas in Tegucigalpa for finding out what had prevented the reception teams from showing up. In the end, the pilots decided to abort the mission and return to Managua, since the planes were running low on fuel. They landed back at Las Mercedes near 1:00AM.

Over dinner, and to top it all off, the project's mechanics informed Brodfrost that the Lightning's electrical system had caught fire while the plane was taxiing for its first test-flight. It wouldn't be available for another couple of days.

CHAPTER 9

THE "SULFATOS"

In the small hours of the invasion's D-day, June 18, worrisome reports began arriving to the Field Command Post at Managua. On the one hand, Pivall had discovered that the number of Castillo Armas' shock troops had decreased considerably yet again, due to desertions and illness.

With the invasion's launching just hours away, Pivall had to improvise and disbanded the "Hornet" guerrilla teams that he had been training since early June, and used its members to augment the main force. Only then the Liberation Army reached 480 troops, which was less than half of the number originally planned.

On the other hand, the inclement weather was delaying the advance of the sole column that had been ordered to infiltrate into Guatemala before H-hour, so it could be in position for attacking the Army garrison at Zacapa -the farthest target from the border- no later than June 19th.

This column, codenamed "HANK", was comprised of 70 men plus

The infamous Cessna 180 "HK-592" of the Liberation Air Force at Esquipulas. The most critical combat air support missions during the invasion were flown in this plane by Carlos Cheesman. The Stinson Reliant seen in the background had brought in a couple of Life Magazine correspondents. (Photo credit: *Life* Magazine.)

A North American AT-6 of the Guatemalan Air Force seen here during a bombing run near Jocotán, Chiquimula. (Photo credit: Guatemalan Air Force.)

a tactical radio operator, and its commanding officer was Col. Juan Chajón Chúa. They had departed Copán Ruinas near midday on June 17, for the town of Florida, where they would cross into Guatemala and proceed "black" (covertly) towards the village of Piedra Blanca to be resupplied; there they would recruit volunteers from the neighboring hamlets and then continue to the vicinity of Zacapa for launching the attack.

That plan was in jeopardy, however, since the four trucks carrying the troops were barely coping with the terrible roads along the mountainous terrain near the border, to the point where Col. Chajón Chúa had decided to continue on foot towards Piedra Blanca, even if that meant that they wouldn't be in the vicinity of Zacapa on the 19th.

That wasn't all, however, since near 6:00 AM, PBSuccess' tactical communications center at Nueva Ocotepeque, codenamed "SALAL", informed the Field Command Post that since midnight, they had noticed considerable traffic between a radio operator attached to one of the Liberation columns and Castillo Armas' headquarters in Tegucigalpa. This group, using the spurious codename "Panchoy", had already crossed into Guatemala and had clashed with an Army reconnaissance squad near the town of El Florido; the Army squad had repelled them for more than two hours, but ended up retreating. This end was confirmed when Pivall's operatives reported that, indeed, the column codenamed "JOHNNY", led by Col. Guillermo Flores Avendaño –Castillo Armas' Chief of Staff- had departed the staging point at Copán Ruinas near 8:00 PM, and had crossed into Guatemala without authorization.

According to the invasion plan, this group, comprised of 96 men and two tactical radio operators, was to cross at El Florido at H-Hour and then advance towards the small village of Caparjá to be reinforced. From there, they would reach Jocotán and split in two groups for attacking Chiquimula, the largest and best defended town in the area.

When Rip Robertson learned about the premature crossing[1], he called Castillo Armas and ordered him to stop Col. Flores Avendaño's column at once. The Caudillo refused, however, alleging that he was in a difficult situation because the Salvadoran President had already backpedalled from supporting him and was threatening to put his troops in jail; additionally, President Somoza was seriously considering withdrawing his support if the invasion wasn't launched as soon as possible. Last, but not least, pulling his troops out of Honduras ahead of schedule was of utmost urgency due to the diplomatic pressure that the Guatemalan government was exerting upon President Gálvez at the OAS and the UN.

Robertson was adamant, however, and threatened to call off The Group's support if Col. Flores Avendaño wasn't stopped immediately. In the end Castillo Armas agreed, but it still took him more than an hour to contact Flores Avendaño, who, at that time, was regrouping his troops at the small village of Shupá after being strafed by a FAG AT-6 that showed up while the column was recruiting volunteers at the town of Caparjá.

By 9:00 AM bad news kept piling up: PBSuccess headquarters informed Robertson that the day before, 52 men of Castillo Armas' forces had been apprehended by the Guardia Civil Salvadoreña (El Salvador's Civil Guard) at a ranch named "San Antonio Abad", in Santa Ana, El Salvador, while preparing to launch yet another premature

A trio of North American AT-6 of the Guatemalan Air Force making a low-pass over the runway of Los Cipresales Air Base, upon returning from a combat mission. (Photo credit: Guatemalan Air Force.)

North American AT-6 "FAG-0930" ready for take off at Los Cipresales Air Base in June 1954. (Photo credit: Guatemalan Air Force.)

infiltration into Guatemala. By then, the U.S. Embassy had already negotiated their deportation to Honduras.

These men comprised the column codenamed "FRANK", led by Cpt. René Fernández. They had orders to cross the border at H-Hour and reach the small village of Asunción Mita to be reinforced. Then, they would attack the garrison at the nearby town of Jutiapa and setup a blockade to contain any Army reinforcements that could be sent to the Chiquimula – Zacapa area.

As soon as Robertson learned about the deportation of Fernández's men, he contacted the captain and ordered him to proceed to Nueva Ocotepeque and join the column led by Col. Miguel Mendoza, Fito Mendoza's older brother.

Col. Mendoza's column, codenamed "DANNY", was comprised of 106 men plus a tactical radio operator. Their orders were to seize the small village of Esquipulas after H-hour, for establishing there the Liberation Army's Field Command Post and to recruit volunteers.

The PBSuccess mechanics who kept the "Sulfatos" flying, posing here before one of their beloved machines at Las Mercedes Airport, in Nicaragua. (Photo: via Dan Hagedorn.)

Then, they would advance towards the town of Quezaltepeque, where the column would split in two, with one group joining Col. Flores Avendaño in a coordinated attack against Chiquimula, and the other advancing towards the village of Ipala for containing any Army troop movements into the area.

The two remaining columns that didn't launch when Castillo Armas gave the order still were at their respective staging points at Macuelizo and Los Tarros, getting ready for H-hour. The first of these, codenamed "BOND", was composed of 116 men led by Major Julián Torres. Its mission would be to set up a blockade at the village of Entre Ríos for isolating the Ejército de Operaciones' logistical center at Puerto Barrios and launch harassment raids on that town, supported by a seaborne assault force of 27 men aboard the schooner "La Siesta", led by the civilian Alberto Artiga.

The last, much smaller column, was codenamed "TOMMY" and was comprised of only 16 men led by Lt. Emilio de Paz; they would throw a supplementary block to Puerto Barrios at the town of Morales, an obligatory stopping point between that port and Zacapa, and cause as much trouble as possible to the military convoys headed in either direction.

Even though the CIA declassified documents do not mention Castillo Armas' reasons for prematurely launching the invasion, the probable cause had to do with the Caudillo's fear of being replaced with an alternate solution for getting rid of Arbenz. His suspicions were based on a series of highly secret meetings that were taking place at Guatemala City between Ambassador Peurifoy and a handful of high-ranking Army officers, all members of the Defense Council, who were willing to stage a coup providing that the CIA could put up a dramatic "show of force" for giving them an excuse to revolt.

Several alternatives had been discussed so far, but the seditious officers believed that the best option was an "air display" over Guatemala City, in which "rebel planes" would buzz the Capital, firing their machineguns and dropping bombs on "safe areas", although in plain view of the population. Once the first bombs had exploded, Army troops would seize the National Palace and capture Arbenz, replacing him with a junta made up of three high-ranking officers.

So, it's possible that Castillo Armas tried to launch the invasion thinking that, once it was on its way, The Group would have to stick with him and disregard the seditious officers' ridiculously simple plan for ending the Communist threat in Guatemala.

What the Caudillo didn't know was that the air display plan was facing fierce opposition from Frank Wisner, who rejected the idea of bombing Guatemala City[2], as it could evolve into a public relations nightmare if someone got hurt or killed by mistake. By then, Castillo Armas' movement had already been labeled as a foreign aggression thanks to the Guatemalan government's diplomatic efforts, and bombing the Capital would only provide a confirmation.

But Peurifoy, who had made the plan his own, was pressing on, alleging that dropping a couple of bombs over the Capital could help resolve the situation faster than the paramilitary campaign, allowing Castillo Armas -or whomever the hell the CIA designed- to enter Guatemala City victorious and without firing a single shot.

The situation between Peurifoy and Wisner turned for the worse when the latter informed all the involved that Rip Robertson had been assigned "*full field command of all CIA controlled PBSUCCESS' assets*" including "*all air operational support activities.*"[3] Wisner's cable added that the fighter aircraft were to fly armed for defense only and "*air fire support authority*" had to be obtained from PBSuccess headquarters, regardless of the urgency.

As it would be expected, the Ambassador found this disposition incompatible with the air display plan and demanded exclusive control over the fighters. "*The shock troops do not need air protection where no air opposition exists*" the determined Ambassador stated in one of the cables[4] he sent to Wisner.

During the morning, Peurifoy's demand reached not only the Secretary of State but also the CIA Director. It didn't take long for them to approve a flight over Guatemala City, during which the Thunderbolts would be limited to drop "harmless" smoke bombs over unpopulated areas and fire their machineguns into the air.

When Brodfrost received the new orders, he was in a quandary. Up until then he and his pilots had been planning a mission that called for buzzing Guatemala City to disband the large number of labor workers and agraristas that were gathering in downtown, despite the government's cancellation of the mass rally they were to attend. But

Wreckage of the AT-6 that Lt. Juan Adolfo Castillo Ralda was flying on a combat mission on June 18, 1954. He crashed near the town of Palin, Escuintla, due to bad weather. (Photo credit: Guatemalan Air Force.)

Lieutenant Juan Adolfo Castillo Ralda, one of the few officers of the Guatemalan Air Force who were willing to fly in combat missions during the invasion. He crashed while trying to return to La Aurora airbase after having aborted a combat mission due to bad weather on June 18, 1954. (Photo credit: Guatemalan Air Force.)

Lieutenant Carlos Lascout Campo, a brave Liberation pilot, was killed by troops of the Guardia Civil after his Cessna 180 crash-landed in Escuintla, while trying to reach Tiquisate, carrying supplies for a resistance cell that had been established there. (Photo credit: Guatemalan Air Force.)

now, headquarters wanted him to load the planes with "*smoke bombs or flares*" to be dropped over "*safe areas*." The problem was that he didn't have any smoke bombs or flares in Managua, nor at France Field, and bringing them from the U.S. could take days.

As there was no time to comply with headquarters' extraordinary requirements, Brodfrost decided to send the fighters without the bombs. The planes needed to depart Las Mercedes no later than 2:30 PM or the pilots would have a difficult time returning to Managua in the dark, without navigational aids.

For this mission, the Thunderbolt's very first sortie, Brodfrost designated Delarm as the flight leader; his wingman would be an ex Marine going by the exotic alias of "T-Bone" Williams, who was one of two newly-recruited pilots that had arrived in Managua earlier that day.

Just before takeoff, Brodfrost had to tackle yet another difficulty: Delarm, standing on his fighter's wing, refused to go if he wasn't paid in advance. The Chief of Air Support had to promise the pilot that he would be paid upon returning, even if that meant doing so out of Brodfrost's own wallet.

The Thunderbolts took off at 2:20 PM and flew up to a waypoint located 90 km Southeast of Puerto de San José, on the Guatemalan Pacific Coast, where they turned north and headed directly to Guatemala City.

Meanwhile, at the Nueva Ocotepeque staging point, a second flight was being prepared: Castillo Armas' Cessna 180, with Carlos Cheesman at the controls, would "bomb" the gasoline tanks of Puerto de San José. For this, two "bombardiers" on board would be dropping explosive contraptions, made of TNT blocks, out of the plane's side doors. This improvised bombing mission, approved by Robertson for augmenting the punch on the first day of combat operations, was the first of many that Cheesman would accomplish throughout the campaign, not only attacking "strategic" targets but also providing close air support for the Liberation troops when the fighters were unavailable.

The Thunderbolts arrived over the Capital near 4:00 PM, making a long low pass over downtown during which the pilots, with their canopies rolled back, tried to drop a handful of leaflets they were carrying in the cockpit. This proved to be impossible, however, since the pamphlets were sucked back in as soon as they were thrown out! (Fearing that the M105 leaflet dispensers could be mistaken for large bombs, Wisner hadn't approved their use.) In the end, the pilots decided to skip that part of the mission, focusing then on putting up the "air show."

During the following 20 minutes, the Thunderbolts buzzed repeatedly not only the Capital's downtown and the National Palace, but also Los Cipresales and La Aurora airbases. This was done virtually unchallenged since the anti-aircraft batteries emplaced around the city remained surprisingly silent. At La Aurora Airbase, instead of getting the aircraft ready to scramble, the mechanics were rushing them into the revetments in the Southeast sector of the airport.

Then, the pilots engaged in terrorizing the labor workers' gathering, firing their machineguns into the air, and raining down hundreds of spent cartridges over the "Justo Rufino Barrios" plaza. As it would be expected, it only took a couple of minutes for the crowd to disperse.

After departing the Capital, the Thunderbolts buzzed the town of Escuintla a couple of times and then headed towards the airbase at Puerto de San José, just to see if there were any FAG aircraft deployed there. After circling the deserted airfield twice, Delarm called off the mission and ordered Williams to join him in formation for returning to Managua, where they landed at 6:20 PM.

According to reports from the CIA station in Guatemala City, the Thunderbolts created a "*strong impression on the populace that neared on panic*"[5], and during the rest of the afternoon, the Capital remained plunged into chaos. The situation got worse when Radio Liberación began announcing that the invasion was imminent and that the population should stay away from military facilities, as they would be attacked. Upon hearing this, many families decided to pack their belongings and head out of the City immediately, sparking an exodus[6] that would increase in the coming days.

The CIA station's report generated a great deal of self-congratulating, both at Opa-locka and at the Field Command Post. The only ones not satisfied with the flight's outcome were the seditious Army officers who deemed it "*pathetic and weak*" or so they told Peurifoy.

It didn't take long for the stubborn Ambassador to contact PBSuccess headquarters once again, demanding a second flight over the Capital, adding that this time the seditious Army officers expected the fighters to drop bombs over military installations. As before, Peurifoy's demands went all the way up to the CIA Director.

At 4:45 PM, Cheesman flew in the Cessna 180 at an extremely low altitude towards the gasoline tanks located on the outskirts of Puerto de San José and bombed them with extraordinary accuracy.[7] Then, he climbed out and headed towards the town of Retalhuleu, some 114 km away, where his companions strafed the gasoline tanks there with the Madsen machineguns they were carrying, puncturing them, and then setting them on fire with hand-grenades.

Only minutes after Cheesman's raid over Retalhuleu, a pair of FAG AT-6s, piloted by Maj. Enrique Valladares Morris and Lt. Juan Adolfo Castillo Ralda, was scrambled from La Aurora to intercept him. The AT-6s didn't get too far, however, as they encountered a heavy storm and Maj. Valladares decided to call off the flight. Unfortunately, Lt. Castillo Ralda didn't make it back to La Aurora airbase, since his plane slammed against a hill near the village of Palín[8], some 30 km south of the Capital. It took almost three days for the FAG's personnel to find the crash-site and recover his body.

At 5:00 PM, a Cessna 180 of Castillo Armas' "A Group", with Cpt. Carlos Lascout Campo at the controls, departed Nueva Ocotepeque for Tiquisate, carrying Cpt. Raúl Secaira, and the civilians Felicito Bolaños and Rafael Méndez, who were going to take over the resistance cell in that town.

As this flight was to be conducted in complete radio silence, it was not until three hours later that the SALAL center noticed that something had gone wrong, because the plane never reached its destination. Near 8:00 PM, the Cessna was declared officially missing.[9]

Sadly, it was not until the campaign had come to an end that a search party was organized and, according to accounts gathered during those search efforts, it seems that the Guardia Civil killed the occupants after they had crash landed at a farm named "San Benito"[10], some 25 km Southeast from the town of Escuintla.

Meanwhile back at Managua, and just before H-hour, Rip Robertson requested PBSuccess headquarters for authority to conduct "*flak suppression*" missions not only over Zacapa and Chiquimula, but also over Guatemala City. Additionally, the Field Commander wanted to start bombing military facilities along the theater of operations "*as example of strength and determination of the anti-Communist forces*" since he feared that the Guatemalan military would find out soon that the strength of the Liberation Army was just a myth.

Wisner rejected Robertson's request initially, stating that the use of air to ground action against any military target within the Capital could engage the Guatemalan Army's honor and prestige and consolidate the majority of the lower ranks in opposition to Castillo Armas. He agreed to start bombing military targets in the Chiquimula – Zacapa area, however, and offered to get the approval from the CIA Director as soon as possible.

At 8:20 PM, the much-anticipated H-hour, Radio Liberación finally went on the air announcing –live- that "*5000 troops of the Liberation Movement were advancing everywhere throughout the country*" with the mission of deposing Arbenz and his "*Moscow-controlled regime.*" A couple of minutes later, and without any ceremony, Robertson ordered the three Liberation columns still in Honduras to cross the border.

The rest of the evening, Radio Liberación kept delivering psychological blows to the population and the government by airing false reports of heavy combats and dramatic acts of sabotage across the country. Then, near midnight, Brodfrost's C-47s buzzed the

Aerial view of the gasoline storage tanks at Puerto San José, which were "bombed" by Carlos Cheesman in the Liberation's Cessna 180 on June 18, 1954. (Photo credit: Life Magazine.)

capital shortly after having parachuted supplies to a resistance cell in the neighboring town of Villa Canales. Within seconds, the Army's gunners began firing at them, scaring the living daylights out of the population with the loud noise and the thousands of tracers filling the night sky. Inevitably, the Capital plunged into chaos yet again.

With the first light of June 19, Brodfrost was ordered to send the Thunderbolts to buzz the Capital for a second time. Wisner had made this decision mostly to appease Ambassador Peurifoy who had spent the night trying to convince everyone in Washington about the necessity of bombing Guatemala City as soon as possible. There was a caveat, however, since the fighters wouldn't be carrying any bombs and the pilots were authorized to open fire only in self-defense.

Thus, the war of nerves on the Guatemalan population resumed at 8:00 AM, when the two Thunderbolts arrived over the City and immediately began buzzing the downtown. As had occurred the previous night, the Army gunners did their best in trying to shoot them down, to no avail. This, however, gave the pilots an excuse to strafe some of the anti-aircraft batteries, forcing their crews to run for cover.

Amid the confusion, a handful of Guardia Civil guards –in civilian clothes- broke into Fito Mendoza's home and set it on fire, with Fito's mother inside! Fortunately, a group of neighbors rescued the old lady in time and took her to the hospital. The fire spread rather quickly, however, and burned down not only Fito's home but also two nearby houses.

Within minutes, and just as Wisner had predicted it, the government issued an official press release saying that "mercenary planes" had bombed various sectors of the Capital, leaving several wounded, including a little girl, and a couple of houses destroyed. Inevitably, the government's statement made it to the world's headlines, and some news reports even stated that the Capital had been razed.

As soon as Wisner got wind of the alarming press reports, he promptly cabled Robertson asking what had really happened. The Field Commander's reply was blunt: "No matter what you read or hear on the radio, we dropped no bombs."[11]

A "Sulfato" in action! This photo was taken at Guatemala City during one of the tactical missions of mid-June 1954. (Photo credit: Via Mario Overall.)

The Thunderbolts' presence in the skies of Guatemala City delivered a profound psychological blow to the population. The roads out of the Capital were now packed with cars, trucks and mule carts carrying worried families looking for a safe place to stay; the streets were deserted and many owners hadn't opened their businesses, while wealthy families were sending their sons and daughters out of the country.

Curiously, the grave situation didn't stop the resilient Guatemalans from coming up with sarcastic jokes about what was happening, and they even began calling the fighters "Sulfatos" -the name in Spanish of a powerful laxative- because whenever they appeared over the Capital,

Guatemalan kids watching the strafing run of a "Sulfato" at Guatemala City during one of the tactical mission of mid-June 1954. (Photo credit: Via Mario Overall.)

the Communists got so scared that they had to change their pants.

The psychological impact on the Guatemalan military was equally profound and revealed the first cracks in their morale, especially at the FAG, where its personnel realized that they were powerless against the fearsome Thunderbolts that buzzed the Capital with impunity.

In fact, of the fifty-one active pilots, only Majors Gustavo Girón Cartagena (brother of the FAG's Commander), Doroteo Monterroso (the FAG's executive commander), Arturo Guirola, Víctor Figueroa, Pedro Granados, Capt. Julio Gálvez Rosales and Lieutenants Fernando Juarez and Rubén Zuchini were willing to fly.

The *coup de grace* to the FAG's morale came when Majors Alberto Posadas Ariza, Luis Urrutia de León, and Ricardo Herrera Llanos, fearing that the government would go after them for refusing to go on combat missions, sought asylum[12] in the Salvadoran embassy.

To make things worse for the Army, the radio operators at the headquarters began having problems in getting their encrypted messages to the troops at the front, as these were being received virtually undecipherable, forcing the recipients to request retransmissions over and over, turning the delivery of a simple order into a nightmarish process that lasted hours.

Inevitably, the troops in the field were practically left to their own devices, with no clear orders but to sit and wait for something to happen, and react to it in the best possible way. The Army's high command also lost sight of the developments in the front, rendering them unable to direct the operations with certainty and accuracy.

Unbeknownst to the Guatemalan military, this severe communications breakdown was being caused by a seldom-documented PBSuccess' sub-project, codenamed "SAHARA"[13], aimed precisely at disrupting the Army's radio channels by garbling the contents of every message that was being transmitted.

19 radio operators, led by a CIA agent going by the *nom-de-guerre* Clifford Marshall, comprised this sub-project, which was based at Nueva Ocotepeque, Honduras, in the same location from where Radio Liberación was broadcasting.

Initially, the Army's Signal Corps tried to secure the government's telegraph network so the headquarters could communicate with Zacapa and Chiquimula. However, as soon as they tried to make the first transmissions, Castillo Armas' saboteurs cut all the lines leading to Guatemala City. Then, the Signal Corps turned to the commercial radio circuits for connecting the headquarters with Zacapa, at the least, but it didn't take long for the SAHARA's operators to discover them and disrupt those channels too. In the end, the Army's high command reluctantly adopted the ancient and slow method of sending its orders with couriers. Fortunately, these brave men were using Jeeps instead of horses!

During the afternoon, the SALAL center began receiving sporadic reports from Castillo Armas' field commanders, who still were en route to their assigned resupplying locations. Robertson expected that the first combats would occur at dawn on the 20th at the earliest, so he didn't worry too much when he heard that the columns were behind schedule. Instead, he decided to take advantage of the present hiatus and resupply a resistance cell that, according to Castillo Armas, was operating near Jutiapa and that could launch a supplementary attack on that town's garrison.

Accordingly, the Field Commander ordered Brodfrost to launch the C-47s, and since this was the first resupplying mission to be conducted under "combat conditions", the Thunderbolts were sent along for escorting them. The fighters' secondary mission would be to buzz Jutiapa, Zacapa, and Chiquimula, as a show of force.

As had become routine by now, the receiving party didn't show up at the drop zone near Jutiapa and after 20 minutes of circling the C-47s returned to Managua, leaving the fighters behind so their pilots could have some "low-level fun" over their assigned targets.

The first town that the Thunderbolts buzzed was Jutiapa, and in the process, they disbanded a large group of militiamen that the government had been training at a sawmill in the town's outskirts. Then, the fighters buzzed Zacapa and it was there where the "low-level fun" came to an abrupt end when a couple of .50 caliber machineguns, emplaced on a hill overlooking the town, turned out to be deadly accurate, hitting both Thunderbolts during their first pass.

Despite the damages, both fighters reached Managua after a couple of hours. However, one of them slammed the runway when its main landing gear collapsed upon touching down. As soon as the plane stopped sliding on its belly, Brodfrost rushed his mechanics to get it

The last surviving pair of Boeing P-26A of the Guatemalan Air Force, photographed at the"Alert Ramp"in La Aurora Airbase, during the invasion. (Photo credit: Peter M. Bowers via Dan Hagedorn.)

back on its feet and out of the way, so the other fighter could land.

Brodfrost's mechanics still were on their way when their Nicaraguan counterparts arrived at the scene and dragged the crippled fighter out of the runway with a tractor[14], causing further damages that put the plane out of commission for the remainder of the campaign.

Even though the second Thunderbolt landed safely, it arrived with its turbo-supercharger system damaged. After an initial evaluation, the mechanics determined that the repairs would take no less than 48 hours, much to Brodfrost's chagrin.

When Rip Robertson got wind of the bad news, his immediate reaction was trying to convince President Somoza about selling them his Thunderbolt, which at the time was still sitting unused at the FAN's main hangar. But Somoza bluntly refused, arguing that they wanted his plane just to put up air shows over Guatemala City and that he wouldn't sell it unless the U.S. provided him with additional aircraft with the same capabilities as the F-47N.

With no other options, Robertson informed Opa-locka about the terrible predicament the project was in, adding that he needed urgently three more fighters[15], whether they were Thunderbolts or F-51D *Mustangs*. Within hours, his request went all the way up to President Eisenhower.

At the close of the day, the SALAL center began querying the different columns about their status. It turned out that none of them had reached their assigned resupplying locations, much less getting near their targets due to the nasty weather. The only news were that Col. Flores Avendaño's column had clashed with an Army patrol near Camotán, but the officer in charge, Cpt. Jorge Jiménez, with 30 troops under his command[16], surrendered as soon as the first shots had been fired. Something similar had occurred near the village of Esquipulas, where an Army reconnaissance squad, led by Cpt. Carlos Maldonado, attacked Col. Mendoza's column for more than an hour and then retreated to safety when the Army officer realized that his troops were facing a superior force.[17]

On their part, Castillo Armas' sabotage groups were engaged in a silent battle against the Army's Engineer Corps along the railroad tracks to Zacapa and Puerto Barrios. As soon as the saboteurs blew up a bridge or caused a landslide to block the railway, the Engineer Corps arrived at the area and cleared the way, sometimes under heavy fire.

Radio Liberación was waging its own kind of war against the government's radio station that night too, airing reports about heavy battles throughout the country that had left hundreds of Army casualties, while the government's TGW radio called the population to calm, denying emphatically that there was an invasion in progress.

On June 20, an exasperated Castillo Armas decided to issue an ultimatum[18] to the Guatemalan officers, and sent his Cessna 180 to drop leaflets over the Chiquimula – Zacapa area, calling them to surrender unconditionally. This flight, which hadn't been authorized by Robertson, came close to a dramatic end since the plane drew considerable ground fire, mainly at Zacapa, where the gunners pulled out all of the stops in trying to shoot it down.

As soon as Robertson learned about this, he immediately ordered Castillo Armas to stop issuing ultimatums to the Guatemalan officers, as it was contrary to the campaign's desired effect, which was precisely to get them to join the Liberation Army against Arbenz. Minutes later the Cessna was ordered to return to Nueva Ocotepeque.

By midday, Brodfrost launched one of the C-47s on a mission for resupplying Col. Chajón Chúa's column at Piedra Blanca and for giving it another shot at dropping arms and supplies for the resistance cell in Jutiapa, which, according to Castillo Armas' operatives, was already positioned at the drop zone.

When the transport arrived over Piedra Blanca, Col. Chajón Chúa's men weren't there, so the pilot began looking for them, as it was a mandatory drop. After more than 20 minutes, the pilot finally found them almost 15km Southeast from where they were supposed to be, and resupplied them. In Jutiapa, and as usual, the receiving parties didn't show up, so the pilot decided to call off the mission.

Regarding the ground operations, during the morning Col. Mendoza's column had seized the village of Esquipulas virtually unopposed. The Liberationists were perplexed when they saw that the population received them as heroes and that more than 600 volunteers wanted to join them. There was no time for celebrations, however, and as soon as the village was secured, Col. Mendoza began preparing the assault on his next target: the nearby town of Quezaltepeque.

At Camotán, Col. Flores Avendaño's column had also taken up many volunteers from the neighboring hamlets and was now preparing to attack the town of Vado Hondo. For this, the Colonel requested air reconnaissance over the target, but his expectations came crashing down when SALAL center replied that, besides Castillo Armas' Cessna 180, no air support was available. The news affected Flores Avendaño deeply, and he began having doubts about going any further without the fighters clearing the way. In fact, that morning a couple of his men heard him say, "*I don't know what the hell we are doing here!*"[19]

After three days filled with uncertainty and rumors of war, the only concrete action that had taken place so far was that the Guatemalan Army had managed to reinforce the Ejército de Operaciones by sending 600 troops on a couple of trains to Zacapa, despite the numerous acts of sabotage.

The FAG had done its part too, since the few pilots still willing to fly, had established a hasty airlift to Puerto Barrios with the only two C-47s on hand, bringing in sorely needed supplies and 200 additional troops. By then, there were more than 1800 soldiers in the theater of operations.

CHAPTER 10
CHIQUIMULA

On Monday June 21, the CIA Director finally made a decision about the fighter aircraft role for the rest of the campaign. Much to Ambassador Peurifoy's chagrin, their primary mission would be to employ maximum firepower against military targets in the Chiquimula – Zacapa area, while providing close air support to Castillo Armas' forces.

Despite Peurifoy's lengthy cables explaining why it was necessary to bomb Guatemala City, Dulles and many CIA analysts still considered it absurd to think that a couple of bombs could spark a major revolt. However, and due to the Ambassador's insistence, the CIA Director approved another round of air attacks against the gasoline storage tanks at Guatemala City and Puerto Barrios, but that would be all he would authorize. If the seditious Army officers wanted something more drastic in order to stage a coup, they would have to look elsewhere for it.

Headquarters notified Rip Robertson about the change of orders near 5:00 AM on that same day, but he did not have any fighters available for conducting the required missions. The Thunderbolt was being repaired from the damages sustained during the last flight, and the P-38L Lightning, which was the only hope for increasing the crippled Liberation Air Force strength, was far from being ready for combat.

As had become painfully the norm, Robertson had to improvise and decided to send Carlos Cheesman in the Cessna 180 to bomb the gasoline storage tanks at Puerto Barrios, achieving thus at least one of the objectives cleared by the CIA Director. During that mission, the pilot would provide some close air support to Maj. Torres' troops during their attack on that town.

Maj. Torres' column had, during the night, secured the villages of Champona and Chachagualilla, where many enthusiastic volunteers had joined them, and arrived in Entre Ríos near 4:00 AM, seizing the town's train station and blocking the railroad tracks leading to Zacapa. An hour later, a large detachment broke away from the column and took up positions a couple of kilometers Southwest of Puerto Barrios, where they set to wait for the signal to begin their attack.

At 6:30 AM, Cheesman approached Puerto Barrios' airfield following the usual landing pattern, and tricked the air traffic controllers into thinking that it was a FAG plane arriving. Upon being authorized to land, the pilot flew over the nearby gasoline tanks where his bombardier dropped a couple of the deadly TNT blocks he was carrying and set the tanks on fire.[1] Within minutes, Cheesman circled back and made a low pass over the airfield's main ramp while his companion tried to strafe a solitary FAG AT-6 that was parked there with his Madsen machinegun, missing it completely due to Cheesman's erratic maneuvering to avoid being hit by the heavy ground fire that the plane was drawing. Then, the Cessna departed the area by diving behind a tree line in the airfield's outskirts and continued flying at a very low altitude towards the Honduran border.

The explosions of the gasoline tanks were the signal that Maj. Torres' men were expecting and immediately commenced their attack on the town. According to field reports, they gained control of over half of Puerto Barrios in less than an hour and seized key installations including the Guardia Civil's barracks, the train station and the telegraph office.

So overwhelming was the assault that the Army officer in charge of the town's defense, Col. Juan Bolaños, thought that he was confronting a much superior force[2], and began calling the Zacapa garrison for reinforcements, but none of his urgent messages went through since the SAHARA team garbled his radio transmissions in no time.

After a couple of hours, Maj. Torres' men ran out of ammunition and had to fall back to Entre Ríos to resupply. This pause gave Col. Bolaños a chance to call on the population, and organized an improvised militia that took upon itself the town's defense while the Army troops set off in hot pursuit of the Liberationists.

During the rest of the morning, Col. Bolaños' troops laid siege to Entre Ríos, prompting Maj. Torres to call Cheesman desperately for air support. The daring pilot wasn't able to respond, however, as he had made an emergency landing in Honduras after a tree branch got stuck in one of the Cessna's elevators during the troubled escape from Puerto Barrios' airfield. With no options left, Maj. Torres resigned himself to hold out until help could arrive.

Less than 40 km Southwest from Entre Ríos, and completely unaware of the developments there, Lt. de Paz's column occupied the town of Morales and blocked the railroad tracks leading to Puerto Barrios.[3] This group had taken up 40 volunteers from the nearby villages of Bananera and Los Amates, which the column had secured

Lt. Col. Carlos Castillo Armas arriving at Esquipulas on June 22, 1954, to lead his forces. (Photo credit: Life Magazine.)

during the night.

In contrast, the operations in the Chiquimula – Zacapa area were unfolding very slowly; Col. Mendoza's column had reached the town of Quezaltepeque and was waiting to be resupplied there before launching a major attack on Vado Hondo, in coordination with Col. Flores Avendaño's group that was also in line to be resupplied at the village of Jocotán.

Vado Hondo was paramount to the Liberationists as the Guatemalan Army's first line of defense was there. As soon as the town could be secured, they would be able to launch a major attack on Chiquimula.

In Piedra Blanca, Col. Chajón Chúa's column was taking up much many more volunteers than expected, forcing the Colonel to delay his advance to Zacapa and request a resupply flight as soon as possible. The majority of these volunteers were members of the resistance cell that had been established in the nearby village of Gualán, where the Army detachment's commander, Capt. Gilberto Aldana, was helping them by turning a blind eye on their activities[4], and eventually providing them with precious intelligence about military movements in the area.

The air operations for the day began at 9:00 AM when the two C-47s arrived over Jocotán to resupply Col. Flores Avendaño's column, escorted by Delarm in the solitary Thunderbolt, whose repairs had been finished early in the morning. The whole resupply process took less that 45 minutes, and as soon as the transports had left, the fighter went looking for targets of opportunity in the area.

Delarm arrived over Zacapa first, and strafed the many machinegun emplacements around the town's garrison, taking out most of them. Then, the pilot headed for Chiquimula, but as he began his first strafing run, several machinegun nests emplaced in the hills North of the town opened fire, hitting the fighter's wings and fuselage. Delarm immediately climbed away from there and not wanting to risk the only available fighter, he decided to call off the mission.

As Delarm was heading for the "emergency escape route" through Honduras, he noticed that a Cessna 180 was making its way to the border, near the village of Esquipulas. Without thinking too much about it, the pilot went after the small plane firing short machinegun bursts across its nose and overtaking it on high-speed passes. It didn't take long for the Cessna's pilot to realize that a menacing fighter plane was trying to shoot him down, so he decided to land at the Esquipulas' airfield.

Hours later the Field Command Post was informed that the plane that Delarm had forced to land was none other than Castillo Armas' Cessna 180, flown by Cheesman, that was returning to its base in Nueva Ocotepeque after having repaired the plane's elevators. Fortunately, the incident didn't have any consequences beyond a little dent on Cheesman's ego and a strong reprimand for Delarm.

Brodfrost's mechanics patched the Thunderbolt up as soon as it arrived back in Managua. Apparently, the bullets hadn't caused major damages and the plane was able take off for a second mission after midday. This flight was aimed at strafing the gasoline storage tanks at Guatemala City, just as Peurifoy had requested. However, after an hour and a half into the flight, the pilot had to turn around due to problems with the engine's carburetor.

The plane hadn't landed at Managua yet when Robertson phoned President Somoza to see if he had changed his mind about selling his Thunderbolt. Unfortunately, he hadn't.

During the afternoon, Robertson informed PBSuccess headquarters that the lack of fighters was jeopardizing the whole operation, and that it was critical to get additional aircraft. This time headquarters' reply was hopeful, however, since President Eisenhower had authorized the CIA Director to "initiate actions to acquire three additional Thunderbolts" from the USAF.[5]

The last flight of the day was conducted by a C-47 that took off at 5:00 PM. Its mission was to resupply Col. Mendoza's column at Quezaltepeque and Cpt. Fernández's group on the road to Ipala, where they would take up positions for containing any Army reinforcements

Liberation troops at Esquipulas, after having received an airdrop from a PBSuccess' C-47. In the background, the legendary Cessna 180 "HK-592." (Photo credit: Life Magazine.)

Liberation troops near Chiquimula, after being resupplied by air. (Photo credit: Guillermo Putzeys.)

Liberation troops of the "JOHNNY" column arriving at Jocotán on June 22, 1954. (Photo credit: Guillermo Putzeys.)

arriving in the Chiquimula – Zacapa area.

Despite it being a nocturnal drop under marginal weather conditions, Col. Mendoza's column was successfully resupplied. The problem began when the C-47 pilots couldn't locate Fernandez's group on the road to Ipala. After half an hour of looking for the light patterns marking the drop zone, a heavy rainstorm rolled in and the crew decided to return to Managua, where the C-47 landed near 9:00 PM.

In the early hours on June 22, the schooner "La Siesta", with the Liberationist seaborne assault force on board, made a spectacular entrance when it ran aground on a beach near Puerto Barrios' airfield. It didn't take long for the Army troops to notice that the Liberationists were disembarking and almost every machinegun emplacement nearby began firing at them, while the schooner was blown to pieces by mortar fire. Surprisingly, the Liberationists were able to split in four guerrilla teams and melted into downtown, where they began wreaking havoc, launching hit and run attacks on the Guardia Civil barracks and other governmental installations.

As soon as the attacks began, the improvised militias, led by the labor union member Alaric Bennett and an activist woman named Aide Godoy, went after the Liberationists and hunted them down block by block across town. The brutal urban battle lasted more than nine days, and all the members of the seaborne assault force were killed or captured.[6]

Meanwhile at Piedra Blanca, Col. Chajón Chúa was facing a complicated situation: By midnight, a party that he had sent to Gualán for retrieving some supplies, returned empty-handed because they had not been able to enter the village. Capt. Aldana, the Army officer who had been helping them, was no longer in charge of the Army detachment there, as he had been replaced by a young Lieutenant named César Silva, who hadn't lost any time in implementing drastic defensive measures. In fact, Lt. Silva had publicly stated that he was determined to crush the resistance cell operating in the village and hunt down the Liberationist column at Piedra Blanca.[7]

Even though PBSuccess' Field Command Post had ordered Col. Chajón Chúa to forget about Gualán and advance towards Zacapa as soon as practicable, the stubborn Colonel decided to regain control over the village. Near 2:00 AM, he sent half of his column to attack the defensive positions that Lt. Silva, with only 30 soldiers, had established near the train station at the village's entrance. The resistance cell's leaders also decided to get rid of the annoying Lieutenant and planned to assault his position from the rear while Chajón Chúa's men were attacking from the front.

Lt. Silva anticipated the enemy's intentions, however, and shortly after the attack began, he pulled his men out of their positions and moved them a couple of hundred meters North of the train station, leaving Col. Chajón Chúa's men facing directly the resistance cell's members. Within minutes, the two groups decimated each other while Lt. Silva observed from a distance.[8]

Just before dawn, Lt. Silva's troops reentered the village and began chasing the few surviving members of the resistance cell. In the process, they discovered that the telegraph operator and a couple of Guardia Civil agents had been massacred at the municipal building. An hour later, and in preparation for the inevitable counterattack, the Lieutenant ordered his troops to establish a security perimeter with the help of the population.

Back in Managua, the air operations for the day began when the Thunderbolt, with a new carburetor, left Las Mercedes for Guatemala City on a second attempt at strafing the Capital's gasoline storage tanks. The flight's secondary objective would be to destroy the shack that housed the government's radio station transmitters.

The strafing of the gasoline storage tanks was successful, as they were left riddled with bullet holes and profusely spilling gasoline. The attack on the radio station failed completely, however, since the pilot machine-gunned the adjacent shack by mistake, destroying the transmitters of the TGNA evangelical radio station, which was owned

Liberation troops of the "DANNY" column, photographed during the attack to Chiquimula on June 23, 1954. (Photo credit: Guillermo Putzeys.)

by an American missionary named Harold von Broekhoven.

Within hours, Ambassador Peurifoy cabled PBSuccess headquarters saying that the seditious Army officers wouldn't stage the coup because the air attack had been deemed "*a fainthearted effort*" and a "*show of incredible weakness*."[9] In addition, he suggested that the pilots should "*work out their technique*" since the Thunderbolt hadn't been lower than 1000ft during the attack. As expected, Brodfrost was furious.

Near 10:00 AM, Cheesman brought Castillo Armas from Tegucigalpa to Esquipulas in the Cessna 180, so he could direct the campaign from the Liberationist Advanced Command Post that had been established there. It was the first time that the Caudillo had been in Guatemala since the beginning of the invasion.

After landing, Castillo Armas made a thorough revision of the campaign's status so far and decided that he would join Colonels Mendoza and Flores Avendaño as soon as they had captured the town of Vado Hondo, where he would take over their columns and launch the offensive against Chiquimula. Then, he went back to the village's airfield and personally oversaw the reception of a large resupply drop from one of Brodfrost's C-47s.

During the rest of the morning, Cheesman conducted what turned out to be the most important flights of the day, bombing the Army artillery emplacements at Vado Hondo and San Esteban with fragmentation grenades and TNT blocks. Later, when Colonels Mendoza and Flores Avendaño finally attacked Vado Hondo, Cheesman provided close air support and reconnoitered the enemy positions.

Back in Managua, the SAHARA team informed Robertson that they had intercepted a series of radio messages from the Army headquarters ordering its troops to secure the railroad tracks from Guatemala City to Zacapa at all costs, since a large convoy, carrying 3000 soldiers[10], had departed the Capital in the early morning. The Field Commander didn't lose any time and sent the Thunderbolt to knock out as many railroad bridges as possible between the Capital and Zacapa to prevent the reinforcements from arriving in the area. The fighter, loaded with three M57 275 lb. demolition bombs, departed Las Mercedes at 11:20 AM with "T-Bone" Williams at the controls.

The very first bombing mission of the campaign turned out to be a complete fiasco, however, since none of the bombs exploded. As soon as Williams got out of the plane after landing at Las Mercedes, he began grilling the armorer for not fusing the bombs properly, but Brodfrost intervened and, after a short investigation, determined that it was the pilot who wasn't familiar with the bombs' arming procedure.

By midday, Brodfrost sent a C-47 to resupply Maj. Torres' column at Entre Ríos. The request had been radioed the day before, but due to the increasing amount of encrypted messages being received from the battlefront, it had not been until then that the SALAL center had been able to forward it to the Air Support Unit.

When the C-47 arrived in Entre Ríos, a reinforced Army company from Puerto Barrios had assaulted the town, and Maj. Torres' men were retreating towards the village of Champona, near the border with Honduras. The pilot tried to drop the supplies close to the Liberationists, but the bundles were seized by a group of soldiers as soon as they hit the ground. Shortly after, Maj. Torres radioed SALAL saying that many of his men had deserted, running away into the jungle.

At 3:00 PM, Colonels Flores Avendaño and Mendoza finally seized Vado Hondo after a long firefight with a couple of Army companies from the Guardia de Honor garrison. In the process, an Army captain and a sergeant were made prisoners, while another officer and 15 men under his command switched sides, joining the Liberationists. Two hours later, when the town was already secured, Castillo Armas arrived from Esquipulas, taking over the command of both columns.

Coinciding with the fall of Vado Hondo, a mysterious event took

Aerial view of Puerto Barrios from the Northeast. In the background, the town's airfield can be seen. (Photo credit: Life Magazine.)

place not far from there, and to this date, it remains unexplained. It began when inhabitants of San Pedro de Copán, Honduras, reported that an unidentified single-engine plane had bombed the town's airfield before escaping in the direction of Guatemala. Of the three bombs that the plane dropped, only two exploded. The third one, a 250 lb. iron bomb, was found stuck nose first in the mud. Hours later, the FAH Commander, Lt. Col. Hernán Acosta, arrived to investigate but wasn't able to determine the bomb's origin.

During the evening, and despite the lack of conclusive evidence, the Honduran government formally accused its Guatemalan counterpart of aggression and threatened to recall its ambassador. At the UN, the incident was chalked up as a maneuver to cast negative light upon the Guatemalan government, and no one gave it a second thought.

In contrast, PBSuccess headquarters launched a full-fledged investigation to determine who was to blame. The first suspect was the Guatemalan government, but it quickly was ruled out since the FAG AT-6s couldn't carry the type of ordnance that had been dropped. Then, CIA security agents descended at Managua and began questioning Brodfrost's pilots, since Opa-locka suspected that during William's bombing mission to destroy the bridges between Zacapa and Guatemala City, the pilot had got lost and had jettisoned the bombs over Honduran soil before returning to his base. In his defense, Williams stated that, indeed, he got lost in bad weather at first, but after a couple of minutes he had been able to find his way and had bombed the assigned targets which, he was sure, were located in Guatemala.

Brodfrost found himself in trouble too, because days earlier, he and Ambassador Willauer had come up with a plan that involved dropping a couple of bombs near the Toncontin Airport in Tegucigalpa, to cause an international incident. The bombing would be conducted by an AT-6 they would borrow from the Nicaraguan Air Force, which would be disguised as a FAG plane.[11] They didn't get too far, however, because Wisner ditched the plan as soon as he was informed about it.

When the Department of State learned about the hare-brained scheme, Brodfrost went under investigation, but the CIA security agents who questioned him found nothing beyond a couple of cables discussing the plan. In the end, the Chief of Air Support was ordered to destroy all the documents and to keep his mouth shut about it.

Meanwhile in Guatemala, the disarray that prevailed among the Army ranks was reflected in the last aviation-related event that took place on that day. At 1:00 PM, two civilian aircraft, a Fairchild PT-26A *Cornell* (MSN FC-223, ex Royal Canadian Air Force serial 10732, U.S. civil registration N9529H) and a Cessna UC-78 *Bobcat* (MSN 5924, ex USAAF serial 43-31896, U.S. civil registration N54458), left Tapachula, Mexico, for El Salvador's Capital. Both planes were on a ferry flight to Chile, and had departed Dallas, Texas, two days earlier.

The crews were well aware of the delicate situation in Guatemala and upon entering the country's territorial waters they opted for flying at a safe distance from the coast. Two hours into the flight, however, a nasty rainstorm caught the planes and got them separated. The Cornell made it to El Salvador safely but the Bobcat, piloted by the Chileans Luis Alberto Núñez Rojas and Iván Bahamonde, developed problems with an engine and was forced to head towards the nearest airfield, which happened to be the Puerto de San José Airbase.

Núñez Rojas, the pilot in command, followed the proper procedure and contacted the airbase's tower, stating that they had an emergency. The tower granted them permission to land, but as soon as the plane touched down, the Guatemalan Army troops guarding the airbase opened fire at the crippled Bobcat, which immediately overran the runway and crashed.[12]

The nervous troops kept firing at the wreckage for more than 10 minutes, until it caught fire. Miraculously, Núñez Rojas and Bahamonde managed to untangle themselves from their seats and escaped the plane's remains, despite the rain of bullets. They didn't get too far though, since a group of soldiers, who mistook them for pilots of Castillo Armas' air force, apprehended them. As it would be expected, the Chilean aviators ended up in jail and it was not until two weeks later that they were able to clear their situation with the

This Cessna 180 was the first airplane acquired by the Liberation Forces. Flown by Carlos Cheeseman, the plane conducted critical close support and "strategic" bombing missions during the campaign.

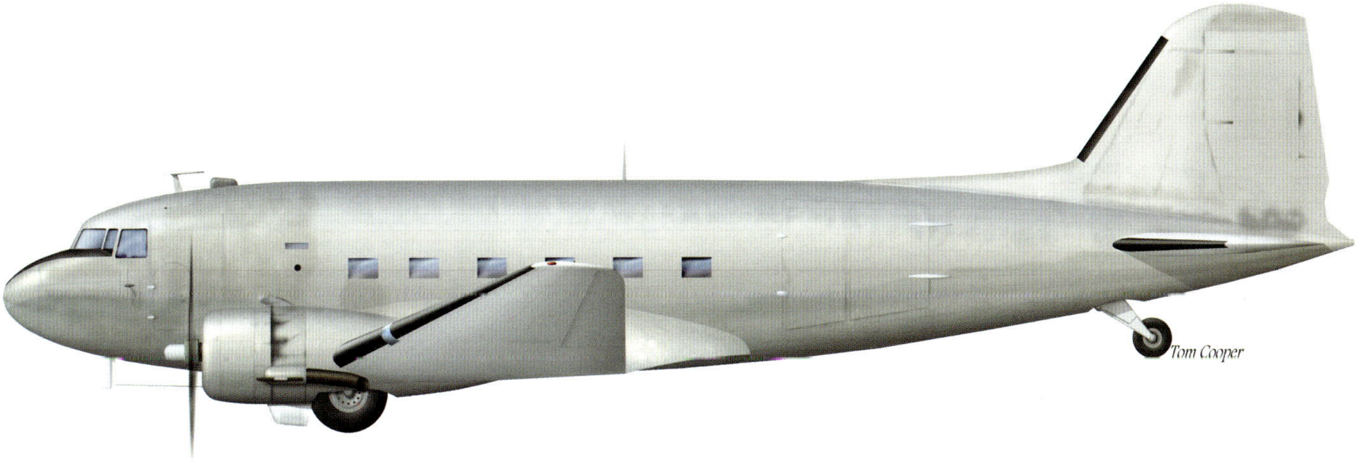

The CIA leased two C-47 transports and purchased an additional one for the Liberation Forces. These planes, which conducted important logistical and psychological warfare missions, were stripped of any markings in order to hide their true origins.

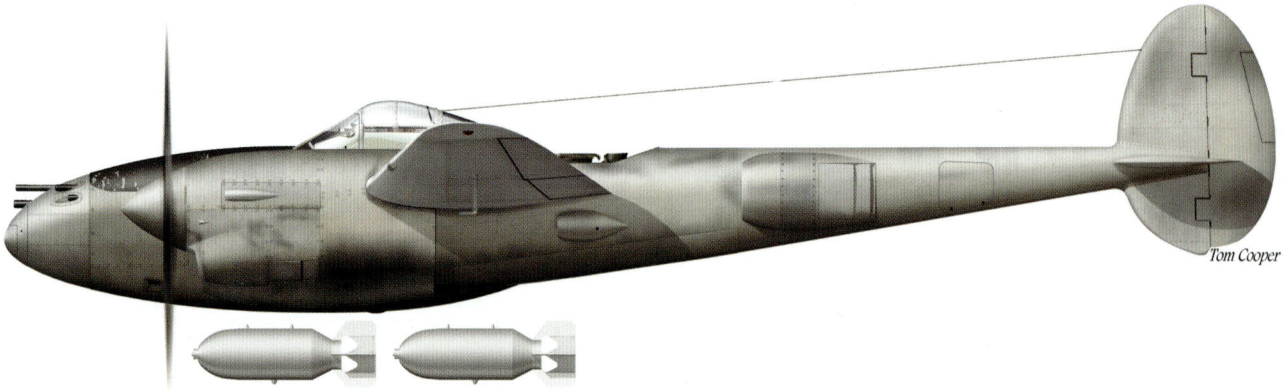

The CIA purchased this Lockheed P-38L from the Nicaraguan Air Force, for conducting psychological warfare and tactical bombing missions during the campaign but only flew in three occasions because it was riddled with mechanical problems. During one of those missions, while flown by Ferdinand Schoup, this plane sank the British ship *Springfjord* at Puerto San José.

The CIA acquired six Republic F-47N Thunderbolts for the Liberation Air Force from the Puerto Rico Air National Guard. Besides conducting close support and tactical bombing missions, these fighters also flew psychological warfare sorties over Guatemala City. The M57 and M64 bombs these fighters and the P-38L carried during the campaign, were painted silver in order to disguise them as fuel drop tanks.

This Cessna 140 was the last aircraft acquired by the Liberation Forces, and was used by Castillo Armas as his personal plane. Flown by Alfredo Silva, the little Cessna conducted a couple of leaflet-dropping missions over Zacapa and Chiquimula near the end of the campaign.

At the time of the campaign, the Guatemalan Air Force had two Douglas C-47 transports, which were used extensively for carrying troops and supplies to the theater of operations.

Although the North American AT-6 was originally designed as a trainer, it had limited offensive capability in the form of two .30 cal machine-guns. It could also carry four 100 lb bombs. The Guatemalan Air Force had six of them at the time of the campaign; three being AT-6Cs and the rest AT-6Ds. All saw considerable action, mainly in attack missions against the Liberation Forces in Chiquimula and Izabal.

Even though considered obsolete at the time, the Guatemalan Air Force had two Boeing P-26As in service during the campaign. The venerable "Peashooters" saw limited action, mainly conducting dangerous patrol missions over Guatemala City.

The Guatemalan Air Force had three Beechcraft AT-11s by June 1954, which formed the "Bomber Squadron." The three airplanes conducted patrol missions during the emergency and one was even captured in Honduras, while flying a highly secret clandestine sortie.

One of the Liberation's F-47Ns ended up with the Guatemalan Air Force after the campaign. Carrying the serial number 0568, it was the very first aircraft to be incorporated into the newly created "Fighter Squadron" that later on, received three North American F-51Ds. In December 1955, this Thunderbolt was traded for a Mustang belonging to the Nicaraguan Air Force.

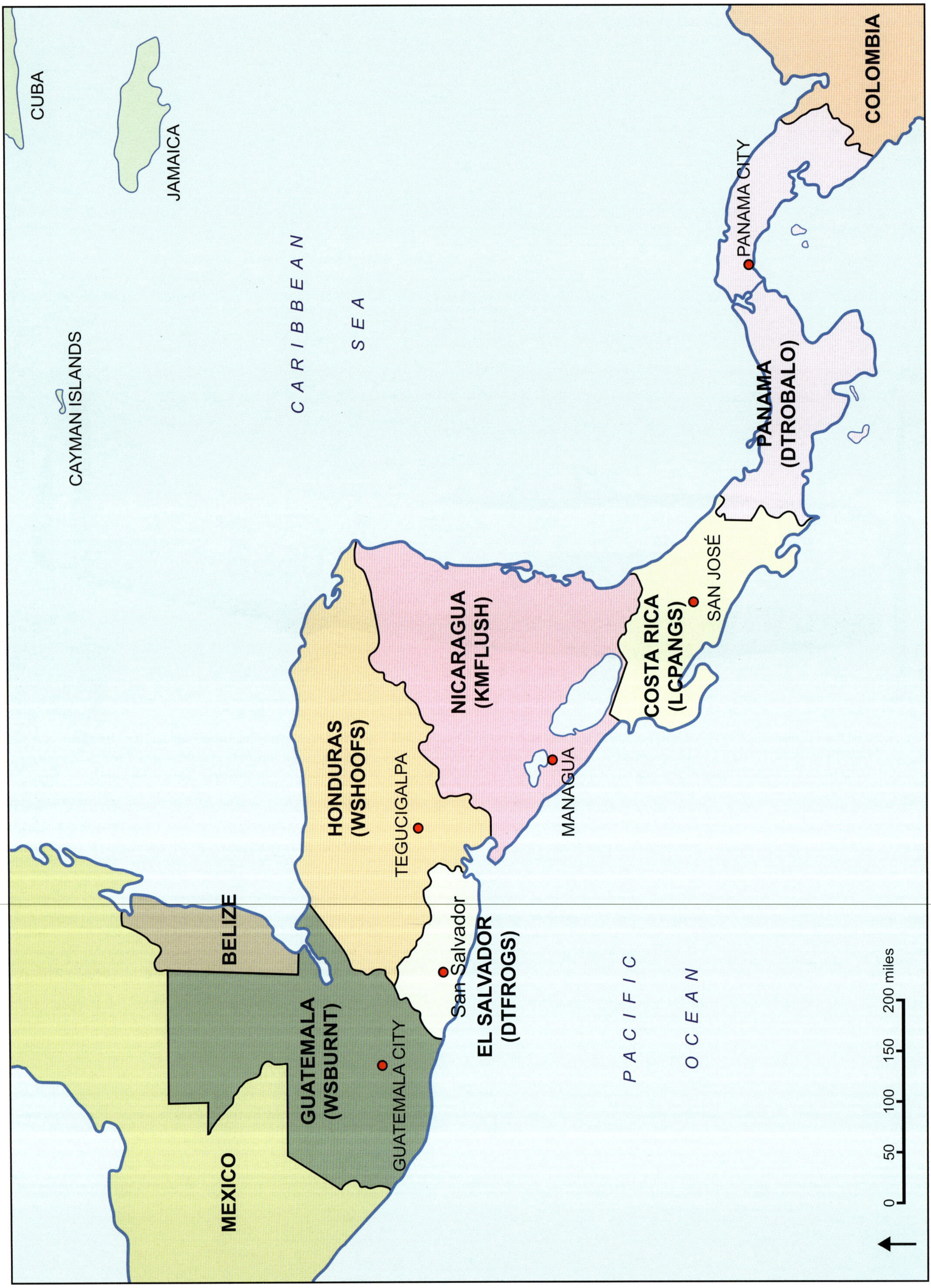

Map of Central America showing the codenames that the CIA gave to the involved countries during Project PBSuccess. (George Anderson)

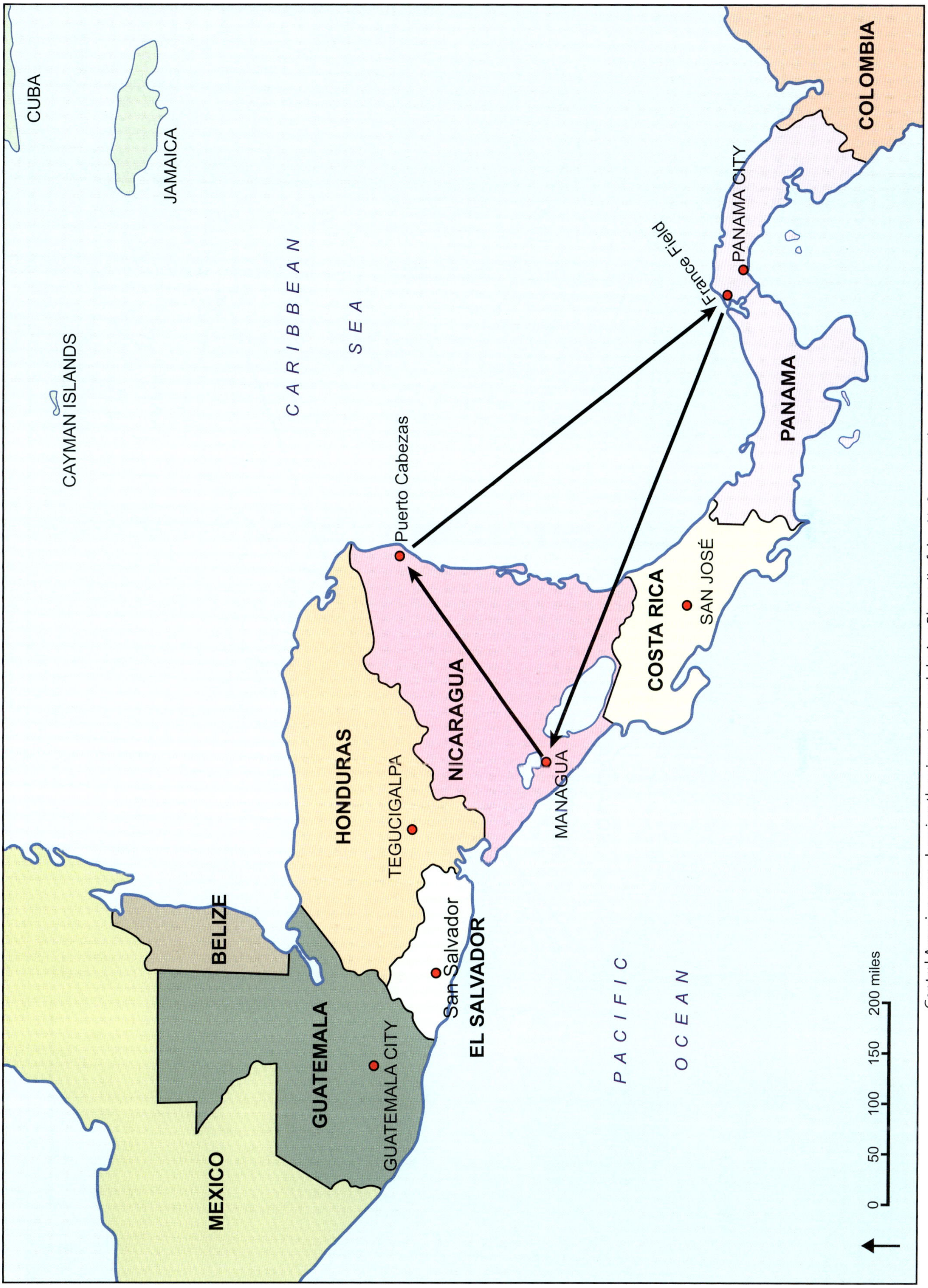

Central America map showing the air routes used during Phase II of the Air Support Plan. (George Anderson)

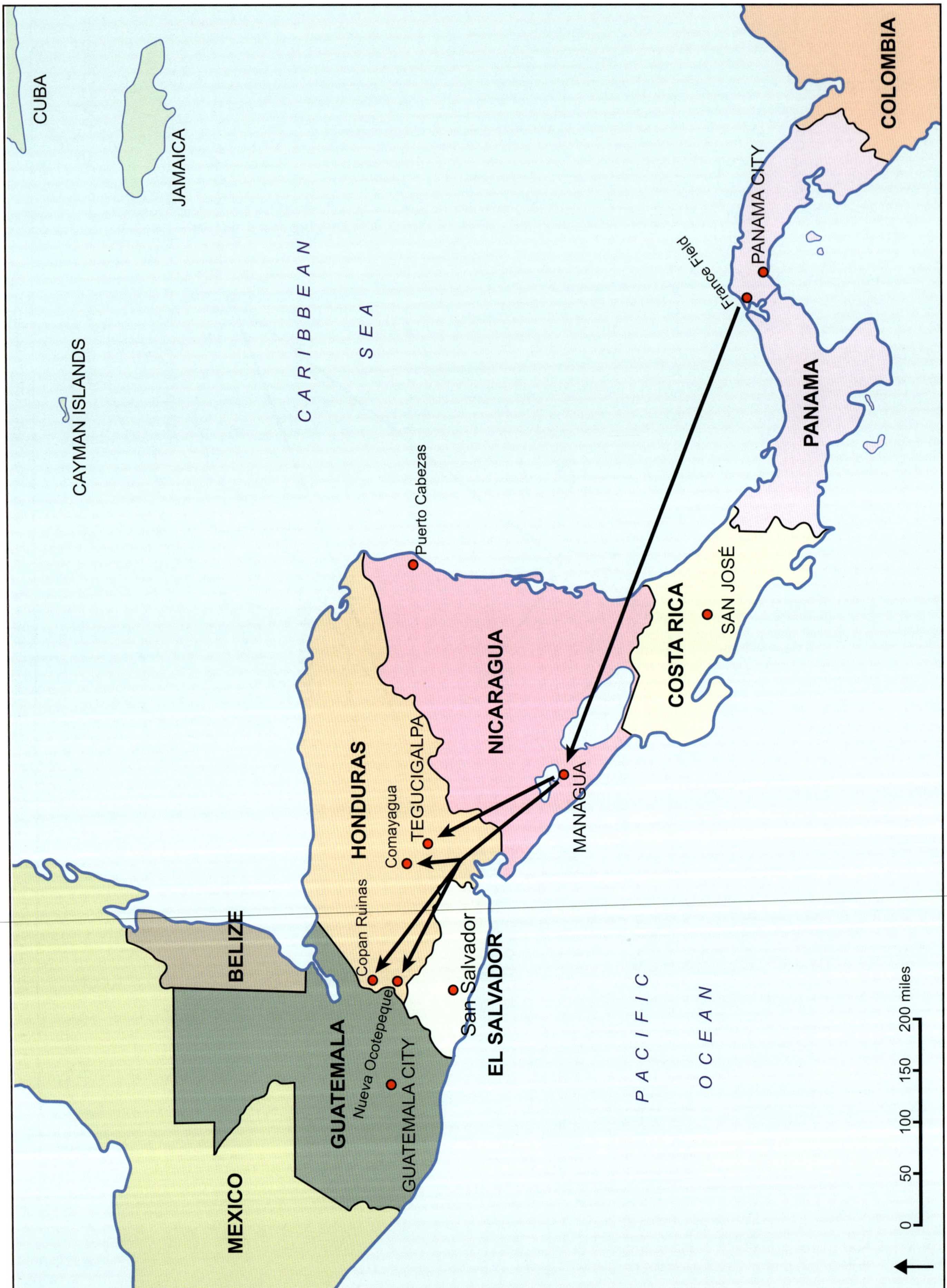

Central America map showing the air routes used during Phase IIIA of the Air Support Plan. (George Anderson)

Central America map showing the common air routes used during the leaflet flights to Guatemala City, as part of Phase IIIB of PBSuccess' Air Support Plan. (George Anderson)

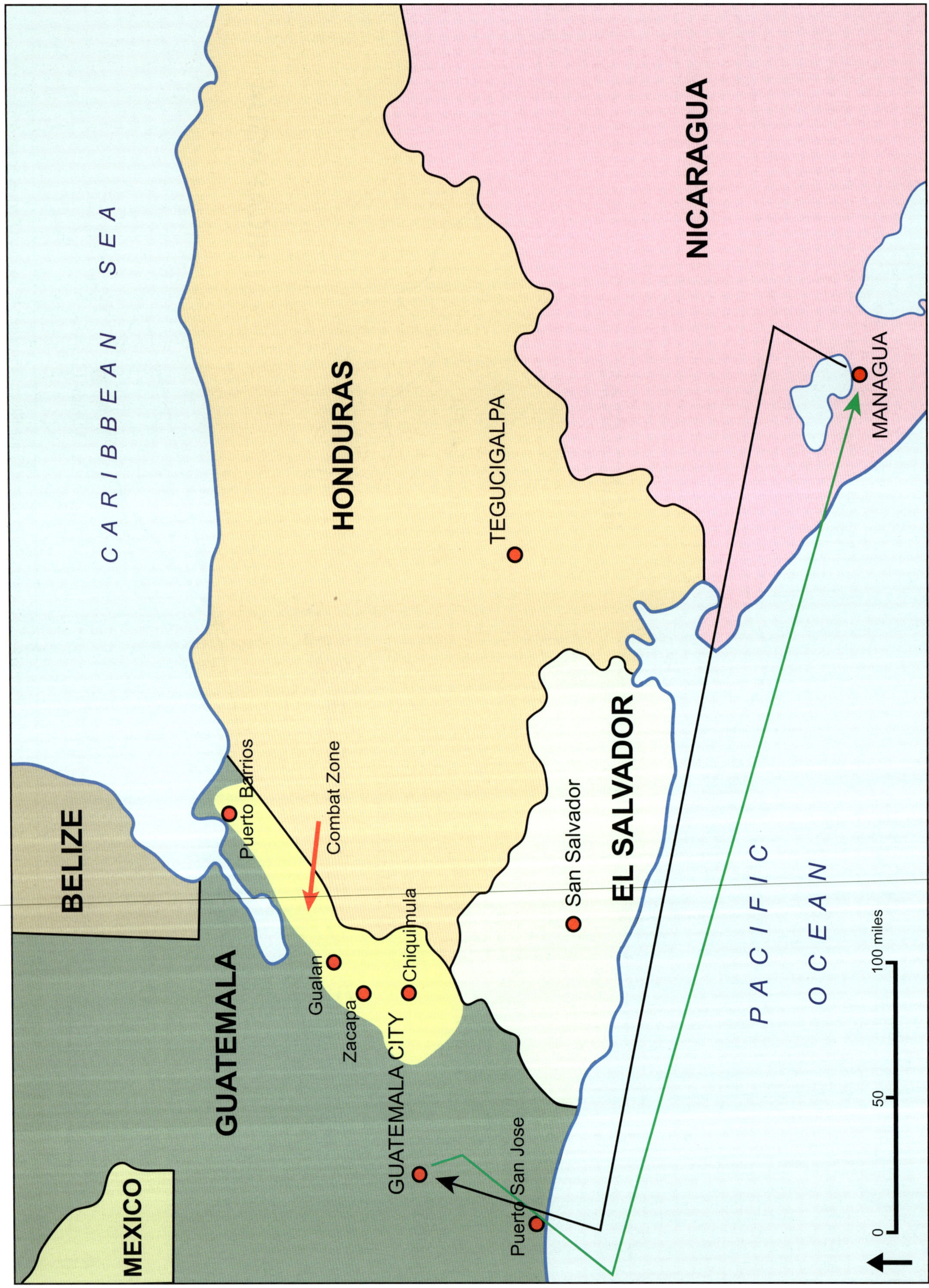

Map depicting the common air routes used by the PBSuccess' Air Unit in tactical missions to Guatemala City, as part of Phase IV of the Air Support Plan. (George Anderson)

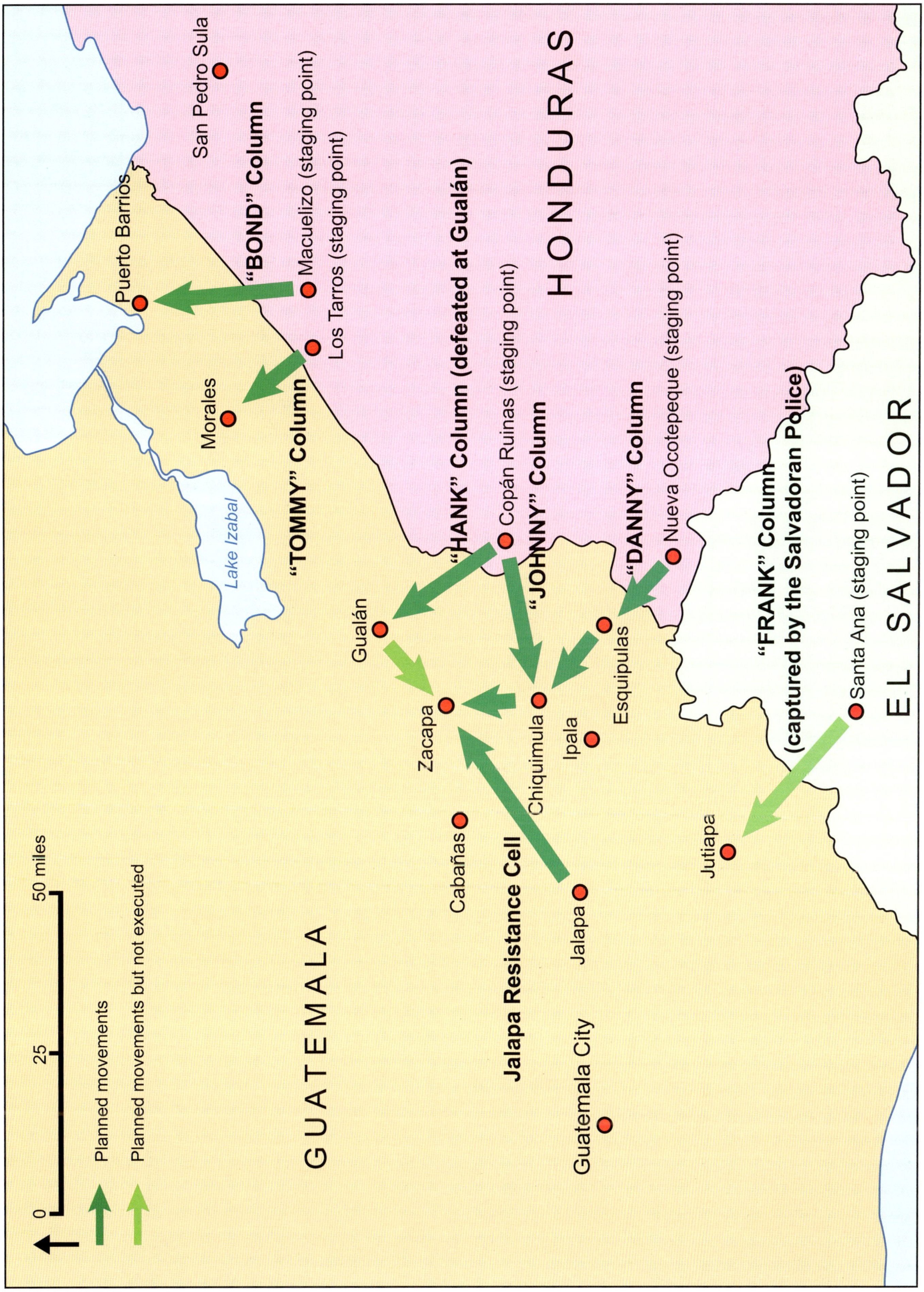

Map depicting the Liberation Offensive. (George Anderson)

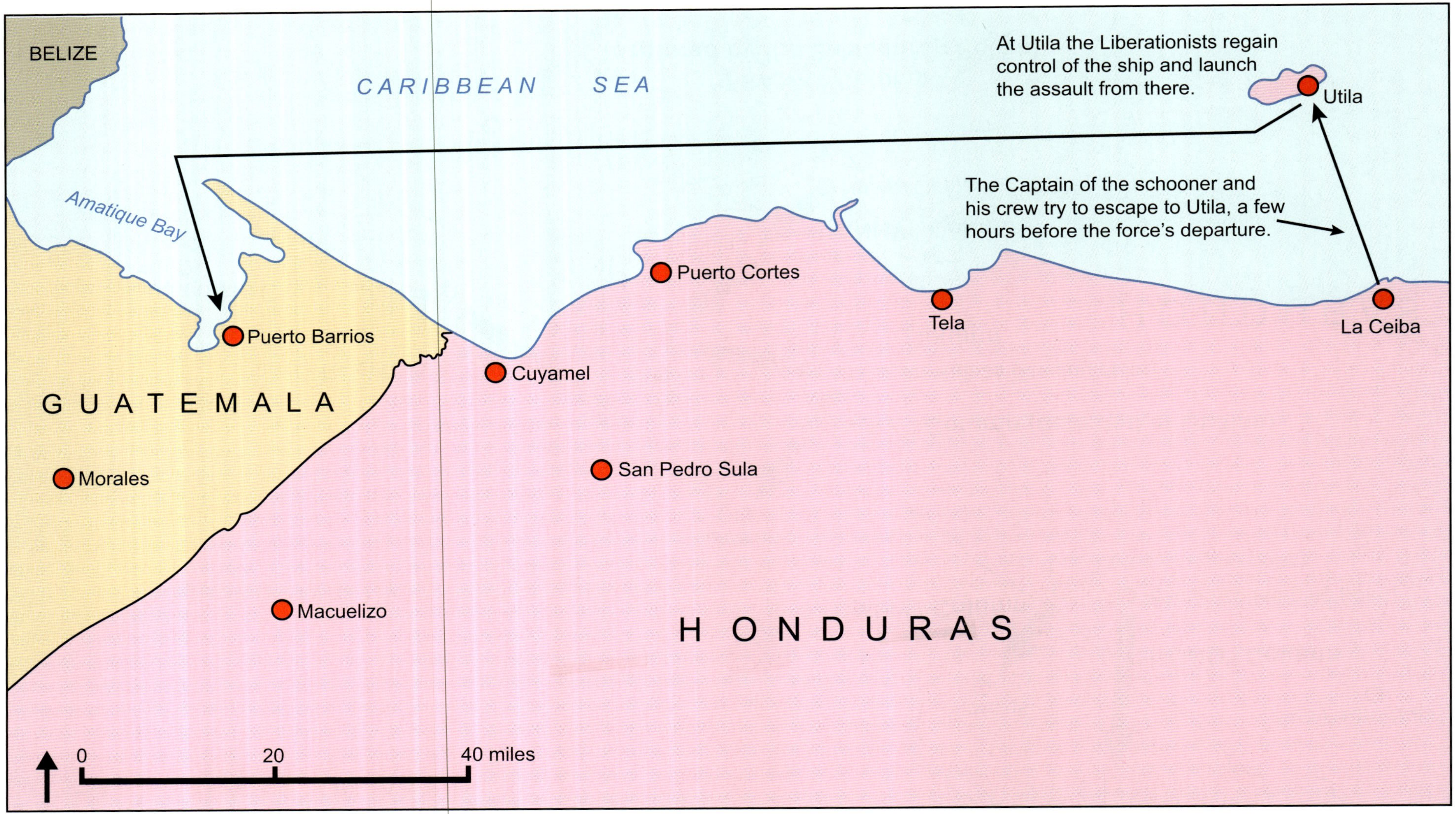

Map showing the "La Siesta" seaborne assault operation of June 22, 1954. (George Anderson)

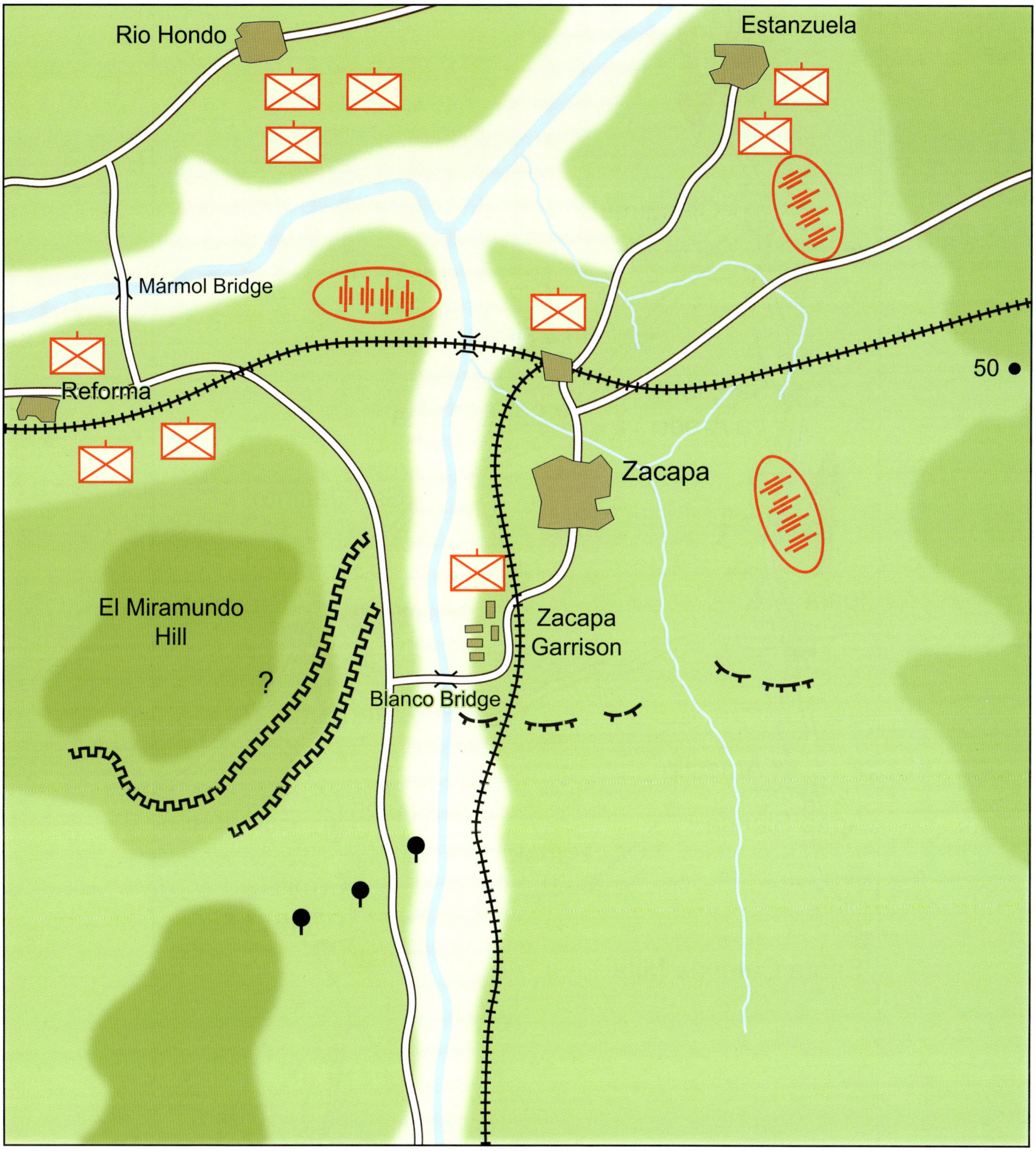

Map showing the disposition of the Ejército de Operaciones' units in and around Zacapa near the end of the invasion. (George Anderson via Guillermo Putzeys.)

Map depicting the Chiquimula area. (George Anderson via Guillermo Putzeys.)

Liberation troops taking a break near the town of Santa Barbara, Chiquimula, during the offensive against Zacapa. (Photo credit: Guillermo Putzeys.)

Guatemalan authorities.

In Managua, and just before midnight, Rip Robertson received a series of cables from PBSuccess headquarters detailing the priorities for the next day. First, he was ordered to move the Field Command Post temporarily to the SALAL center at Nueva Ocotepeque[13], as the campaign was approaching a critical phase and Wisner wanted him to exercise maximum control over Castillo Armas' forces.

In addition, he would take with him one of the RS-1 "spy radios" and an operator, so he could issue orders directly to the Air Support Unit without the intervention of the SALAL center. This was decided so because Castillo Armas was complaining about the inefficient radio communications network. Urgent messages requesting air support were being delivered by the SALAL center more than six hours after they had been transmitted. The Caudillo went as far as to demand that Robertson hand him the frequencies and encryption codes required for contacting the Air Support Unit directly. Obviously, PBSuccess headquarters didn't approve this, as it would give the Caudillo complete control over the aircraft.

Brodfrost also received a cable detailing the rules of engagement for the next day. It said that only Robertson could determine the tactical missions to be flown within the Chiquimula – Zacapa area. Other targets outside this zone would have to be authorized by headquarters regardless of the urgency. On the other hand, the missions against targets considered "strategic" would be determined by PBSuccess headquarters and would have top priority, even over urgent tactical requests. Finally, yet importantly, psychological warfare missions over the combat zone would take precedence over all others, since it was necessary to convince the Ejército de Operaciones' officers to join Castillo Armas in his fight against Arbenz as soon as possible.

The fifth day of the invasion, Wednesday June 23, began with excellent news for Robertson and Brodfrost: Headquarters informed them that three F-47Ns had departed Ramey AFB, in Puerto Rico, and would arrive in France Field the next day at the latest.[14]

As in the case of the three Thunderbolts previously acquired by the CIA for PBSuccess, the USAF serials of these fighters haven't been conclusively established. There are four candidates though, these being 44-88548, 44-88974, 44-89136 and 44-89439.

Interestingly, the USAF was treating the ferry flight as a highly classified operation, unlike the previous delivery, which had been disguised as a transfer to Nicaragua under the U.S. Reimbursable Aid Program. In fact, a cable that Brodfrost received stressed that "every effort should be made to keep the fighters under cover at FJHOPEFUL and minimize the number of personnel having direct or indirect knowledge of their existence."[15]

Accordingly, the Air Support Unit's second in command, Capt. Wallace C. Cowden, was ordered to take the planes into hangars as soon as they had arrived. Not even the USAF C-47 accompanying the fighters would be allowed to land at France Field, and would have to do so at Albrook AFB on the Pacific side of the Canal Zone.

PBSuccess headquarters had also arranged to send two CAT pilots to France Field, who would ferry two of the Thunderbolts to Managua no later than June 26, while the third plane would be kept there as backup. It was expected that these pilots would arrive early the next day.

As soon as President Somoza got wind of the additional Thunderbolts, he promptly allowed Brodfrost to use his fighter[16], which up until then had been off-limits for PBSuccess' pilots. This sudden display of generosity on the part of the Nicaraguan President was because he believed that the newly acquired fighters would end up being transferred to his air force. What he didn't know was that the CIA had the obligation of returning them to the USAF as soon as they were no longer needed. In the meantime, however, Brodfrost decided to use the Thunderbolts as the carrot at the end of the stick for keeping Somoza's support.

The day's air operations began at 4:30 AM with a briefing in which Brodfrost detailed the situation in the combat zone to his pilots.

According to reports from Castillo Armas' field commanders, the Guatemalan Army was preparing a pincer move with two battalions[17], one coming from the North by rail to Zacapa and the other from the South by road to Ipala, which would converge over the Liberationists in the Chiquimula area.

Therefore, their mission would be to isolate the combat zone by preventing the reinforcements from arriving, and to soften the Army positions near Zacapa and Chiquimula, so Castillo Armas' forces could launch the much-anticipated attack on the latter and consolidate its position there before advancing towards Zacapa.

At 5:00 AM, one of the C-47s departed Las Mercedes for resupplying Castillo Armas at Vado Hondo and Col. Chajón Chúa near Gualán. 40 minutes later, the Thunderbolt, piloted by Delarm and loaded with three 275 lb. bombs, took off on a mission to bomb the Zacapa garrison. Then, Brodfrost's mechanics began preparing Somoza's F-47N for a second bombing mission that would take off at 6:30AM.

At 7:30 AM, the C-47 resupplied Castillo Armas' columns at Vado Hondo and a small reserve detachment that Col. Flores Avendaño had left at Jocotán. Then, the transport went to the drop zone near Gualán and began looking for Col. Chajón Chúa's group. After circling for more than 20 minutes without finding them, the pilot decided to see if the Liberationists were in Gualán. However, upon approaching the village, the C-47 began taking small arms' fire and had to climb away while the pilot called Delarm so he could take a closer look.

Unbeknownst to the C-47 pilots, the reason why Col. Chajón Chúa's men hadn't showed up at the drop zone was that the column no longer existed. Just before dawn, the Liberationists had stormed Gualán in three trucks, arriving in the central plaza, shooting right and left, completely unaware that during the night, Lt. Silva's small detachment had been reinforced with more than 300 troops from Zacapa.

The ensuing clash was short but bloody, and the majority of Chajón Chúa's men were killed within minutes. Only the Colonel and a handful of his men were able to escape, but the Army troops were now after them in hot pursuit.[18]

When Delarm received the call from the C-47 pilot about going to Gualán, he had just bombed the ammunition storage dump at the Zacapa's garrison. The huge explosion produced a dense smoke cloud that obscured most of the town, and prevented him from making another run. Thus, he decided to go check what was happening at Gualán while the smoke dissipated.

Delarm arrived over the village 10 minutes later and made a low pass over downtown, during which almost every soldier on the ground fired at his plane. Then, he circled back and strafed the central plaza and the Army detachment.

In his third pass, Delarm dropped a bomb over a couple of machinegun emplacements near the train station, but it didn't detonate. Minutes later, the pilot spotted a train that was approaching the village from the Northwest and dropped the last bomb he was carrying right in front of the locomotive. As soon as the train stopped, he began strafing the cars, knocking down a couple of them.[19] Sadly, what Delarm thought to be a military train, was packed with civilians and many of them were wounded, including a 12-year-old child named Julio César Romero Peralta, who died shortly after. Minutes later, a rainstorm rolled in, and Delarm had to call off the mission, landing back in Managua at 9:15 AM.

Somoza's Thunderbolt, flown by Williams, took off from Las Mercedes at 7:10 AM with the mission of providing close air support to Castillo Armas during the attack on Chiquimula, which would begin near 8:30 AM. It was expected that by the time the Liberationists had the town surrounded, the Thunderbolt would show up.

However, by 10:00 AM, which was more than an hour after the fighter's estimated time of arrival, it hadn't made it to the area and Castillo Armas had to call Cheesman, who was at Esquipulas awaiting orders, for providing them with air coverage in the Cessna 180.

It was not until 10:30 AM that Williams reappeared in Managua, stating that, despite the extremely bad weather, he had "knocked out the biggest bridge between Zacapa and Chiquimula."[20] Brodfrost knew better though, and after a thorough debriefing, the pilot confessed that he hadn't made it to Chiquimula because he got lost trying to get under the clouds that covered the area.[21] To orient himself he had gone to Guatemala City and followed the railroad tracks back to Zacapa. Near El Jícaro, a small village located more than 40 km Northwest of Chiquimula, the pilot had dropped "accidentally" the M64 555 lb. bomb his plane was carrying, and a couple of minutes later, he depleted his ammunition on two civilian trucks near the village of Cabañas.

After wreaking havoc in an usually peaceful area, Williams realized that his plane was running low on fuel, so he climbed over the clouds and headed towards the "emergency escape route" that would take him to San Marcos Ocotepeque, Honduras, and then to Managua.

In contrast, Cheesman and his bombardier spent most of the morning strafing artillery positions around Chiquimula, and bombing the town's garrison repeatedly, while Castillo Armas called the SALAL center every half hour, requesting desperately that the Thunderbolts be sent to the area as soon as possible.

At 3:00 PM, the two Thunderbolts finally arrived over the combat zone, but instead of supporting the attack on Chiquimula, they began attacking the railroad bridges South of town. According to Castillo Armas' reports, many of his men deserted when they saw that the planes were not covering them and had gone to attack other targets.

By the time the fighters were done bombing the bridges and retuned to Chiquimula, it was a little too late, since the town's garrison had been reinforced with 300 troops from Zacapa, which arrived carrying .50 Cal machineguns, 47 mm mortars tubes, and heavy artillery. Under the command of Col. Eduviges Pérez Morales, these troops pushed the Liberationists back to the nearby village of San Esteban.[22]

As soon as the Field Command Post learned about the Liberationists' predicament, Castillo Armas' was ordered out of the area for safety reasons. Thus, the Caudillo returned to Esquipulas, while Colonels Mendoza and Flores Avendaño were left at San Esteban to contain the Army's advance. By 5:00 PM, they began calling SALAL for help as they were about to be overrun.

Then, an absurdity took place: As the Army troops were about to storm San Esteban, the Ejército de Operaciones' Commander, Col. Víctor León, radioed Col. Pérez Morales, ordering him to return with his troops to Zacapa at once. Pérez Morales was also ordered to leave only a small detachment of 32 men, under the command of Lt. Col. Jorge Hernández, at Chiquimula.

When the Liberationists noted that the Army troops had gone, they launched a successful counterattack on Chiquimula, seizing most of the town except for the garrison, where Col. Hernández's men were holding out. At this point, the Commander of the Ejército de Operaciones ordered the troops defending Gualán to go to Chiquimula and reclaim the town.[23]

The Thunderbolts arrived over Gualán just when the Army troops were boarding a couple of trucks to carry them to Chiquimula. The planes bombed and strafed them, destroying the train station in the process, but weren't able to prevent their departure. A couple of hours later the scared troops arrived in Chiquimula and took up positions on a hill overlooking the town. Then, another absurdity occurred:

Cheesman's Cessna 180 shortly after having been forced to land at Esquipulas by one of the Sulfatos. (Photo credit: Life Magazine.)

The officer in charge, Maj. Enrique Villatoro, ordered the soldiers to deplete their ammunition by firing randomly at the town.[24] When the Liberationists noted their presence and returned the fire, Maj. Villatoro's troops turned around and headed for Zacapa.

Meanwhile, at the town's garrison, Lt. Col. Hernández and his men had managed to keep the Liberationists at bay, but they were running out of ammunition. Desperate, Hernández began calling for help, but the only reply from Zacapa was: "Hold your position, we'll send reinforcements in the morning."

During the evening, the SALAL center began querying Castillo Armas' field commanders about their situation and the reports that arrived were not reassuring. The Army had pushed the remnants of Maj. Torres' column out of the country, and they were now at the town of Correderos, in Honduras, waiting to be resupplied.[25] In Morales, Lt. De Paz's column had been attacked with artillery fire and a FAG AT-6 had bombed their positions twice, forcing them to retreat into the hills nearby. In Chiquimula, Colonels Mendoza and Flores Avendaño were still trying to seize the town's garrison. They even phoned Col. Hernández a couple of times[26], trying to convince him to surrender, to no avail. As for Col. Chajón Chúa's column, the only information that SALAL had was that they still were in the Gualán area, advancing towards Zacapa.

The news coming from Opa-locka was not encouraging either. At 8:00 PM, Robertson received an urgent cable from headquarters saying that there had been a change of plans and now he was required to achieve an earliest victory or failing that, to get Castillo Armas' forces in the most advantageous position as soon as possible. This was necessary because the Guatemalan government's diplomatic maneuvering at the UN was succeeding and there was a serious possibility that a cease-fire could be enforced in the next 72 hours. In addition, the OAS was about to send a peace committee to Guatemala, Honduras, and Nicaragua to determine the causes of the conflict. In both cases, the CIA would have to suspend immediately all support to the Liberation forces.

By then, PBSuccess headquarters was considering two possibilities for achieving a quick victory.[27] The first was to embrace Ambassador Peurifoy's plan of bombing military targets in Guatemala City with the hope of forcing the Army to switch sides and stage a coup. In the process, Castillo Armas' would launch an airborne operation to seize and hold the National Palace. The other was to induce the Ejército de Operaciones to switch sides, and together with Castillo Armas' forces, launch an offensive against the Capital. A third plan, to be implemented only in case of emergency, involved an airborne operation to seize and hold Puerto Barrios, where Castillo Armas would establish a provisional government.

In the meantime, Brodfrost's pilots were authorized to conduct bombing attacks against the Matamoros Fort[28], the largest military target in the Capital, while Radio Liberación would start encouraging the Army to stage a coup.

As it would be expected, when Ambassador Peurifoy got wind of the change of plans, he was delighted. Shortly before midnight, he got in touch with the seditious Army officers and told them to get ready for toppling Arbenz within the next 48 hours.

On Thursday, June 24, air operations in the combat zone began when one of Brodfrost's C-47s arrived in Chiquimula at 8:15 AM, and dropped a large amount of ammunition for the Liberationists, who had spent the night unsuccessfully trying to seize the town's garrison. Five minutes later, the Thunderbolts arrived on the scene

Wreckage of the Cessna UC-78, U.S. civil registration N54458, which was machine-gunned by Guatemalan Army troops at the Puerto San José airbase upon landing. Miraculously, the occupants walked away with only minor injuries. (Photo credit: Via Álvaro Romero.)

and immediately began bombing the railroad bridges between the town and Zacapa. The first to be blown to pieces was the one that Williams had failed to destroy the day before. Delarm hit it with a 555 lb. demolition bomb on the first pass.

Then, both fighters returned to Chiquimula where Delarm spent more than 20 minutes strafing the garrison, while Williams dropped two 275 lb. fragmentation bombs on a large group of Army reinforcements that were taking up positions on a ravine Northwest of town. Minutes later, he dropped his last bomb over a heavy artillery emplacement that Army troops had set up on a hill overlooking the town's cemetery. Just before departing, both fighters strafed the town's airfield, hitting a couple of machinegun nests located at the end of the runway and the airfield's gasoline deposits.

As soon as the impressive air attack ended, Colonels Flores Avendaño and Mendoza seized the town's garrison, capturing Lt. Col. Hernandez and the 32 soldiers under his command. Near 10:00 AM, Chiquimula was declared officially under Liberationist control and the Field Command Post authorized Castillo Armas to go there, so he could take over his forces and start preparing an all-out attack on Zacapa.

During the morning, Colonel Mendoza sent a couple of reconnaissance squads to check the town's surroundings, and what they found was extremely shocking: The Army troops had retreated to Zacapa as soon as the air attack had begun, leaving behind only a couple of reserve battalions, comprised mostly by ill-armed peasants, to cover their retreat.

Octavio Reyes, a Communist activist sent by the PGT to secretly observe the Army's operations in the combat zone[29], had witnessed this cowardly act and didn't hesitate in going to Zacapa to question the Ejército de Operaciones' Commander. However, upon arriving in that town, he was promptly captured and jailed. Hours later, he was able to escape, and without losing any time, headed for the Capital to inform the party members about his findings.

At 12:00 PM, Brodfrost launched one of the C-47s on a mission to find and resupply Col. Chajón Chúa's column near Gualán. Up until then, no one at the Field Command Post knew that this group had been decimated and that the 15 survivors were having a hard time trying to evade the Army troops that were after them near the town of La Unión. Obviously, the transport had to return to Managua with the supplies still on board.

After midday, the fighter missions were cancelled much to Castillo Armas' chagrin, because both Thunderbolts blew their tail tires while taxiing prior to take off, and wouldn't be repaired until the next day. To make things worse, the three additional fighters still were en route to France Field and their estimated time of arrival was anyone's guess.[30]

Meanwhile in Guatemala City, President Arbenz assumed direct control of the Army's combat operations after delivering a strong reprimand to the high command for having lost Chiquimula to the enemy. Then, he phoned the Ejército de Operaciones' Commander and ordered him to reclaim the town as soon as possible. To aid in this effort, Arbenz ordered the FAG Commander, Col. Girón Cartagena, to launch air strikes against all the enemy positions in Puerto Barrios, Zacapa, and Chiquimula.

Minutes later, at La Aurora Airbase, Col. Girón Cartagena summoned the few pilots still willing to fly and briefed them on the situation in the combat zone and the targets they were going to attack. Before sending them away, the FAG Commander gave them clear instructions in case they ran across the Liberationist fighters: "reduce your speed and lower your landing gear; then wave your wings and let the enemy pilot know that you are surrendering."[31]

The first pair of FAG AT-6s, led by Maj. Pedro Granados, strafed Esquipulas near 3:00 PM[32], scaring the hell out of the Caudillo and his men, as they were caught by surprise. During the attack, the Texans dropped four 100 lb. bombs over the village's airfield, which caused more noise than damages.

A second pair of AT-6s, led by Maj. Víctor Manuel Figueroa, attacked Lt. De Paz's positions in the hills near Morales, causing him to retreat to the Honduran border. Then, the Texans went to Puerto Barrios to refuel and returned to the area, spending most of the afternoon strafing and bombing Lt. De Paz's column, until driving them out of the country.[33]

In the evening, Arbenz sent to Zacapa and Ipala almost all the remaining troops that the Army had in the Capital, so the Ejército de Operaciones could execute the pincer move on Chiquimula.

Since Guatemala City was going to be defenseless with all the Army troops gone, the President ordered the mobilization of more than 1500 labor union members, who would take up defensive positions around the Capital.[34] In addition, 500 labor workers were taken to military training camps that the Guardia Civil had established at the Campo de Marte and the Country Club, while 500 more were sent to Zacapa, also for training.

When Castillo Armas was informed by his intelligence operatives about the impressive Army movement that was taking place, he radioed SALAL saying that having fighter air support would be critical during the next 72 hours, whether it was for holding out at Chiquimula or for covering his forces' during the attack on Zacapa. He went as far as to state that without fighter coverage, he would abandon everything and go home.

The CIA station in Guatemala confirmed the Army's movement that same evening. Two trains packed-full of troops from the Guardia de Honor and La Aurora garrisons were on their way to Zacapa, while Ministry of Public Works' trucks were also hauling a couple of companies to Ipala. So massive was the operation that the seditious officers told Ambassador Peurifoy that they had lost half of the troops they planned to use in the coup, as they had been moved to the front.

That night, Peurifoy cabled Opa-locka saying that the Field Command Post had to stop sending the Thunderbolts to support Castillo Armas' forces, as it had resulted in the depletion of the Army effectives in the Capital due to the maximum effort the government was making to dislodge the Liberationist in the Chiquimula – Zacapa area.[35]

To make things worse, Arbenz's militias would soon overshadow the Army's strength in Guatemala City, giving the Communists a chance to take over the government. Thus, to counterbalance this delicate situation, the Ambassador suggested that the Thunderbolts should be sent to bomb –repeatedly- as many military targets in the Capital as possible.

This time PBSuccess headquarters listened, and shortly after midnight, Robertson was ordered to send the Thunderbolts to "Bomb Matamoros and strafe all gas tank targets at 8:00 AM on June 25 or thereafter as weather permits. Attacks should be followed immediately by C-47's leaflet drop. Pilots must be carefully cautioned to avoid loss of civilian life. Accurate bombing of vital importance."[36]

The cable that PBSuccess' Field Commander received also stated: "This mission has precedence over any other tactical requirements due to the imminence of diplomatic action that could halt all external support to Castillo Armas' forces. In addition, this will be a calculated effort coinciding with a probable revolt of the Guatemalan Army's high command. Plan carefully."

Shortly after, Robertson phoned Brodfrost to tell him about the change of orders. However, the Chief of Air Support replied that he couldn't fulfill the requirement, since he didn't have any fighters available. Two Thunderbolts were grounded in Managua without tail tires, the recently acquired ones had arrived in France Field with their main landing gear and tail tires in a sorry state too, rendering them unusable.

Robertson informed Opa-locka about this new predicament, and requested that spare tires be sent to France Field as soon as possible. In addition, he requested approval for using the CAT pilots, who would ferry the Thunderbolts to Managua, for tactical support missions. "The ground units will need all the support they can get during the next three days," he added.

PBSuccess headquarters approved the use of the CAT pilots that same night.[37] There was a caveat though, this measure would be only temporary, and the Chief of Air Support would have to recruit eligible pilots anywhere he could. Fortunately, one of the CAT pilots at France Field offered to contact four aviators who were friends of his, and who were willing to fly on combat missions.

Robertson was advised also to hire additional mechanics, since using those of the U.S. Air Mission in Managua could turn problematic when the OAS peace committee arrived in the Nicaraguan capital. Fortunately, Brodfrost moved fast and, through a friend, he managed to hire two adventurous mechanics and an armorer in the Florida area.

CHAPTER 11

ZACAPA

Shortly after midnight, on June 25, PGT activist Octavio Reyes, who had witnessed the Army troops retreat from Chiquimula, arrived in Guatemala City and immediately went to see Jose Manuel Fortuny, Arbenz's minister without portfolio, to inform him about his findings. Less than an hour later, Fortuny called for an urgent meeting with the President at the National Palace, during which he informed Arbenz that the Ejército de Operaciones officers were avoiding combat. At first, Arbenz didn't buy it, but at Fortuny's insistence, he decided to appoint Col. Anselmo Getellá as Inspector General of Combat Operations[1] and sent him to Zacapa to find out what was really happening.

Meanwhile at the U.S. Embassy, Peurifoy had been ordered by the Department of State to start pressuring Arbenz to resign and to openly assist anyone willing to oust him. The CIA Director had also authorized John Doherty, the Guatemala Station's Chief, and case officer Enno Hobbing, to help the Ambassador in any way they could.

The plan was to take advantage of the deep cracks that the Army was showing by then, since there were two groups that wanted to get rid of Arbenz. The first of these, led by Colonels Élfego Monzón, José Luis Cruz Salazar and Mauricio Dubois, had been in contact with Peurifoy during the previous several weeks and were the ones clamoring for the Capital to be bombed so they had an excuse to revolt. The other group, led by Colonels Carlos Enrique Díaz, Chief of the Armed Forces, and José Ángel Sánchez, Minister of Defense, was loyal to Arbenz but wanted him to resign in order to defuse a potentially disastrous situation with the U.S. They had also held meetings with Peurifoy, but the Ambassador disliked them because

The aftermath of the bombing of Fort Matamoros, on June 25, 1954. (Photo credit: Life Magazine.)

they didn't want to deal with Castillo Armas in any way. In both cases, however, the officers were hesitant about making a definitive move, since they lacked the courage to face the imposing Arbenz persona.

Unbeknownst to all involved, a third seditious group had emerged during the preceding 24 hours, and in contrast with the other two, this one had considerable firepower, enough troops, and all the motivation required for tipping the political balance. Arbenz's Inspector General of Combat Operations was the first to come face to face with them.

Col. Getellá arrived in Zacapa near 8:00AM in a heavily guarded jeep, and immediately went to supervise the defensive positions established around the town and along the road to Chiquimula. In the process, he learned that the troops were extremely frightened by the constant airstrikes, while the junior officers were doing their best to contain the numerous desertions. Many of these officers were eager to fight but so far, they had received only contradicting orders from their superiors.

On his way back to the Zacapa garrison, Getellá spoke with an intelligence officer who had arrived from the Capital during the night, and he informed the Colonel that the trains and trucks bringing the reinforcements had spent the night outside Guatemala City. Someone from the Ejército de Operaciones had ordered them to advance towards their destinations only during the daylight hours. Obviously, this absurd disposition made them extremely vulnerable to air attacks.

At the Zacapa garrison, Getellá met with Col. León and his staff, and questioned them about their plans to defeat the enemy, but the Commander of the Ejército de Operaciones replied that they didn't have any. They had limited themselves to contain the Liberationists by encircling and harassing them, and their priority was to achieve the most advantageous tactical position in order to force a negotiation.

Furious, Getellá reminded Col. León that negotiating with the enemy was an act of treason and told him that he would recommend the President to relieve the Ejército de Operaciones' staff if they refused to rout the Liberationist as soon as possible. Nonchalantly, Col. León replied, "*Arbenz can go to hell. We no longer follow orders from him.*"[2] Then, he added that as soon as they had the situation under control in Zacapa and Puerto Barrios, they would march upon the Capital to oust him. Surprisingly, Col. León allowed Getellá to leave the garrison, and within minutes, the Colonel was on his way back to the Capital.

Meanwhile at Chiquimula, Brodfrost's C-47s arrived to resupply the Liberationists in preparation for the assault on Zacapa, which would be launched by midday. The bundles with food and ammunition were dropped in four passes, since low clouds were obscuring the drop zone. Minutes later, the transports repeated the operation near Jalapa, where a resistance cell would attack that town's garrison in order to draw the attention of the Army reinforcements headed for Chiquimula via Ipala. Escorting the C-47s was one of the recently acquired Thunderbolts, which had been fitted with a tail tire from one of the fighters still grounded at France Field, and that had been rushed to Managua during the night.

At 7:30 AM, the C-47s were done with the resupplying and the Thunderbolt, piloted by Williams, was released to conduct the day's first combat mission. Initially, the pilot reconnoitered the areas North and Northeast of Chiquimula, looking for enemy troops, but he didn't find any. Then, he went to Zacapa and from there, followed the railway to Guatemala City, looking for any trains carrying reinforcements.

Williams caught one 5 km West of El Jícaro and hit it with two 275 lb. fragmentation bombs, which didn't detonate. Then, he made another pass and dropped a 555 lb. demolition bomb over the locomotive, but it didn't detonate either. Unabated, the pilot began strafing the train, setting the locomotive on fire and knocking down three cars. As it

Another view of the destruction caused by the 555 lb. bomb dropped by Jerry Delarm over Fort Matamoros on June 25, 1954. (Photo credit: Douglas Larsen.)

would be expected, it didn't take long for the scared Army troops to leave the train and run to the hills nearby. As soon as the Thunderbolt left, they continued on foot towards Zacapa. Williams, on the other hand, landed in Managua near 9:20 AM.

In Nueva Ocotepeque, where Robertson had temporarily moved the Field Command Post, worrying news arrived from Opa-locka: The much-anticipated bombing of the Matamoros Fort, which had been delayed due to bad weather over the Capital, was on the brink of being cancelled. The Department of State wanted that the fort to be attacked by any other "less spectacular" means.[3] Wisner and Peurifoy had spent the morning trying to convince Henry Holland, the Assistant Secretary of State, that there was no other way to deliver such an important psychological blow, at least on time. The worst part was that Robertson had been ordered to keep the fighters on the ground until the situation was resolved, even if they were needed for defending Chiquimula in case of a counterattack. In any case, the hiatus had given Brodfrost's mechanics the chance to repair a second Thunderbolt, using a patched up tail tire that had been brought from France Field on the night's cargo run.

It was not until midday that Holland finally approved the bombing of Matamoros and accordingly, the repaired plane and the one that had accomplished the morning's mission, were launched from Las Mercedes at 12:10 PM[4], piloted by Delarm and Williams. Their primary mission however, would be to check for enemy troops around Chiquimula and then destroy the remaining trains that were advancing towards Zacapa. Once these two important tasks had been accomplished, they would set course to the Capital for bombing the fort.

The Thunderbolts arrived over Chiquimula at 1:30 PM and immediately began looking for enemy activity in its surroundings. Incredibly, the pilots missed the two Army columns assembling near the village of Agua Blanca, some 10 km North of the town, obviously for a major counterattack.

In any case, just before departing for Zacapa, the fighters buzzed the town repeatedly, noting where the Liberationists had established their defensive positions, since Robertson wanted to have a clear picture of what was happening.

Upon reaching Zacapa, the fighters followed the railroad tracks to the Capital. It only took a couple of minutes for the pilots to spot the first train near Cabañas, and strafed it until the locomotive exploded. Then, they finished the train that Williams had attacked near El Jícaro in the morning, blowing the locomotive to pieces with machinegun fire. The third and last train was caught near the town of El Progreso, and the Thunderbolts strafed it until it stopped. However, to make sure that the train couldn't continue to Zacapa, Williams circled back and destroyed a bridge two kilometers ahead of it, with a 555 lb. demolition bomb. In all cases, the troops had continued on foot, sometimes following the railway or through the nearby hills and ravines.

The fighters reached Guatemala City at 2:20 PM, and the first to make a pass over Matamoros was Williams, but the two 275 lb. fragmentation bombs he was carrying didn't release. Delarm went next, and dropped a 555 lb. demolition bomb right over the fortress' ammunition depot, blowing it to pieces and causing large secondary explosions.

As the Thunderbolts were circling back for a second pass, Delarm's plane began taking anti-aircraft fire and the cockpit filled with smoke. Desperate, the pilot rolled open the canopy and immediately set

The plume of smoke rising from Fort Matamoros after being bombed by Jerry Delarm in one of the Sulfatos. (Photo credit: Via Mario Overall.)

course to Managua. Williams, on his part, jettisoned his two bombs at a ravine 10 km East of the Capital and then escorted Delarm back to Las Mercedes. After landing, Brodfrost's mechanics determined that 40mm shrapnel had damaged the left wing spar and the turbo-supercharger of Delarm's plane, rendering it unusable for at least three days while it was repaired. It also meant that the Air Support Unit was down yet again, to just one fighter.

Back in Guatemala City, Peurifoy contacted Col. Monzón's group as soon as he learned that Matamoros had been bombed, and urged them to stage the coup as soon as they could, but the officers refused. The few remaining troops in the Capital, which they had planned to use for the revolt, were about to depart for Jalapa to reinforce that town's garrison, which was under heavy attack. As it could be expected, the Ambassador was furious.

As soon as PBSuccess headquarters learned that Col. Monzón's group had called off the revolt, Wisner decided to shelve the plan of seizing the Capital and focused on implementing "Plan Beta" instead[5], which involved an air assault on Puerto Barrios where Castillo Armas would establish a provisional government. Wisner also expected to move there the project's Field Command Post and the Air Support Unit once the town had been occupied. Accordingly, PBSuccess headquarters urged Robertson to capture Zacapa and secure its airfield within 24 hours, since it would be necessary to launch the air assault from there, and from the Chiquimula airfield. In addition, Robertson ordered Maj. Torres and Lt. De Paz to join what was left of their columns at Correderos and proceed to Puerto Barrios for launching harassment attacks against the town's garrison and airbase, in order to soften their defenses in preparation for the air assault.

Also, as part of the implementation of "Plan Beta", Robertson urged Brodfrost to procure additional fighters since he would need eight of them, for operating six at all times, while the other two would be used for spares. Additionally, a fourth transport would be required so the third C-47, currently flying supplies between France Field and Managua on a daily basis, could be used on tactical missions.

Brodfrost cabled the urgent request to Opa-locka that afternoon, and within a few hours, headquarters replied that the remaining Thunderbolts the USAF had in Puerto Rico were not combat-ready and required a minimum of 12 days of work before delivery. Other fighters, stored in the U.S., were not in flying conditions and would take no less than 60 days.[6] Therefore, Brodfrost was advised to shift to North American F-51D *Mustangs* for increasing the fighter fleet, since the USAF could provide three of them in less than a week.[7] As for the additional transport, the CIA would borrow a Douglas C-54 from CAT, which would be sterilized at Andrews AFB before being sent to France Field.

The Chief of Air Support reluctantly accepted the three Mustangs, even though operating mixed fighter types could turn into a maintenance nightmare. To be on the safe side, however, he promptly requested that three additional mechanics and a planeload of spare parts[8] for both, the Mustangs and the Thunderbolts, be sent to France Field as soon as possible.

Meanwhile at Chiquimula, the much-anticipated Army counterattack finally materialized at 3:00 PM, in the form of a two-pronged assault with fire support from heavy artillery positions emplaced on a hill named "El Ingeniero", 5 km Northeast of town. Just as Robertson feared, it occurred at the worst possible time since the Thunderbolts still were en route to Managua after having bombed Matamoros.

Unable to provide Castillo Armas with adequate air support, Robertson ordered Carlos Cheesman to depart Esquipulas in the Cessna 180, and bomb and strafe as many enemy troops as he could while he worked something out. Then, he phoned Brodfrost and ordered him to refuel and reload the Thunderbolts as soon as they arrived, and send them back to Chiquimula. However, the Chief of air support came up with a much more expeditious solution: He would use one of the C-47s as an improvised bomber. Robertson approved the idea in no time.

Within minutes, Brodfrost's mechanics loaded one of the transports

The fearsome *Solothurn S-18/1000* 20 mm anti-tank rifles played an important part during the invasion. Here, two Liberationists can be seen carrying one of those heavy weapons near Chiquimula, during the offensive against Zacapa. (Photo credit: Life Magazine.)

with 24 20 lb. and two 260 lb. fragmentation bombs and instructed the cargo kickers on how to roll them out of the cargo door when the pilot signaled them to do so. Shortly before departing, Brodfrost briefed the crew on the current situation in the combat zone and the areas they would have to bomb. The other C-47 was loaded with ammunition and supplies for the Liberationists so they could withstand the assault, and for the resistance cell at Jalapa, which by then was about to overrun that town's garrison. At 3:25 PM, both transports took off from Las Mercedes.

The improvised bomber arrived over Chiquimula near 5:00 PM and immediately began dropping its deadly cargo on the Army columns that were advancing towards the town from the North and Northeast. However, the heavy bombardment didn't prevent the Army troops from advancing further and by 5:45 PM, they engaged the Liberationist's first line of defense. At this point, Cheesman was brought into the fight and his gunner began strafing the enemy soldiers, trying to stop them, to no avail. Meanwhile, the C-47 began bombing the artillery positions emplaced on "El Ingeniero" hill, which were causing heavy casualties among the Liberationists, but wasn't able to silence them. Minutes later, the transport had to depart the area, as it was running low on fuel.

By 6:15 PM, several Army fire squads took up positions in the town's Eastern edge, setting up mortars and heavy machinegun nests between the airfield and the train station, and began firing at the Liberationists guarding the town's main entrance. Overwhelmed by the Army troops' firepower, they retreated into downtown and informed Col. Mendoza, who was in charge of Chiquimula's defense, that they were about to be overrun. Shortly after, the Colonel escaped[9] to San Esteban, leaving his men behind.

When the Liberationists realized that their commanding officer had left in the face of the enemy, many of them deserted or headed for the nearby hills. However, a young Lieutenant named Antonio Beteta, took over the remaining troops, and after an intense firefight, managed to stop the assault and forced the Army soldiers to retreat to Zacapa. About this episode, in his daily field report Robertson stated, "*Beteta's weapons placement and leadership definitively won the day.*"[10]

Meanwhile near Ipala, Capt. Fernández's group had spent much of the afternoon waiting for a major offensive from the Army reinforcements that had been arriving in that town during the day, but it never materialized. It turned out that these troops had been redirected to aid in the defense of Jalapa, just like Robertson had planned it.

Despite the relative success at stopping the counterattack on Chiquimula and defusing a major offensive from Ipala, albeit temporarily, the Liberationists' situation was precarious, and Robertson had serious doubts about whether they would be able to seize Zacapa. By the end of the afternoon, the Field Commander met with Lt. Col. Pivall for making plans on how to proceed. What puzzled them, however, was why the Ejército de Operaciones was delaying the closing of the pincer move on Castillo Armas' forces, which essentially, were sitting ducks at Chiquimula. Robertson suspected a trap, but Pivall believed that the Ejército de Operaciones' officers didn't have a clue on how to end the campaign. Little did they know that the Guatemalan officers were just buying time while a negotiated solution could be reached.

Robertson wasn't the only one worried, however, since President Somoza had been informed about the status of the operation and how it was on the brink of failure. Therefore, by 6:30 PM, he went to Las Mercedes and stormed the Air Support Unit's hangar, demanding to speak with The Group's leader immediately.[11] Brodfrost tried to calm him down, explaining to him that that couldn't be possible, at least in the short term. Unabated, Somoza ordered him to arrange a meeting with The Group's higher authority within 24 hours, or he would kick them out of the country. Before leaving, the Nicaraguan

Liberation troops setting up a mortar position near Zacapa. (Photo credit: Guillermo Putzeys.)

President yelled that he was sick of feeling like "*a guest in his own house*" and that he no longer would tolerate not having a say about the manner in which the operation was being conducted, specially when his government could end up being seriously compromised if it failed.

As soon as Somoza left, Brodfrost informed Opa-locka about the awkward incident, but surprisingly, Wisner urged him to play it down until Puerto Barrios had been secured and everything that they had in Managua, including the aircraft, had been relocated there. In the meantime, he would order Al Haney to send "someone", preferably a senior intelligence officer, to appease the raving President.[12]

At 7:15 PM, Castillo Armas, accompanied by Colonels Flores Avendaño and Mendoza, arrived in Chiquimula and established the Liberation's Advanced Command Post at the Hernández Hotel, near the town's central plaza. Despite the prevailing demoralization among his troops, the Caudillo began planning an all-out attack on Zacapa, scheduling it for the next day. Then, he contacted the Field Command Post and requested that the Zacapa garrison be bombed continuously during the morning and that the fighters keep constant air reconnaissance over Ipala in order to anticipate any offensive from that area.

Minutes later he tried to contact Col. Chajón Chúa's group on the radio, to make sure that they would join the assault on Zacapa. However, a resident radio operator at Teculután, informed him that Chajón Chúa and a couple of his men had been captured by Army troops near the village of La Vainilla and had been taken to Guatemala City. The remainder of the column, less than 10 men, was hiding in a ravine 8 km West of La Unión. Incredibly, it was until then that the Caudillo learned that this group had been defeated at Gualán six days earlier.

Saturday, June 26, began with worrying news for Robertson. Despite the previous day's airstrikes on the trains, more than 1300 troops had reinforced the Zacapa garrison during the night. Moreover, five M3A1 Stuart tanks had been brought in by rail and they were being readied for another counterattack on Chiquimula. The situation in the South was similar, since 2000 soldiers of the Guardia de Honor had disengaged from the battle at Jalapa during the night, and were advancing towards Ipala, from where they would launch a major offensive against the Liberationist rearguard in Quezaltepeque.

Without a doubt, Robertson needed to force a decision in the Chiquimula – Zacapa area urgently, but it was more than evident that the Liberationists were not up to the task. Thus, he requested Opa-locka for authorization to form an "*Advance liaison, advisory, communications and support detachment*" that would join and follow Castillo Armas and would provide him with advice and guidance for the remainder of the campaign.[13] Lt. Col. Pivall, his assistant officer going by the *nom-de-guerre* Mathew Ontrich, and two CIA radio operators would conform this detachment.

PBSuccess headquarters approved Robertson's request[14] but with reservations, since the presence of any Americans among the Liberation forces was considered a major security breach. Therefore, Pivall and his companions were to avoid being captured at all costs, and if there were signs of an impending defeat, they would have to "*fade into the bush*" and return to Honduras as soon as possible. Hours later, Pivall and his team departed Nueva Ocotepeque for Chiquimula in a truck, while Castillo Armas was informed about the new plan.

Near 4:30 AM, Radio Liberación began broadcasting the Liberation

Jerry Delarm (left, with sunglasses) and Fito Mendoza (center, with hands in his waist) with Castillo Armas at Chiquimula, on June 26, 1954. (Photo credit: Guillermo Putzeys.)

Movement's conditions for a cease-fire.[15] The message, which would be repeated every half hour, urged the Army officers to oust Arbenz and establish a temporary military junta as soon as possible, which would negotiate with the "Liberation Council" the conformation of a new government that would include Castillo Armas.

The announcement caught the Caudillo by surprise and he didn't lose any time in radioing Robertson asking what was it all about. The Field Commander explained that it was a "*political propaganda maneuver*" for encouraging the Army officers to stage a coup and avoid "*a pointless bloodshed.*"

The Ejército de Operaciones' officers also were surprised by the announcement, and soon began making plans for contacting Castillo Armas. In the meantime, Col. León ordered his troops to tighten the encirclement around Chiquimula.

Back in Managua, Brodfrost met with his mechanics at 4:45 AM to see what was the status of the fighters, since the airstrikes would be decisive during the assault on Zacapa. Within minutes, the Chief of Air Support learned that the situation wasn't promising: Of the three Thunderbolts at Las Mercedes, only one was available. One was being repaired from the damages sustained during the Matamoros mission and the other was lacking the tail tire. At France Field, the situation was similar, since the spare tires hadn't arrived yet and the two Thunderbolts still were grounded. The good news was, however, that a USAF C-124 packed with spare parts would arrive in the Canal Zone during the day and the P-38L *Lightning* had finally been repaired.

At 5:00 AM, the cargo kickers finished loading one of the C-47s for the day's first resupplying mission. It was carrying 10 Italian *Mortaio da 81/14 Modello 35* 81 mm mortar tubes, several crates of 15 lb. high explosive shells, and 10 *Solothurn S-18/1000* 20 mm anti-tank rifles, which were going to be used by Pivall for supporting the assault on Zacapa. Robertson believed that this relatively heavy weaponry, plus the airstrikes, would assure the Liberationist a quick victory.

The C-47 arrived over Chiquimula at 7:15 AM, escorted by the only Thunderbolt available, piloted by Williams. Since clouds were obscuring the area, it took five passes for the transport to drop all of its cargo, and when it was done the fighter broke its patrolling pattern and headed for Zacapa.

Upon arriving over the town, Williams discovered that five trains, packed with supplies and reinforcements, were being unloaded at the marshaling yards. The pilot radioed this information to the Field Command Post and requested authorization to attack the trains instead of the town's defensive positions. It only took a couple of minutes for Robertson to give him the green light.

During the first pass, Williams placed two 275 lb. fragmentation bombs adjacent to the outside train, damaging three cars and wounding many of the soldiers who were still inside them. Then, he circled back and destroyed one of the locomotives with the 555 lb. bomb he was carrying. When he made sure that the trains were immobilized, he began strafing the artillery emplacements and heavy machinegun nests scattered over the town's Southwestern edge and along the road to Chiquimula. 20 minutes later, the Thunderbolt departed the area and landed at Las Mercedes near 10:00 AM without any problems.

Since it was necessary to determine if Chiquimula's airfield could

The "El Portillo" storage tanks leaking gasoline after being strafed by one of the Sulfatos on June 22, 1954. (Photo credit: U.S. Embassy to Guatemala.)

be used for the airlift to Puerto Barrios, Fito Mendoza and Delarm were sent to check it on a C-47. Additionally, they would be carrying 10 gasoline drums for Castillo Armas' forces and six additional 81 mm mortar tubes for Pivall. They took off at 8:00 AM.

Near 10:30 AM, the C-47 landed[16] at Chiquimula's airfield and while it was being unloaded, Delarm and Fito examined the runway carefully, but deemed it too short for a fully loaded C-47 to take off. Then, Castillo Armas arrived and picked them up to take them to the Hernández Hotel where Fito had the chance to speak with his brother and with Col. Flores Avendaño. In his after-mission report, Fito stated that, by then, more than 1500 volunteers had joined the Liberation forces, and that the population was very happy about having been "liberated."

Around the same time, the P-38L, flown by Ferdinand Schoup, was making its way towards the combat zone, with the mission of destroying a bridge near Jalapa, and attacking the troops that were advancing towards Ipala. However, as he began descending near the Salvadoran Coast, one of the engines developed problems and he had to abort the mission. While crawling back to Managua, Schoup jettisoned at sea the two 555 lb. bombs he was carrying.

The second airstrike on Zacapa was carried out by one of the Thunderbolts, flown by a CAT pilot. At 10:45 AM, the fighter began strafing artillery emplacements around the town and the trains that Williams had bombed earlier, setting two of them on fire. Then, before departing, the pilot destroyed the town's train station with a 555 lb. bomb and took out a couple of machinegun nests emplaced near the marshaling yards with two fragmentation bombs.

Shortly after the airstrike, six 81 mm mortar tubes that Pivall had emplaced on a hill named "El Miramundo", 4 km Southwest of Zacapa, began shelling the Ejército de Operaciones headquarters and the defense positions along the town's Southern and Western edges. Meanwhile at Chiquimula, Castillo Armas ordered his troops to start assembling for the assault on Zacapa.

Near 11:00 AM, Arbenz met with the Army high command and members of the Defense Council at the National Palace to hear Col. Gettella's report about the situation in Zacapa. According to eyewitnesses, the President was an emotional wreck when the meeting began; something had happened during the night that had crushed him completely, and upon hearing about the Ejército de Operaciones' rebellion, he became deeply demoralized. The Defense Minister hammered the last nail in the coffin when he reported that the Ejército de Operaciones' officers had cut the communications with the Army headquarters and the "La Aurora" Military Base had done the same.

Then, Col. Díaz took advantage of the President's sorry state and told him that the majority of the Army officers wanted him to step down. He also mentioned that a certain group of seditious officers was about to stage a coup and then negotiate with the Liberationists the establishment of a military junta that surely would include Castillo Armas. Therefore, Díaz suggested that the best option for preserving the gains of the October Revolution was for him to resign and let a "loyal" junta take over the government. In the end, Arbenz agreed to resign the next day, on the condition that the Army high command promised to keep fighting Castillo Armas' forces.

What Arbenz didn't know was that earlier that morning, Col. Díaz had met with Peurifoy to let him know about his plan to take over the government; and even when Peurifoy had been ambiguous during such meeting, Díaz had left convinced that he had the Ambassador's acquiescence.

President Arbenz had another chance to avoid a debacle when

A trio of C-47s of the Guatemalan national airline Aviateca at the La Aurora international airport. At least two of these transports were sent to Mexico City on a secret mission aimed at acquiring arms and ammunition for the Guatemalan Army. (Photo credit: Guatemalan Air Force.)

the Chief of the Guardia Civil, Col. Rogelio Cruz Wer, arrived at the National Palace carrying a list with the names of Col. Monzón's group members and a complete report about their nefarious intentions.[17] Upon presenting them to Arbenz, Cruz Wer asked if he should apprehend them or even execute them immediately. The President however, only thanked him for the information and then locked himself in his office, spending the rest of the day there.

The third mission for bombing Zacapa, to be conducted by Williams in one of the Thunderbolts, took off from Las Mercedes at 11:25 AM. It would signal the Liberationists to commence the assault on the town. However, 36 km West of Mechapa, Nicaragua, the fighter's engine began sputtering and the pilot had to jettison the three bombs he was carrying before returning to Managua. Minutes later, Robertson radioed Castillo Armas telling him to begin the assault without air cover, and promised to send another fighter during the afternoon.

As the first trucks carrying the Liberationists were leaving Chiquimula, Robertson received a cable from President Somoza saying that if Castillo Armas managed to seize Zacapa, he would lend them his A-20 attack plane, two armed AT-6s and 150 trained troops for supporting the air assault on Puerto Barrios. Robertson took Somoza at his word and assured him that Zacapa would be seized within 24 hours.

Far from being a clash of epic proportions, as many at the Field Command Post expected it, the Liberationists began the assault by timidly probing the Army's defense lines along the town's Southern areas, while Pivall's 81 mm mortar tubes kept pounding the garrison. Then, Col. Mendoza, who was in charge of the operation, sat to wait for the air cover to arrive.[18]

Despite Pivall's devastating mortar fire, the Ejército de Operaciones managed to reinforce its defenses and began assembling a major counterattack at the garrison. Col. León also ordered the Army troops at Ipala to assault Quezaltepeque immediately and then close the pincer move by attacking Chiquimula from the South. As it would be expected, when Capt. Fernández noticed the sudden advance of the Army troops at Ipala, he began calling urgently for air support.

The first to arrive in the area was the P-38L[19], flown by Schoup. After studying Fernandez's situation for a couple of minutes, the pilot decided to destroy a bridge 12 km West of Quezaltepeque to prevent the trucks carrying the Army troops from reaching that town. Then, he strafed the convoy for more than 30 minutes, destroying five trucks and forcing the soldiers to retreat to Ipala.

At 3:45 PM, one of the Thunderbolts, with Delarm at the controls, scooted under the heavy overcast and flying dangerously close to the mountains, began the third attack on Zacapa. First, the pilot strafed a couple of Army columns that were climbing the El Miramundo hill to silence Pivall's mortars. After a couple of passes that left many casualties, these soldiers retreated into the town in a rush. Minutes later, Delarm dropped two fragmentation bombs on the large contingent that was assembling at the garrison and strafed the artillery emplacements in the town's Southwestern edge. Only then did Col. Mendoza order his men to get closer to the town and engage the Army's first line of defense.

After an hour of continuously pounding Zacapa, Delarm set course for Guatemala City following the railway, to check if any trains were approaching. He didn't find any, but near El Jícaro, he thoroughly machine-gunned a couple of military jeeps that were racing towards Zacapa.

Delarm finally reached the Capital at 5:00 PM. His objective was to bomb the Matamoros Fort for a second time, but the heavy anti-aircraft fire prevented him from getting near it. Unabated, he decided to conduct some "flak suppression" runs and during one of them, dropped a 555 lb. demolition bomb over a pair of Oerlikons that were emplaced at the Country Club, 600 meters Southeast from the fort. Then, the pilot made a strafing run over the "El Portillo" gasoline storage tanks in the Southern part of the City, setting one of them on fire. Shortly before departing, Delarm decided to check on La Aurora Airbase, but as he was approaching it from the North, his plane began taking anti-aircraft fire, which damaged the fighter's left wing and aileron, and tore a 10 cm hole in the left wing's fuel tank. The pilot immediately climbed away and headed back to Managua, where he landed at 6:10 PM. On his report about this mission, Brodfrost stated, "*this is the pilot's major accomplishment to date.*"[20]

At the Nicaraguan Capital, President Somoza was about to propitiate one of the most embarrassing episodes of the entire operation. It began when he phoned Robertson urging him to send the fighters to sink the M.S. *Springfjord*, a British ship that had just docked at Puerto de San José. According to Somoza's intelligence operatives, the ship was carrying a large amount of arms and ammunition for Arbenz's militias. Robertson immediately requested Opa-locka's authorization to bomb it[21], but PBSuccess headquarters refused, as the CIA couldn't confirm what was onboard. In fact, Wisner advised the Field Commander to "*wait for specific targets of importance and avoid any indiscriminate attacks.*"[22]

Minutes later, Somoza phoned Robertson and once again urged him to sink the ship before it began to be unloaded. When the Field Commander told him that The Group hadn't authorized the attack, the President yelled: "*If you use my airfield, then you do as I say! Bomb the damn ship!*"[23] and hung up.

Robertson was about to discard the awkward incident as just another of Somoza's bravados when a string of urgent cables, which apparently confirmed that Arbenz was trying to acquire arms for the militias, began arriving at the Field Command Post.

First, a cable from the CIA station in Guatemala[24] stated that Jorge Toriello, brother of the Guatemalan Foreign Minister, had arrived in Mexico City to purchase all the weapons he could; and for transporting them, two C-47s of the Guatemalan government's airline AVIATECA (civil registrations TG-AHA and TG-AJA, according to CIA declassified documents) were parked at Mexico City's Central Airport. In addition, the USAF attaché in the Mexican Capital had received unconfirmed reports stating that the Mexican President, General Adolfo Ruiz Cortines, was about to send a handful of Republic P-47D *Thunderbolts* to Guatemala[25], for increasing the FAG's airpower. Finally, yet importantly, Ambassador Peurifoy reported that Carlos Manuel Pellecer, a leading Communist, had taken over the militias and that arms and ammunition were being passed to them clandestinely, so they could be deployed to Zacapa and Jalapa as soon as possible.

What finally sent Robertson into "crisis mode" was a cable from the Department of State saying that the much-anticipated OAS' inspection team was set to depart Washington the next day, and would visit Guatemala, Honduras and Nicaragua, spending three days in each country. It meant that the CIA's support to the Liberationists would have to end within 72 hours or less if Castillo Armas wasn't able to force a decision in the combat zone. Therefore, now more than ever, it was imperative to seize Zacapa as soon as possible, since it would enable the air assault for taking Puerto Barrios. Once the latter had been occupied, the Field Command Post and the Air Support Unit would relocate there, ending the project's dependence on the neighboring countries. It would also allow Castillo Armas to establish his provisional government and defuse the complicated diplomatic situation in which the Liberationists were being labeled as "foreign aggressors."

Thus, to hasten the seizing of Zacapa, Robertson requested of the CIA Director that a "*special operations group*"[26] be formed exclusively with CIA paramilitary specialists for conducting tactical combat missions completely independent from Castillo Armas' forces. Such group would be infiltrated into the Chiquimula area, but as soon as Zacapa had been taken, they would redeploy to Puerto Barrios, to support the air assault on that town.

In addition, Robertson wanted to add a naval component to the air assault on Puerto Barrios, and for this, he requested that two civilian vessels be procured.[27] One of them would have to be equipped with four M45 Quadmount .50 Cal batteries, four M20 75 mm recoilless rifles, and four 2.36 in. rocket launchers. Its primary mission would be to attack coastal targets and provide fire support to the Liberation troops. The other ship would have to be packed with communications gear for serving as a temporary command and control platform. Both ships would have to be in the Guatemalan Caribbean waters no later than July 2, since Robertson planned to launch the air assault the following day.

Back in Managua, Somoza had got wind of the Mexican President's intentions of sending a handful of fighters to Guatemala, and didn't lose any time in putting Las Mercedes on high alert, as he was sure that as soon as Arbenz had those planes, he would launch them to bomb Managua. Accordingly, the FAN Commander, Col. Carlos Venegas, was ordered to emplace anti-aircraft batteries at both ends of the runway and Brodfrost was urged to scatter the PBSuccess' aircraft all over the airport.[28]

Brodfrost got worried about the possibility of the FAG acquiring equivalent fighters of the model they were using, and cabled Opa-locka requesting that the Mustangs be sent immediately to Las Mercedes and not to France Field as it had been originally planned. Additionally, he requested that three Douglas A-26 *Invader* attack planes[29] be procured from the USAF inventory, not only for supporting the assault on Puerto Barrios, but also for increasing the airpower in case the FAG decided to put up a fight in equal terms.

Then, amid the turmoil that prevailed, both at Nueva Ocotepeque and Managua, one of the SALAL radio operators received an urgent message from Castillo Armas saying that Col. Víctor León, Commander of the Ejército de Operaciones, had sent a group of officers to parley and a temporary truce had been agreed. Minutes later, the Caudillo reported that negotiations for enforcing a definitive cease-fire were taking place at a bend on the road between Zacapa and Chiquimula named "Vuelta del Tuno."

No one paid attention to those messages at first, and it wasn't until Pivall radioed further details that Robertson realized what was happening. According to Pivall, the continuous airstrikes and constant shelling had discouraged the Zacapa officers and now they were seeking a negotiated -yet honorable- solution. Thus, for a couple of hours, everyone at the Field Command Post held their breath, expecting to see what would be the outcome of the ongoing talks. Robertson even cabled the Caudillo urging him to offer Col. León to join the two forces and march upon the Capital to oust Arbenz, but to no avail. By midnight, the negotiations fell apart due to the intransigence of both parties. Castillo Armas wanted an unconditional surrender, while Col. León was demanding the same. In the end, the truce was called off and Castillo Armas requested of Robertson that the Army's defensive positions South of Zacapa be bombed continuously, as he was about to try assaulting the town once again.

Shortly before dawn, on Sunday June 27, Brodfrost received a cable from Opa-locka detailing the air operations to be conducted during the day, which would include the bombing of Zacapa, just as Castillo Armas had requested it, and continuous attacks on the Army troops

Wreckage of the British ship M.S. *Springfjord* at Puerto de San José. It was bombed –without authorization- by the PBSuccess Lockheed P-38L on June 27, 1954. (Photo credit: Via Mario Overall.)

advancing towards Quezaltepeque from Ipala. In addition, PBSuccess headquarters wanted the gasoline storage tanks at Puerto Barrios and Puerto San José bombed to cause a general shortage of fuel in the country, but mainly to force the hesitant Guatemalan military to stage a coup.

By then, the Air Support Unit's situation had improved considerably, since the spare parts had arrived at France Field, allowing the mechanics to repair the two Thunderbolts that were grounded there. During the night, two CAT pilots had ferried them to Managua, where they had joined the only F-47N available there, and the P-38L. In total, Brodfrost had four operational fighters.

At 4:00AM, while the aircrews began arriving at Las Mercedes for conducting their pre-flight checks, Robertson phoned Brodfrost and ordered him to change the flight plan for the mission that Schoup would conduct in the P-38L. Instead of bombing the Puerto San José gasoline storage tanks, the pilot would attack the *Springfjord*. The Chief of Air Support asked if Opa-locka had approved the airstrike, to which he replied that due to the circumstances, they would "*shoot first and give explanations later.*" Then, it was Somoza who phoned Brodfrost to make sure he was aware of the change in the mission, adding that the Nicaraguan Intelligence had spotted at least five crated Supermarine *Spitfire L.F. IXe* fighters being unloaded from the ship.

The first aircraft to depart Las Mercedes that morning were two C-47s loaded with ammunition, food, and gasoline drums for the Liberationists at Chiquimula and Quezaltepeque. Both took off at 5:15 AM, escorted by one of the Thunderbolts. Minutes later it was the turn for the third C-47, which had arrived in Managua after being replaced by the CAT C-54 on the daily runs from France Field. The plane departed loaded with 24 20 lb. fragmentation bombs for attacking Zacapa, followed by the second Thunderbolt flown by one of the newly recruited pilots.

The plan was that the much faster Thunderbolt would arrive first over Zacapa to commence the bombardment and an hour later, the C-47 would take over. Mother Nature however, got in the way, and the fighter got lost in bad weather near the Salvadoran Coast. The pilot had to jettison the bombs before calling off the mission. More familiarized with the terrain, the C-47 crew flew under the low overcast and managed to arrive in Zacapa where Pivall began directing them towards the targets, marking them with smoke grenades.

According to the after-mission report, the plane bombed the Army positions along the railway leading to Chiquimula and damaged a bridge 2 km Northwest of Zacapa. Then, it circled over the town for more than an hour, trying to draw fire so Pivall could locate and mark other heavy machinegun emplacements that could be hiding on the town's outskirts, but the Army troops were so scared that they ran for cover instead of shooting at the plane.

At 7:30AM, the P-38L reached Puerto San José and immediately buzzed the *Springfjord* as a warning for the crew that they were going to be attacked. Then, the fighter circled back and dropped on the ship the two 555 lb. demolition bombs it was carrying, but only one hit it, causing a large explosion. Minutes later, the *Springfjord* began sinking, engulfed in flames.

As the fighter climbed away, the anti-aircraft batteries emplaced at the San José Airbase opened fire and almost shredded its left tail boom and tore off completely the left rudder.[30] During the flight back to Managua, Schoup had a hard time trying to keep the fighter together. However, he was able to land at Las Mercedes near 9:10 AM, where Brodfrost's mechanics began the repairs on the plane immediately, using spare parts from another P-38 that was sitting at the FAN's junkyard.

The "official" after-mission report of flight "F-25"[31], as it was recorded in the CIA declassified documents, does not mention the attack on the *Springfjord*. In contrast, the brief document states that the mission was a complete fiasco since the pilot had tried to strafe and bomb the gasoline storage tanks at Puerto San José, but the machineguns had jammed and the bombs didn't release.

In any case, the P-38L hadn't landed yet when news about the sinking of the ship reached Washington. Wisner had the embarrassing task of going to the British Embassy to apologize. It turned out that far from carrying arms for Arbenz's militias, the ship was being loaded with coffee and cotton sacks destined for the European market.

To no one's surprise, the CIA Director grilled Brodfrost over the phone for having disobeyed a direct order. Then, it was Robertson's turn, but when Dulles tried to reach him at Nueva Ocotepeque, he was informed that the Field Commander had gone to Chiquimula to personally direct the combat operations. This, besides being a major security breach that could compromise the entire operation, was also an act of disobedience on the part of Robertson, as he had gone to the combat zone without authorization. Dulles was furious and the only thing that prevented him from firing the Field Commander was the extremely complicated overall situation.[32]

Completely oblivious of the developments at Washington and Opa-locka, Robertson arrived in Chiquimula about 9:30 AM in a Cessna 140 that had been recently acquired in Honduras for Castillo Armas, as he had requested a small plane for liaison duties over the combat zone.

As soon as Robertson reached the Liberation's Advanced Command Post, Castillo Armas briefed him about the ongoing situation. The Army troops at Ipala were already moving for a major showdown at Quezaltepeque and Col. Mendoza, who had been sent to the area, had requested that the fighters attack them as soon as possible, since his men wouldn't be able to withstand their advance. Additionally, there were intelligence reports stating that the Army troops at the Zacapa garrison were slowly regrouping for yet another assault on Chiquimula. To make things worse, the Thunderbolt that had been sent to attack them, had been unable to reach the combat zone due to the bad weather.

Despite the complications, Robertson ordered Castillo Armas to launch another assault on Zacapa. Thus, by midday, two columns led by Colonels Ernesto Neiderheitmann and Flores Avendaño attacked the town from the Southeast and Southwest, supported by Pivall's mortar fire.

As it had happened before, when the Liberationists were repelled by the Army's first line of defense, they pulled back and began requesting air support, even when the weather conditions prevented any plane from reaching the area. In fact, one of the C-47s loaded with fragmentation bombs, had almost crashed near Chiquimula while trying to fly under the overcast. Therefore, near 3:00 PM, the Field Command Post informed Robertson and Castillo Armas that all the fighter missions had been cancelled for the remainder of the day.

Not surprisingly, it didn't take long for the Liberationist columns to suspend the attack and retreat to Chiquimula. Finally, at 5:00 PM, Opa-locka ordered the Liberation forces to sit tight and delay any engagements until air support could be available. They were also instructed to switch to guerrilla warfare if the Army decided to close the pincer move on Chiquimula.

Meanwhile at the Puerto Barrios area, things weren't looking good for the Liberationists either, since an entire company had ambushed Maj. Torres' column near Champona, pushing them back to the Honduran border.[33] By 5:00 PM, a pair of FAG AT-6s arrived on the scene and began bombing and strafing them, and they had to retreat to Quimistán, Honduras. Later on, Maj. Torres informed the Field Command Post that it was impossible to penetrate the area due to the presence of a major enemy force, and that "Plan Beta" was not advisable.

During the evening, Castillo Armas had an intense argument with Robertson about the campaign's serious situation and the lack of adequate air support. By then, it was more than obvious that an all-out attack from Zacapa and Ipala was imminent. The Caudillo was so angry that he declared,

> If tomorrow there is not a crushing bombardment during the entire day on the two fronts, I shall be obliged to abandon everything attained. If this assistance so anxiously requested today is not given, I shall decline all responsibility.

Minutes later, he cabled[34] the exact same words to the Field Command Post.

At 8:30 PM, Ambassador Peurifoy informed the CIA Director about the outcome of a daylong meeting he had sustained with the Army high command. The good news was that the majority of officers had agreed on letting Col. Díaz assume the presidency that same night. On his part, Díaz had promised the Ambassador to jail all the Communists in the government as soon as he had been appointed president. The bad news was that he refused to deal with Castillo Armas and had declined the "good offices" of the U.S. government for enforcing a cease-fire, as he was determined to defeat the Liberationists as soon as possible. In his report to Dulles, Peurifoy stated:

> It is my opinion that once Arbenz is out tonight, Díaz should be forced to deal with Castillo Armas. I personally do not wish to become a part of another Mihailovich – Tito deal.[35]

Then, at 9:00 PM, the Guatemalan government's radio station began broadcasting President Arbenz's resignation speech, during which he openly accused the U.S. and the UFCO of having financed, trained and equipped Castillo Armas' forces. Minutes later, as Arbenz was stepping into the Mexican Embassy where he had been granted political asylum, Col. Díaz took the microphone and proclaimed that the gains of the October Revolution were going to be preserved by his regime, and promised to continue the fight against the Liberationists at all costs.

Wreckage of the Thunderbolt that crashed at the Chiquimula airfield after sustaining heavy damage while strafing the Zacapa garrison on June 29, 1954. (Photo credit: Guillermo Putzeys.)

CHAPTER 12

CEASE FIRE!

A couple of minutes after midnight, on June 28, Col. Díaz took the first steps to secure the new regime by decreeing a "*state of siege*" that suspended the civil rights and allowed the Guardia Civil and the Policía Judicial to go after anyone deemed to be an enemy of the government. Subsequently, he decided to placate Peurifoy and the Army officers who still wanted to stage a coup, by calling for the conforming of a governing junta that would be comprised by him, as President, Col. José Ángel Sánchez, as the representative of the pro-Arbenz wing of the Army, while the seditious officers would be represented by Col. Élfego Monzón.

By then, however, both the Department of State and the CIA had deemed Díaz unfit for taking over the presidency, since the prevailing feeling was that the he would pick up Communism where Arbenz had left it. Accordingly, Wisner was ordered to facilitate Díaz's ousting as soon as possible, and replace him with Col. Monzón, who had a proven anti-Communist background and was relatively more amiable to Castillo Armas.

Hence, by 1:00 AM, John Doherty, the Guatemala Station's Chief, and case officer Enno Hobbing, arrived at the Army headquarters with Col. Monzón in tow[1], for an urgent meeting in which they would try to force Díaz out of the presidency and transfer executive power to Monzón.

After two hours of intense negotiations, however, Col. Díaz stood his ground saying that his government had Ambassador Peurifoy's approval and that under no circumstances would he walk away. Furious, the CIA operatives called Peurifoy, who, by 4:00 AM, arrived at the Army headquarters.

There are varying accounts of what happened next. According to the available CIA documentation, Peurifoy told Díaz that he had "lost all rights to a favorable treatment" from the U.S. government, since he had allowed Arbenz to make "a straight Communist farewell speech, openly attacking the U.S." Therefore, accepting him, or the junta that he was going to form, would make the U.S. government look ridiculous in the eyes of the world.

In contrast, Guillermo Toriello, Arbenz's Minister of Foreign Affairs, in his book "La Batalla de Guatemala" (The Battle for Guatemala) describes the scene very differently, as Col. Díaz recalled it:

> Peurifoy waved a long list of names of [Communist] leaders. He was going to require Díaz to shoot those who were on that list within 24 hours. When Díaz asked why the Ambassador wanted them dead, Peurifoy replied, because they are Communists!"

In any case, the negotiations stalled and the meeting was adjourned at 6:30 AM. Minutes later, an obscure Lt. Colonel named Jorge García Calderón, who was a member of Col. Monzón's group, summoned the remaining 200 Army officers that were left in the Capital, for a meeting at the National Palace. They would discus the country's situation and take the "appropriate course of action."[2]

Meanwhile at Chiquimula, the Liberation forces were being resupplied by two C-47s in preparation for an offensive against the Army troops that were approaching Quezaltepeque in order to close the pincer move. Robertson's plan was to launch a 200-men contingent for a frontal attack over the road to Ipala, while several fire squads were to be positioned South and Southwest of Chiquimula to protect the town. The final assault on Zacapa, on the other hand, would be suspended until the rearguard could be secured. In the meantime, the Thunderbolts would bomb the town and the Army positions around it, in staggered attacks during the day. In addition, the resistance cell that had attacked Jalapa, now under the command of Cpt. Emilio Chacón, was instructed to move to Cabañas to be resupplied and then head for Zacapa for launching harassment attacks from the West and eventually support Castillo Armas' final assault on the town.

The survivors of Col. Chajón Chúa's column, now reinforced with 28 Hondurans who had been recruited in the Los Tarros area, were also ordered to launch harassment attacks on Zacapa from the East. Accordingly, they were positioned over the road between La Unión and Camotán to be resupplied before moving to the Zacapa vicinity, 16 km away.

About 7:20 AM, the third C-47 landed at the Chiquimula airfield, bringing even more 81 mm mortar tubes and sorely needed ammunition. However, the crew had strict orders to take Robertson back to Managua, since Wisner had decided to relocate the Field Command Post there, mainly to keep the rambunctious Field Commander under close supervision. By then, the sinking of the *Springfjord* was causing a commotion in Washington, and many were demanding Robertson's head.

Near 7:30 AM, Delarm, in one of the Thunderbolts, approached Zacapa from the West, under marginal weather conditions, and began strafing the hills along the road to Chiquimula, where several Army troops had set up defensive positions. Minutes later, he made a low pass over the garrison, dropping a 555 lb. demolition bomb on a "*large gray building*" which apparently was an ammunition dump, because there were several large secondary explosions after the "500 pounder" hit it. Then, shortly before departing, the pilot made a second pass over what was left of the building, and dropped on it two 250 lb. fragmentation bombs, which finished the job.

After climbing away from Zacapa, Delarm spotted in the distance what seemed to be a C-47 "dodging in and out of the clouds" over the Ipala area, and immediately decided to intercept it. As he was getting closer, Delarm fired short burst across the transport's nose, in an attempt to get the crew's attention, to no avail.

Sure that it was a FAG transport trying to escape, Delarm latched onto the plane and shifted his nose towards it, pushing his throttle forward, while trying to center it in his gun sight. However, when he was about to pull the trigger, the C-47 dove out of the clouds, and Delarm was able to see clearly that the transport had USAF markings on it.

Not surprisingly, Delarm cut the chase and as some sort of strange apology, the pilot circled the C-47 twice, while rocking the fighter's wings before heading in the direction of the Salvadoran Pacific Coast and then to Managua. In his after-mission report, Delarm declared that he "could not positively identify the plane until it dove out of the clouds."[3]

As for the mysterious C-47 that Delarm almost shot down, it was conducting the first of several missions to evacuate American citizens from Guatemala City[4] due to the grave situation that had developed there. In the following days, however, the USAF crews were advised to use alternate air routes when entering Guatemala, preferably away from the Southeastern region of the country, as there were "mercenary aircraft" operating in the area. For the record, the C-47s involved in the airlift were based at Albrook AFB, in the Panama Canal Zone, while the American civilians were being taken to Southern stateside cities, like New Orleans, Miami, and Houston.

Around 8:35 AM, the second Thunderbolt, with Williams at the controls, arrived over a surprisingly quiet Zacapa. The pilot decided to make several low passes trying to draw ground fire, but the Army gunners refused the invitation and limited themselves to watch the impressive airshow that Williams was putting up. Not even the heavy machineguns emplaced on the hills overlooking the town fired a single shot. With nothing better to do, Williams decided to cut the railway leading to Chiquimula with a demolition bomb and then dropped two fragmentation bombs on a branch line Southwest of Zacapa. Minutes later, the fighter climbed away and returned to Managua.

The third Thunderbolt, flown by a newly recruited pilot named Robert "Bob" Wade, approached the Salvadoran Pacific coast at around 9:15 AM and tried to scud under the heavy overcast ahead, but he soon realized that it was impossible to reach Zacapa with the prevailing weather conditions. The ceiling was too low and a fierce rainstorm was rolling in. Thus, he tried approaching the combat zone from the North but was unable to find a hole in the clouds through which he could make his letdown. In the end, Wade decided to call off the mission and jettisoned his three bombs at sea before heading back to Las Mercedes. About 10:00 AM, Brodfrost decided to suspend all flights until weather improved.

By 11:00 AM, the Field Command Post was reestablished at PBSuccess' hangar in Las Mercedes and Robertson was contacted by Opa-locka for assessing the ongoing situation. Wisner was worried that despite the current political changes and the evidence of the Guatemalan government's confusion, Castillo Armas' forces still were in a precarious position due to the Ejército de Operaciones greatly superior forces. In addition, the impending international intervention would force the termination of the external support to the Caudillo. Therefore, it was imperative to execute Plan Beta without wasting any time.

Robertson was about to articulate a reply when President Somoza arrived in the hangar and joined the discussion, anxious to get into the act. He and Robertson then discussed three possibilities for ending the campaign successfully. The first was executing Plan Beta as it was conceived, that is, seizing Puerto Barrios by means of an air assault; then they considered a variation of the plan that involved a rapid redeployment of Castillo Armas' forces by foot from Chiquimula for seizing Puerto Barrios. The last possibility, which was christened "Plan Zeta", involved an air assault on Guatemala City, launched from the Jutiapa and Zacapa airfields. In all cases, however, it was necessary to seize Zacapa first. Shortly after departing, Somoza told Robertson that if Castillo Armas managed to accomplish any of the three plans within 48 hours, he would recognize his provisional government as soon as he established it, whether it was at Puerto Barrios or Guatemala City.

Around 11:45 AM, Robertson began imparting new orders to Castillo Armas' field commanders, so any of the three plans could be implemented. First, he contacted Maj. Torres, who still was at Correderos, and instructed him to attack and seize the Army detachments at Champona, Chachagualilla, and La Manga, and then proceed to set up blockades along the railway leading to Puerto Barrios. To accomplish this, 200 Hondurans recruited in the Los

Guatemalan Army Captains Juan Martínez and Marco Juarez arriving at the "Vuelta del Tuno" with a white flag, in order to begin negotiations with the Liberation forces, on June 29, 1954. (Photo credit: Life Magazine.)

Tarros area, would join his group. Subsequently, he radioed Castillo Armas and ordered that the 200 men currently at Quezaltepeque, engage the Army troops advancing towards that town over the road from Ipala as a deceptive move aimed at forcing the Ejército de Operaciones to deploy troops from Zacapa to reinforce that front. Then, in the middle of the night, these Liberationists would have to pull out of the Quezaltepeque area and join the entire Liberation Army at Chiquimula for an all-out attack on Zacapa, which would have to be launched by mid-morning on June 29.

By midday, Col. Díaz went ahead with his plan of establishing a governing junta and made it official through an announcement that was broadcast by the government's radio station. Without losing any time, Peurifoy, Doherty, and Hobbing rushed to the Army headquarters to try to convince Col. Díaz –yet again- about enforcing a cease-fire and establish negotiations with Castillo Armas. After more than two hours of heated exchange, the junta members declared that they needed to consult with the Army high command before making such an important decision.

Shortly before the meeting was adjourned, Peurifoy asked Díaz about the composition of the new cabinet, to which the Colonel replied that almost every minister would be replaced, with the exception of Augusto Charnaud McDonald, Arbenz's Minister of the Interior and a leading Communist. This decision obviously contravened the agreement that Díaz had reached with Peurifoy during the morning's meeting. The straw that broke the camel's back was, however, a general amnesty that the junta was about to decree, which would set free all of the political prisoners, both Communists and anti-Communists, as a humanitarian gesture.[5]

Furious, Peurifoy left the Army headquarters, and as soon as he arrived at the embassy, he cabled the following to the PBSuccess headquarters: "We have been double-crossed. Díaz, Sánchez, and Monzón formed a junta and announced it over TGW at 11:45. Díaz renounced presidency, but still is the Chief of Armed Forces. Sánchez is the Minister of Defense. Monzón is Minister of Interior. Díaz asked Charnaud McDonald to remain. This is a complete violation of the agreement reached 7 hours earlier. Urgently recommend bombing [the Capital] this afternoon. Next meeting is at 17:30, with the same participants. Bombs would persuade them fast."[6]

At 4:20 PM, Opa-locka ordered Brodfrost to "Bomb Matamoros and the TGW transmitter at once."[7] By then, two Thunderbolts, piloted by Delarm and Wade, had departed Las Mercedes to bomb Zacapa. Thus, the Chief of Air Support got on the radio and notified them about the change of orders, as well as the appropriate information about their new targets.

The fighters arrived over Guatemala City at 5:20 PM, that is, a scant ten minutes before the beginning of Peurifoy's meeting with the governing junta. Without losing any time, Delarm attacked Matamoros and despite the extremely low ceiling, he managed a direct hit on the fort's main building with a demolition bomb, which caused several secondary explosions. On his part, Wade made a couple of strafing runs over the government's radio station shack and antenna, causing only minor damages. Then, he circled back and dropped his two fragmentation bombs over the building, but both drifted and exploded within 20 meters of the structure.

Despite the chaos sparked by the airstrikes, Ambassador Peurifoy was able to navigate the city streets and reached the Army headquarters, where Colonels Díaz and Sánchez were already awaiting him. Not surprisingly, both junta members were now more than willing to accept the U.S. government's good offices and begin negotiations with Castillo Armas. They even offered to declare illegal the Communist PGT and round up its members. What caught the Ambassador's attention was, however, that Col. Monzón was not present. In any case, Peurifoy left the premises and went back to the embassy to inform the Department of State about the meeting's outcome and to begin organizing the talks between the junta and Castillo Armas.

By then, the 200 officers that Lt. Col. García Calderón had summoned at the National Palace during the morning, had agreed on forcing Díaz and Sánchez to resign and replace them with their own representatives. Col. Monzón on the other hand, would be the president of the new junta that they would form. To overcome the lack of troops, which were needed for seizing the Army headquarters and capture Díaz and Sánchez, Col. Mauricio Dubois offered to provide soldiers from his own unit, the Guardia Presidencial (the Presidential Guard.) First, however, it was necessary to make sure that the commanding officers of the military bases in the Capital would support them or at least wouldn't intervene. Hence, two groups of officers were sent to inform them about the plan.

About 7:30 PM, Col. Monzón was told that all the Army commanders in the Capital had agreed on disavowing Díaz and Sánchez. Even the staunchly pro-Arbenz FAG commander, Col. Girón Cartagena, had acceded and rushed Maj. Arturo Guirola to the National Palace to represent him. Minutes later, the entire Guardia Presidencial was sent to the La Aurora garrison to pick up ammunition and supplies before marching upon the Army headquarters located a couple of hundred meters West of the National Palace.

Near 9:30 PM, and completely oblivious to the ongoing developments, Ambassador Peurifoy returned to the Army headquarters to let Díaz and Sánchez know that the negotiations with

Castillo Armas were going to take place in El Salvador's Capital where President Osorio had offered to host them. As Peurifoy was going over some minor details regarding the negotiations, the U.S. Army Attaché called him out of the meeting because Col. José Luis Cruz had arrived and wanted to see him in private.

As soon as Peurifoy stepped out of the conference room, Col. Cruz informed him that himself, Monzón and Dubois had formed a new junta and urged him to get out of the building immediately, since troops of the Guardia Presidencial were on their way to seize it, but Peurifoy refused.

As the Ambassador was about to step back into the conference room, Col. Monzón phoned him saying that it wasn't safe for him to be there and that he should go to the National Palace as soon as possible. When Peurifoy declined, Monzón said that he would join him at the Army headquarters right away. Then, Peurifoy returned to the room, but the meeting never resumed. Díaz and Sánchez excused themselves and went to confer in an office nearby for couple of minutes. When they came back, Díaz informed the Ambassador that they had decided to resign. Shortly after, the Guardia Presidencial cordoned off the Army headquarters and the new junta members, accompanied by a handful of armed officers, stormed the conference room and captured Díaz and Sánchez, consummating in that way Peurifoy's long-awaited coup.[8]

An hour later, an avalanche of Communist leaders and former members of Arbenz's cabinet overwhelmed the Argentine, Chilean and Salvadoran embassies, seeking political asylum. Some of them had been permitted to escape from jail by Col. José Luis Morales Melgar, whom Díaz had appointed as Chief of the Guardia Civil shortly after Arbenz had resigned. Others chose to flee the Capital and were heading out of the country, mainly to Mexico and El Salvador.

At about 11:00 PM, the 200 men that Castillo Armas had deployed to Quezaltepeque during the morning began pulling back to Chiquimula after having successfully stopped a force comprised of 880 soldiers from the Guardia de Honor, considered to be the best troops in the country. The relative victory came at a price, however, since the Liberationist column, led by the civilian Mario Quiñónez, had sustained heavy casualties and according to field reports, 17 men were killed in action. During the clash, Castillo Armas' Cessna 180, flown by Cheesman, was heavily damaged while providing air cover to Quiñónez's troops, but the daring pilot was able to make it in one piece to Chiquimula's airfield, where his plane was quickly repaired.[9]

On the other hand, the Cessna 140, with Alfredo Silva Romero at the controls, had spent the afternoon dropping leaflets over Army positions in and around Zacapa. The pamphlets warned the Ejército de Operaciones that they had until 10:00 AM on June 29 to join Castillo Armas' forces. Also, Opa-locka had ordered Radio Liberación to repeat constantly the ultimatum, hoping that the Guatemalan military would accept it before the final attack on Zacapa was launched.

By midnight, Castillo Armas ordered his troops at Chiquimula to advance to their respective points of departure.[10] Accordingly, 150 men led by the civilian Luis Buchhalter took up positions near the town of Santa Rosalía, some 4 km South of the Zacapa garrison, while another column of 150 men, led by the civilian Felipe Villegas, was placed near Puente Blanco, less than a kilometer Southwest of the garrison's main entrance. These two groups would execute a pincer movement over the military facility at H-hour, which had been set for 10:00 AM.

In addition, a column of 100 men under the command of Lt. Antonio Beteta was sent to reinforce the Liberationist positions at the El Miramundo hill that were providing protection to Pivall's artillery. Another column of 100 men, led by Arturo Oliva, took up positions near Cabañas, where Cpt. Emilio Chacón's group would join them before launching harassment attacks on the town and throw up blockades along the road to the Capital. Lastly, yet importantly, a reserve column comprised of 200 men under the command of Cpt. René Fernández was positioned near the Matasano Bridge, 4 km east of Zacapa, where the survivors of Chajón Chúa's group would join them near H-hour.

The most dangerous mission to be conducted, however, involved five trucks that would storm the garrison during the initial phase of the assault. These trucks, which had been fitted with steel plates and sandbags as some sort of armoring, would be carrying 50 men armed to the teeth, who would seize the garrison's main building and capture the Ejército de Operaciones high command. The well-known troublemaker Cpt. Fernando Romero, who had arrived recently from El Salvador after being released from CIA's custody, would lead this group. (Back in March, Romero had led a mutiny at the troops' training camp in Nicaragua, and Pivall had ordered his immediate removal.) Once Romero's group had taken over the garrison, 150 men under the command of Rogelio Olavarrueth would occupy and secure Zacapa. This was easier said than done, since by then the Ejército de Operaciones had more than 2900 well armed troops scattered along the town and its surroundings.

The last group to leave Chiquimula was led by Cpt. Eduardo Taracena and was comprised of 30 men. Their mission was to reconnoiter the shores of the Shusho River in search of enemy patrols approaching Chiquimula and then take up defensive positions at the "Vuelta del Tuno." For some strange reason, Castillo Armas was obsessed with controlling that forsaken bend of the road to Zacapa, and on several occasions, he mentioned that whoever held that position, could control the entire Zacapa area.

At the break of dawn on Tuesday, June 29, Ambassador Peurifoy met with the new governing junta, as its members were ready to begin negotiations with Castillo Armas. At first, Col. Monzón asked Peurifoy to try his best to end the Liberation Air Force's airstrikes against the Capital and convince the Caudillo about ceasing the hostilities. Peurifoy refused saying that the only acceptable solution was a cessation of the activities on both sides. It didn't take long for the junta to agree on meeting Castillo Armas in El Salvador as soon as possible, if the Papal Nuncio and the Salvadoran President could be the "guarantors" of the negotiations. Thus, by 5:00 AM, Peurifoy notified Opa-locka and the Department of state about the new junta's decision and asked Al Haney to determine if Castillo Armas was willing to attend the meeting at San Salvador and establish a joint cease-fire.

When Robertson got wind of the ongoing developments, he immediately cried hoax. What the new junta was saying didn't match the intelligence that Castillo Armas' operatives had collected about the Ejército de Operaciones during the last couple of hours. The Zacapa officers had refused to recognize the new junta and still were trying to achieve an advantageous tactical position before establishing their own negotiations with the Liberationists. Therefore, the Field Commander tried to convince Wisner about not enforcing a cease-fire just yet, because it would put the Liberation forces in a vulnerable position and would allow the Ejército de Operaciones to launch a counterattack at any time while the negotiations with the new junta were taking place.

Ambassador Peurifoy confirmed Robertson fears when he informed Opa-locka that a FAG plane, carrying two envoys of Col. Monzón, had been unable to land at Zacapa, since as soon as it had approached the garrison's airfield, a couple of anti-aircraft guns emplaced near the runway had opened fire. Miraculously, the old AT-

11 had managed to climb away and return to La Aurora in one piece. By then, however, Col. Monzón's only hope was to reach a negotiated solution with Castillo Armas and only then deal with the Ejército de Operaciones.

By 5:00 AM, and still without a definitive answer from Wisner about the inconvenience of a cease-fire, Robertson decided to take matters into his own hands and ordered Brodfrost to launch staggered airstrikes against the Zacapa garrison during the morning to convince the Ejército de Operaciones officers to negotiate with Castillo Armas. Accordingly, less than 15 minutes later, one of the C-47s departed Las Mercedes, carrying two 250 lb. iron bombs and 20 – 24 lb. fragmentation bombs.

At about 7:00 AM, Wisner finally cabled Robertson ordering him to suspend the final attack on Zacapa immediately[11], and use the fighters for reconnaissance missions over the combat zone only. Additionally, the cable instructed the Field Commander to ask Castillo Armas if he was willing to meet the new junta for establishing the joint cease-fire. Not surprisingly, Robertson decided to sit on the cable and let the airstrikes continue for the rest of the morning. He didn't even notify Castillo Armas that a new junta had been conformed and that its members wished to meet him.

By 9:00 AM, while the Liberation troops were reaching the assigned attack positions around Zacapa, Brodfrost's C-47 began bombing the garrison and several machinegun nests emplaced South and Southwest of the town. The crew even managed to destroy a military convoy that was approaching Cpt. Taracena's position at the "Vuelta del Tuno."

An hour later, Williams, in one of the Thunderbolts, arrived at the scene and dropped a cluster bomb over an Army column that was about to engage Lt. Antonio Beteta's group in the slopes of the El Miramundo hill. Then, he destroyed a couple of artillery positions emplaced at the airfield with a fragmentation bomb and shortly after, the pilot dropped the last cluster bomb he was carrying over an Army column that was approaching Cpt. Fernández's position near the Matasano Bridge.

As the Thunderbolt was establishing a strafing pattern over the garrison, Cpt. Romero's trucks stormed the garrison's main gate and managed to reach the barracks, where several fire squads repelled them, forcing them to turn around and seek cover along the road just outside the garrison's fence. Minutes later, the Thunderbolt departed the area, as it was running low on fuel.

The third airstrike of the day began at 11:15 AM when Wade, in one of the Thunderbolts, dropped two cluster bombs over an Army column that was attacking Felipe Villegas' position near Puente Blanco, which was providing cover for Cpt. Romero's men positioned along the road leading to the garrison's main gate. Then, he dropped a 250 lb. bomb over a couple of .50 Cal machineguns emplaced inside the base. Minutes later, Wade established a strafing pattern over the garrison during which he took out a couple of artillery pieces and dispersed the troops that were taking up positions around the main building. During the tenth pass, however, an Oerlikon anti-aircraft gun that had been emplaced at the base's Northern area, opened fire and managed to hit the fighter repeatedly.

As Wade began climbing up from the strafing pass, the fighter's engine began sputtering and the cockpit filled with smoke. Sure that his plane was beyond salvation, the pilot jettisoned the canopy and set course for Chiquimula's airfield, where he attempted an emergency landing, but upon touching down, the main landing gear collapsed and the massive Thunderbolt began sliding on its belly until it fell into a drainage ditch at the end of the runway.[12]

Minutes later, a group of Liberationists arrived and helped the battered pilot out of the cockpit. Incredibly, Wade had only minor bruises and was able to walk away unassisted from the wreckage. Then, during the morning, one of the trucks took him to Nueva Ocotepeque, where Alfredo Silva Romero would pick him up in the Cessna 140 and fly him to Managua. As for the Thunderbolt's remains, Castillo Armas' men destroyed it with dynamite.

At 12:20 PM, Robertson finally got on the radio to inform Castillo Armas that a new junta had been organized and that its members wished to meet him to discuss the terms of a cease-fire. The Field Commander told him also that The Group was ordering him to call off the attack on Zacapa so peace talks could be initiated in El Salvador as soon as possible.[13] Deeply confused, the Caudillo replied that he would let the Field Command Post know his decision in two hours.

Ten minutes later, at 12:30 PM, Delarm arrived over Zacapa for conducting the fourth airstrike of the day in one of the Thunderbolts. According to his after-mission report, he bombed the Zacapa garrison and reconnoitered the Army positions South of town for more than 45 minutes, but he wasn't able to see any troop movements. Then, he went to Chiquimula and made a couple of low passes over the airfield to check that the remains of the crashed fighter had been destroyed. Shortly after, he set course to Managua, where he landed at 1:15 PM.

By then, Wisner had been informed about the unauthorized airstrikes that Robertson had ordered during the morning and that one of the Thunderbolts had been lost to enemy fire. Therefore, he promptly cabled the Field Commander ordering him that from then onwards he would use the fighters for reconnaissance and defensive purposes only. As for the C-47s, he was authorized to use them for resupplying Castillo Armas' forces "to the extent necessary to maintain effectiveness while awaiting a final decision."

At about 2:45 PM, Castillo Armas radioed the Field Command Post saying that his troops were retreating to their pre-attack positions and that "he accepted to meet the new junta with the understanding that his attendance would not bind him to come to an agreement if the conditions didn't satisfy the plans and ideas of the Liberation Movement."[14]

Fifteen minutes later, the Cessnas departed Chiquimula's airfield for dropping leaflets over both the Liberation and the Ejército de Operaciones positions, announcing that a cease-fire had been agreed with the new junta. Then, Robertson asked Castillo Armas to mark his troops' most advanced positions with large fires, for signaling that they had received the order to cease the hostilities.

By 3:00 PM, the very last combat mission of the campaign, conducted by Williams in one of the Thunderbolts, had to be aborted due to bad weather. His mission would have been to mark on a map the fires that the Liberationist had started and to make sure that the Ejército de Operaciones would not attempt a counterattack.

Near 3:30 PM, the Ejército de Operaciones Captains Juan Martínez and Marco Juarez arrived at the "Vuelta del Tuno", where the Liberationists had set up an advanced position, and requested to see Castillo Armas, as they were carrying an important message from Col. León and the Ejército de Operaciones high command. Shortly after, the officers were escorted to the Hernández Hotel in Chiquimula, where they informed Castillo Armas that Col. Léon wanted a truce for negotiating the unification of both Armies. The Caudillo accepted the proposal and offered to meet Col. León right away.

At 5:00 PM Castillo Armas, and Colonels Flores Avendaño, Neiderheitmann and Mendoza arrived at the "Vuelta del Tuno" where Army Colonels León, Víctor Rodríguez, Jorge Medina, and Major Manuel Sosa Ávila were already waiting for them to begin the negotiations. In the skies above them, and despite the heavy rain, Cheesman established a tight patrolling pattern with the Cessna 180,

A still reticent Castillo Armas arriving in El Salvador for the peace talks with the Guatemalan Junta, on June 30, 1954. (Photo credit: Life Magazine.)

ready to attack in case there was any suspicious movement.[15]

At about 7:45 PM, Robertson sent a cable to Castillo Armas informing him that the new junta had agreed on enforcing a cease-fire that would begin at 8:00 PM. In addition, a C-47 would arrive at Esquipulas' airfield the next morning to pick him up and take him to San Salvador for the meeting with Col. Monzón. Robertson finished the cable with a rather corny sentence: "Colonel, you have earned the glory today."[16]

By 10:00 PM, Castillo Armas interrupted the negotiations for a brief moment and cabled Robertson informing him that a truce had been agreed and that the conversations with the Ejército de Operaciones high command were proceeding well.[17] However, he didn't want to make it public yet and asked the Field Commander to keep it secret while a final arrangement could be worked out.

It wasn't until 4:00 AM on June 30 that Castillo Armas and Col. León drafted and signed a formal agreement for the unification of the Liberation Army and the Ejército de Operaciones. The document stated that Castillo Armas would be the "supreme leader" of both forces and that they would continue the fight against Communism in Guatemala by any means.[18] Accordingly, the Liberation field commanders and the Ejército de Operaciones' officers began making plans for an all-out assault on the Capital. They now had more than 5000 well-equipped troops and seizing Guatemala City would be like a walk in the park.

At dawn's break, however, Castillo Armas announced to his men that he would go to San Salvador to meet the new junta and begin negotiations. Many Liberation senior officers received the news with deep dissatisfaction and tried to convince the Caudillo about not going. They wanted to end the campaign by seizing the Capital as soon as possible.[19] Robertson and almost everyone at the Field Command Post believed that this was the best course of action too. As it would be expected, Castillo Armas became hesitant.

Inevitably, the Department of State intervened and urged Ambassador Peurifoy to arrange a visit of the U.S. Army Attaché and a representative of the Papal Nuncio to Chiquimula, for convincing Castillo Armas to negotiate with the new junta and avoid any unnecessary bloodshed. Simultaneously, Wisner contacted Pivall and Ontrich directly, and ordered them to discourage the Liberation field commanders from undertaking any offensive action against the Capital. Lastly, yet importantly, by 5:30 AM, The Group informed the Caudillo that their financial and military support would be discontinued if he insisted in prolonging the hostilities.

Overwhelmed, Castillo Armas agreed to negotiate with the new junta and went to Esquipulas where one of Brodfrost's C-47s picked him up at 6:15 AM. As soon as the transport took off, the crew set course to Managua instead of San Salvador, since Thomas Whelan, the U.S. Ambassador for Nicaragua, had arranged a meeting with President Somoza, who wanted to make sure that the Caudillo would accept a negotiated solution.

Robertson got in the way, however, and as soon as Castillo Armas stepped down from the C-47 at Las Mercedes, the Field Commander locked him in the Air Operations Office at the PBSuccess' hangar.[20] The CIA documentation doesn't mention what was the intent of Robertson's action, but it seems that he tried to convince the Caudillo about continuing the fight. When a Somoza representative arrived to pick up Castillo Armas, Robertson told him that due to security measures, he wouldn't be able to meet the President. The envoy returned minutes later, but yet again Robertson refused to let him see Castillo Armas. It wasn't until Ambassador Whelan arrived that Robertson released him.

Meanwhile at the Puerto Barrios area, Maj. Torres' group had managed to capture the town of Champona virtually unopposed and was requesting to be resupplied so they could continue to Puerto Barrios. Up until then, Robertson had avoided informing the Liberationist commander about the ongoing developments so his group could seize the port in case the negotiations with the new junta fell apart and the fighting had to be resumed. Therefore, at 7:10 AM, one of Brodfrost's C-47s was dispatched with ammunition and supplies for Maj. Torres' group.

The mission failed, however, because the crew wasn't able to find the receiving party, even after searching for them for more than an hour and a half. The plane landed back at Managua at 11:45 AM with the cargo still onboard.

By that time, the Cessna 140, piloted by Alfredo Silva Romero, had picked up Robert Wade at Nueva Ocotepeque and was on its way to Managua. According to the pilot's after-mission report, while flying over the Gulf of Fonseca, near the Nicaraguan and Salvadoran coasts, he spotted the wake of a submarine's periscope. Curious, the pilot descended to take a better look, but the submarine "*made a crash dive*" while heading in the direction of the open sea.[21] As soon as Brodfrost was informed about the incident, he contacted the U.S. Navy attaché, as he believed that it was a Soviet submarine sent to pick up Guatemalan Communists exiled in El Salvador or to disembark sabotage teams in Nicaragua. In the end, the origins of the mysterious submarine were never determined, nor its whereabouts.

At 12:45 PM, one of the C-47s, with Delarm and Fito Mendoza at the controls, departed Las Mercedes carrying Castillo Armas and his assistant, Maj. Enrique Trinidad Oliva, to San Salvador for the peace talks. This flight turned out to be Project PBSuccess' very last mission.

Minutes later, and in view of an early political solution, Opa-locka ordered all the CIA personnel involved in Project PBSuccess to end the "active phase" of the project and initiate their respective withdrawal plans. Only the Air Support Unit would maintain operational readiness until further notice, in case the negotiations failed and the fighting had to be resumed.

CHAPTER 13

CREATING THE MYTH

With the opening of the negotiations at San Salvador, the U.S. Government was finally able to openly intervene, offering its "good offices" through Peurifoy who, from then on, began directing the peace talks with an iron hand, supported by the U.S Ambassadors to El Salvador, Honduras and Nicaragua. Beneath the surface, the Department of State took over all the political aspects of Project PBSuccess –which so far had been handled entirely by The Group- to make sure that Castillo Armas became the next president of Guatemala.

The talks didn't go well, however, since both Castillo Armas and Monzón constantly threatened to resume the fighting if their respective demands were not met. Ambassador Peurifoy had to exert a considerable amount of pressure to keep the rambunctious officers at the negotiations table, and it wasn't until 24 hours later that both parties agreed to form a temporary junta comprised by Castillo Armas, Col. Monzón, Lt. Colonels José Luis Cruz, Mauricio Dubois, and Maj. Enrique Trinidad Oliva. This new junta would be dissolved as soon as law and order had been reestablished across the country

Members of the governing junta that was established during the peace talks in El Salvador. Seated, from left to right: Lt. Colonels José Luis Cruz, Carlos Castillo Armas, Élfego Monzón, Major Enrique Trinidad Oliva and Lt. Colonel Mauricio Dubois. (Photo credit: CIRMA collection.)

Castillo Armas arrival at La Aurora airport, on July 2, 1954. (Photo credit: U.S. Embassy to Guatemala.)

The entire Liberation Air Force's fighter component at Las Mercedes air base. When this photo was taken, President Somoza had seized the aircraft and was refusing to let the PBSuccess pilots get near them. (Photo credit: CIA.)

and a new Constitution had been drafted. It was also agreed that both the Liberation Army and its Guatemalan counterpart would march in Guatemala City on a "victory parade" that would end in a public event where they would be formally merged into a single force.

Meanwhile, the Field Command Post focused in covering the Agency's tracks by getting rid of any evidence that could denote its participation during the liberation of Guatemala. Accordingly, the radio network was terminated and the communications equipment was handed over to the Nicaraguan Guardia Nacional. The SAHARA team also shut off their radio-interception devices and delivered them to the Honduran government as a present for its collaboration. Simultaneously, the operatives in charge of the paramilitary program crated the remaining 10 tons of armament and ammunition -still stored at the Nueva Ocotepeque staging point- and trucked it to Chiquimula where it was handed over to Castillo Armas' field commanders.

In Managua, the Air Support Unit was ordered to airlift to France Field the remaining ordnance and the Field Command Post's equipment, using for this the C-54 that the CAT had provided and one of Brodfrost's C-47s. Then, the majority of the PBSuccess personnel began departing their assigned posts, with some of them returning to Opa-locka via commercial flights while some others were flown in one of Brodfrost's C-47s to France Field. Thus, in a matter of hours, what had been a rather complicated clandestine operation that had required the participation of at least 600 CIA operatives, was stripped down to the bones, leaving in place only the essential personnel, just in case something went wrong with the peace talks.

Despite the CIA's best efforts, the notion of a U.S. intervention in Guatemala was taking hold of the public opinion, both locally and across the World, fueled by what Wisner described as an "*unprecedented campaign*" on the part of international Communist organizations that were accusing the U.S. of having invaded the Central American country to overthrow its President. Therefore, Wisner set out to launch his own propaganda campaign to counteract the widespread accusations.

Initially, David Atlee Phillips and the two announcers of Radio Liberación, Leonel Sisniega and José Torón, were dispatched to Guatemala City with orders to take over the government's radio

One of the "Sulfatos" now sporting the colors and insignia of the Nicaraguan Air Force. (Photo credit: William Martin via Dan Hagedorn.)

station as soon as possible. Their mission would be to "*build up Castillo Armas as a popular hero, and extol the virtues of justice and free speech.*"[1] Subsequently, CIA intelligence operatives were dispatched to the Guatemalan Capital with the mission of obtaining the testimonies of all the victims of torture and other terror acts during the Arbenz administration. Special emphasis was placed in getting the "*complete story*" from the prisoners of the Salamá Revolt, who had been mercilessly tortured and some were even executed as a reprisal whenever the Arbenz's regime had felt threatened by the anti-Communist organizations. Other operatives focused on collecting documentary evidence that proved the Communists' control over the government and labor unions, and their intervention in neighboring countries.

Processing the documentary evidence proved to be a monumental task, however, since the CIA operatives soon found themselves overwhelmed by the amount of documents that was discovered at the government offices and at the Communist organizations headquarters. The worst part was that they only found a fraction of the papers that had ever existed, because the rest had been destroyed or stolen shortly after Arbenz's resignation.

Deeply worried about not having enough time to screen and process all the documents and produce solid evidence against the Arbenz regime, Wisner requested of the CIA Director funds and additional personnel for manning a new clandestine operation, which was codenamed "PBHistory"[2], and that would collect, analyze and distribute to the media outlets the contents of the documents found. PBHistory would also feed the world's public opinion an "official" account of the events that had taken place during the military campaign to liberate Guatemala. Obviously, such account would not mention any foreign involvement, and would emphasize the "indigenous origins" of the Liberation movement. The project would work with the Department of State in arranging the appearing of prominent

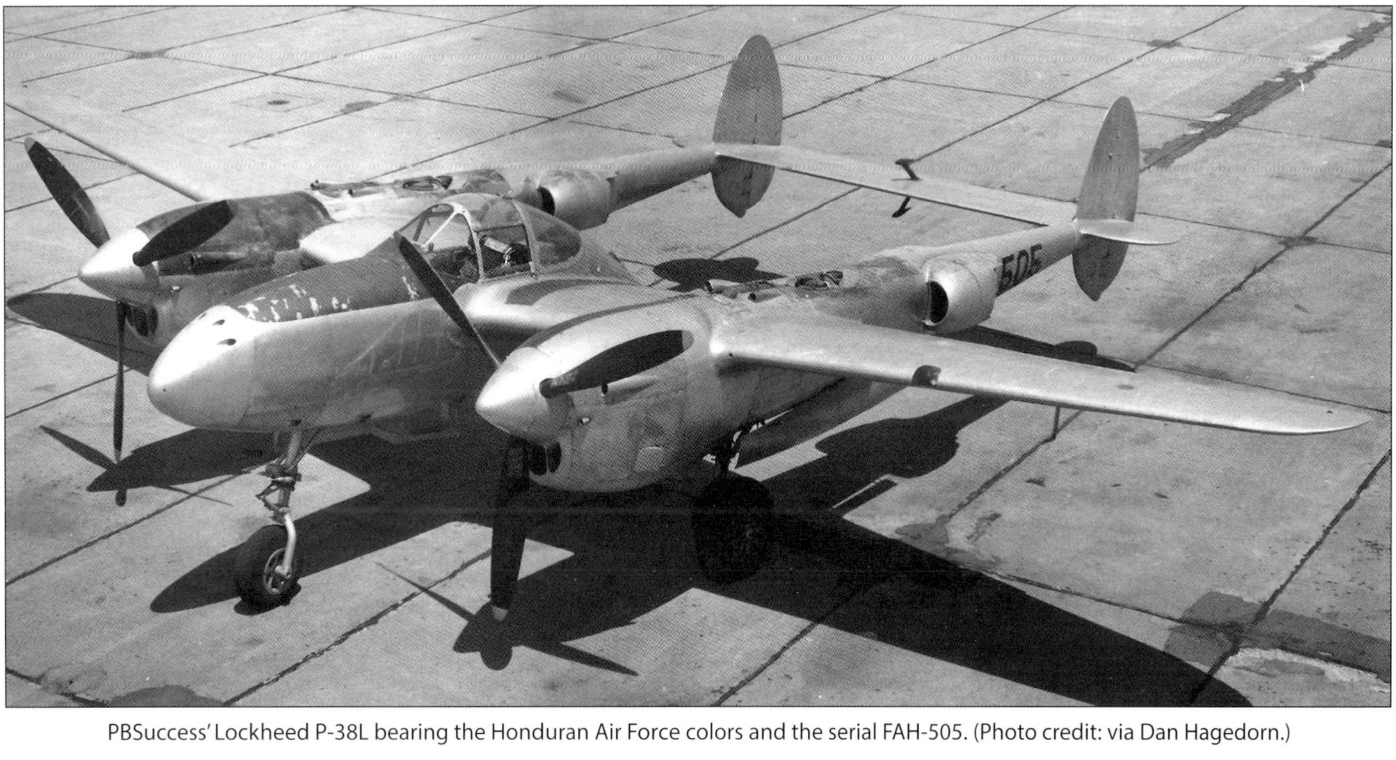

PBSuccess' Lockheed P-38L bearing the Honduran Air Force colors and the serial FAH-505. (Photo credit: via Dan Hagedorn.)

Castillo Armas' C-47, painted in the Guatemalan Air Force colors and sporting the serial FAG-0515. (Photo credit: Guatemalan Air Force.)

FAG-0515 alongside the other two C-47s of the Guatemalan Air Force. (Photo credit: Guatemalan Air Force.):

representatives of the Guatemalan government before the UN and the OAS to publicize the official version, while delegations of suitable international bodies would be invited to attend public hearings on the Communists' misuse of labor unions and the Agrarian Reform during the Arbenz administration.

Lastly, yet importantly, PBHistory would provide funds and assessment to the Guatemalan government for the publication of a "White Book" containing all the pertinent evidence of the Communist activity in the country, as well as the official version of the Liberation campaign. Such book, which would be translated to several languages, would be given mass distribution in the continent and in Europe.

At this point, the use of combat aircraft during the Liberation campaign turned to be a controversial issue, because it didn't mesh with the official version that Wisner and the CIA analysts were fabricating. A couple of weeks earlier, Castillo Armas had stated publicly that he had acquired his planes with the financial help of anti-Communist sympathizers across the continent, but that cover story had grown old and the press wasn't buying it anymore. In fact, the Communists worldwide were presenting the use of airpower during the campaign as proof of the U.S. involvement. Inevitably, the Department of State got in the act and urged Wisner to get rid of the planes as soon as possible, by ferrying them to France Field where they would simply "disappear."

As soon as Brodfrost was informed about this, he got in contact with Wisner and reminded him that PBSuccess had the obligation of turning over to the Nicaraguan Air Force the three Thunderbolts that The Group had purchased through Somoza. In addition, Brodfrost desired to give Castillo Armas the fourth Thunderbolt plus one of the C-47s, so he could have an embryo of an air force upon his return to Guatemala City.

The CIA Director cabled Wisner also, suggesting that as soon as Castillo Armas had taken over the Guatemalan government, Fito Mendoza, and the "loyal anti-Communist pilots of the Liberation Air Force", should join him in the Capital in "their own aircraft." Dulles' cable also stated, "It would be a mistake for them not to have at least a few planes of their own, especially after the important role that the Liberation Air Force has played during the hostilities."[3] Therefore, the CIA Director wanted that at least two Thunderbolts and a C-47 be turned over Castillo Armas. Besides -Dulles reasoned- the absence of the Liberationist aircraft in the Capital could be suspicious and would denote an U.S. involvement.

Wisner and his analysts still were trying to come up with an

The only Republic F-47N that Castillo Armas received after the invasion, seen here at La Aurora air base in July 1954. (Photo credit: Herbert Erdmenger.)

After the arrival of the only "Sulfato" at Guatemala City, it became the center of attention for the Guatemalans and everyone wanted to be photographed with it. (Photo credit: Guatemalan Air Force.)

appropriate solution when the Department of State sent a cable urging him not to send any of the project's aircraft to Guatemala City while the OAS peace committee was there. The cable reiterated that the planes should be taken immediately to France Field, where they would be kept until their safe disposal had been arranged. Meanwhile, the cable added, Castillo Armas would have to decline making any comments to the press about the whereabouts of the Liberation Air Force's planes, stating that it was a military secret and that their location would be disclosed in the near future, at which the airfield where they were could be declared a "national shrine."

To further complicate the situation, during the early hours of July 1, President Somoza decided to intervene and sent a couple of heavily armed platoons of the Guardia Nacional to Las Mercedes Airbase to cordon off the PBSuccess hangar and the tarmac where the project's aircraft were parked.[4] At dawn break, when Brodfrost and his pilots arrived to Las Mercedes, a Nicaraguan officer informed them that no Americans were allowed near the planes or the hangar. Wasting no time, Brodfrost went to see Col. Carlos Venegas, the Nicaraguan Air Force Commander, to try to convince him of at least letting him in to retrieve sensitive documents pertaining the air operations and the safe where the encryption pads were stored. As it would be expected, Col. Venegas refused, saying that he had direct orders from Somoza. Then, Brodfrost appealed to the close friendship they had and begged him for only 15 minutes inside the hangar, to no avail.

It wasn't until midday that the FAN Commander felt pity and allowed Brodfrost inside the airbase. As soon as Brodfrost reached the hangar, he radioed Opa-locka about the problem and Al Haney ordered him to destroy all the Air Support Unit's files and the encryption pads, since copies of almost everything were kept at the PBSuccess headquarters.

During the afternoon, Robertson and Brodfrost went to see President Somoza and tried to convince him about releasing the aircraft. The stubborn President refused, nevertheless, and said that due to the impending visit of the OAS peace committee, he needed

The only Thunderbolt that Castillo Armas was assigned after the invasion, can be seen here sporting the colors of the Guatemalan Air Force and the serial "FAG-0568." (Photo credit: Guatemalan Air Force.)

Fito Mendoza and Lt. (USAF) Don "Red" Ryder, one of the pilots who ferried the first North American F-51Ds to La Aurora Air Base, in August 1954. By then, Fito was serving as an advisor to the Guatemalan Air Force. (Photo credit: Dell Toedt.)

the four Thunderbolts parked at Las Mercedes, so he could show them as proof of the purchase his government had made in early June. It wasn't until Ambassador Whelan intervened that Somoza agreed on releasing some of the planes, these being the P-38L, one of the Thunderbolts and the two leased C-47s. The remaining three F-47Ns were immediately incorporated into the FAN's inventory and were assigned the serials GN-70, GN-72, and GN-73 (ex USAAF serials 44-89439, 44-89265 and 44-89131, respectively.)

In the following days, proposals on what to do with the rest of the Liberationist aircraft began piling up at Opa-locka. The USAF wanted their fighters back, while the Department of State insisted on scrapping all the aircraft used by the project. Meanwhile, the CIA accountants were trying to determine how the planes had been obtained and who would have to pay for them, so that their books could reflect the financial transactions accurately before getting rid of them.

It wasn't until Wisner sent a long cable to the CIA Director and the Department of State that the issue was put to rest. The document stated,

> Either the absence or presence of Castillo Armas' aircraft in Guatemala City would be conspicuous. Aircraft could bear scrutiny but would only engender additional questions that could be most embarrassing, like how many aircraft were involved, where they were obtained, how they were armed, who flew them, who bombed this target or that target, etc. Acceptable answers to these questions would require an elaborate story which all the involved would have

Arrival of the first three North American F-51Ds of the Guatemalan Air Force at La Aurora Air Base, in August 1954. (Photo credit: Guatemalan Air Force.)

Carlos Cheesman (left) and Fito Mendoza (with sunglasses) receiving the honorary Guatemalan Air Force wings in September 1954. (Photo credit: Guatemalan Air Force.)

to stick to and that could stand up under detailed investigation that surely will follow. The use of air power during this campaign, while a key to the success of the project, was also one of the most controversial issues. The press has played up the bombing of open cities and, in general, has made it look like some ruthless force was using flamethrowers to discipline unruly children. Therefore, we should let this issue die if possible by having the airpower disappear. Few, if any, outside PBSuccess are aware of the full extent of our airpower. There are many conflicting stories in the press and from Guatemalan officials. I feel that it would be better to let the issue remain confused and perhaps let it grow into a legend of what happens when little boys play with Communism.[5]

Surprisingly, everyone involved agreed with Wisner and the PBSuccess analysts were able to finish crafting the "official" story, not only about the use of combat aircraft but also about the entire campaign. From then on, Castillo Armas and his men were to proclaim that they had acquired "only two Sulfatos", which had been based at a "secret airfield in Honduras." Regarding the aircrews who flew the planes, the Liberationists would say that it had been Fito Mendoza, the Chief of the Liberation Air Force, and his brave pilots Jerry Delarm, Carlos Cheesman, and Alfredo Silva, who from then on, were to be praised as heroes by the Guatemalan population.

As for the final disposition of the remaining PBSuccess aircraft, it was Brodfrost's proposal that prevailed. Therefore, the only Thunderbolt that Somoza had released was given to Castillo Armas together with the C-47 that the Caudillo was already using. To explain the presence of only one of the fighters in the Guatemalan Capital,

Alfredo Silva Romero receiving the honorary Guatemalan Air Force wings in September 1954. (Photo credit: Guatemalan Air Force.)

Jerry Delarm taking off in the "Sulfato" somewhere in Southern Nicaragua, during the failed invasion of Costa Rica in January 1955. (Photo credit: Life Magazine.)

Castillo Armas and his pilots would say that the other had crashed in Chiquimula during a combat sortie. In return for their extraordinary services, the Cessna 180 was handed over to Carlos Cheesman and the Cessna 140 was given to Alfredo Silva Romero, while the two remaining C-47s were to be returned to their respective owners as soon as the airlift of the PBSuccess operatives out of Nicaragua and Honduras was completed.

Getting rid of the P-38L proved to be difficult, though, because neither Castillo Armas nor Somoza wanted the fighter, as it was linked to the sinking of the *Springfjord*, and they feared that whoever owned it would have to pay the British for the damages caused. Therefore, Brodfrost decided to hand it to the Honduran Air Force[6] in return for its collaboration during the campaign. It was flown to Toncontin on July 8, 1954, by one of Brodfrost's pilots. According to witness accounts, the fighter arrived at Toncontin freshly repaired, but lacking the turbo superchargers and the nose machineguns. Upon entering service with the FAH, it was assigned the serial FAH-506. After a couple of weeks, however, it was secretly re-serialled as FAH-505 (which makes it ex USAAF 44-53232), in order to hide its true origin and identity. Ironically, this fighter flew a couple of ground attack missions against the Nicaraguan Guardia Nacional during the so-called "Mosquitia conflict" in February 1957. It is currently preserved at the National Museum of the U.S. Air Force in Wright-Patterson AFB, Ohio, the staff of which excellent institution have virtually no idea of the provenance of their otherwise pristine aircraft.

Due to their clandestine origins, tracking the final fates of the Liberationist aircraft has proven to be extraordinarily difficult. For many years, aero-historians have been on a wild goose chase thanks to the extreme measures that the recipients of those planes took for hiding their identities. The Cessnas given to Cheesman and Silva Romero are a good example, since both entered the Guatemalan Civil Registry lacking essential information like their manufacturer serial numbers or any reference to their previous identities. In the case of Silva Romero's Cessna 140, it was registered as TG-BOH early in 1955, but the records of the Guatemalan Civil Aeronautics Directorate do not have any other data about it. As for the Cessna 180 given to Cheesman, it doesn't even appear in the Guatemalan Registry, although it is well known that the plane ended up in the country. Perhaps the fact that Cheesman was appointed Civil Aeronautics Director after Castillo Armas became president may explain why there are no records about these planes.

Something similar occurred with the C-47 given to Castillo Armas. The transport was incorporated into the FAG's inventory late in July 1954 with the serial 0515. Less than a month later, Lt. Col. Luis Urrutia de León, the newly appointed FAG Commander, ordered that the four-digit system used for the serials of the air arm's aircraft to be dropped in favor of a completely random three-digit system. In the process, new serial numbers were assigned to all of the airplanes in service. Unfortunately, no records of the previous serials were kept, making it virtually impossible to determine which four-digit serial corresponded with the new three-digit number. To further confuse the issue, early in 1955, a new and more coherent three-digit numbering system was introduced, and again, all the airplanes received new serials. Thus, Castillo Armas' C-47 ended up in the 5XX range of serials, which had been assigned to all the GAF transports.

Regarding the sole Thunderbolt given to Castillo Armas, its history is fascinating: It was flown by Delarm to Guatemala City on July 8, just in time for putting up an impressive air show during the victory parade that the Liberationist organized. Then, the fighter was formally incorporated into the Guatemalan Air Force with the serial 0568. During the following days, many fortunate citizens who had friends or relatives in the FAG had the chance to go to La Aurora Airbase and take or have their photos taken with the fearsome "Sulfato." What no one expected was to see the fighter firing its machineguns in anger once again. However, in the early morning of August 2, the Thunderbolt –with Delarm at the controls- was scrambled to protect a large contingent of Liberationists, which was based temporarily at the Roosevelt Hospital in the Southern sector of the Capital, since a company comprised of senior cadets of the Escuela Politécnica was attacking them.[7] Despite spending most of the morning strafing the cadets' positions, Delarm was unable to prevent them from taking the hospital and capturing the Liberationists who, thanks to the mediation of Monsignor Mariano Rossell, were put on a couple of trains bound for Chiquimula. However, as soon as the cadets surrendered and were disarmed by Army officers loyal to Castillo Armas, the Liberationist troops debarked the trains at "La Ermita" station, on the Capital's outskirts, thus breaking the agreement made just a few hours earlier. The cadets, on the other hand, were sent to exile, mostly to South American countries, where many of them managed to complete their military studies.

Near midday, Delarm returned to La Aurora Airbase to refuel, but a handful of FAG officers, who felt pity for the young cadets, seized the Thunderbolt and retained Delarm until the dust settled and the cadets had regrouped at the Escuela Politécnica.

Four days later, on August 6, the Thunderbolt was scrambled again,

Wreckage of a North American P-51D of the "Costa Rican Air Force", which crashed during the failed invasion to that country in January 1955. For many years, Jerry Delarm claimed that he had shot down this fighter (Photo credit: Guatemalan Air Force.)

because a group of pro-Arbenz Army officers tried to spark a revolt at the Matamoros Fort.[8] As soon as the fighter arrived, however, the rebels surrendered and Delarm spent the rest of the afternoon patrolling the skies above the Capital, bringing back nefarious memories to the frightened Guatemalans who still had vivid recollections of the Sulfatos' airstrikes.

During the first week of August, the FAG acquired its first three North American F-51D *Mustangs* that, together with the Thunderbolt, were incorporated into the newly created Fighter Squadron. However, the F-47N only served with the Guatemalan air arm for a brief period because in late November, the FAG traded it for one of the P-51Ds that the Nicaraguan Air Force had purchased from Sweden. Delarm, who flew it to Managua[9] on December 15, 1954, also stayed there, since by then, Somoza was planning his own clandestine operation against the government of neighboring Costa Rica, which also involved a rag-tag army comprised of Costa Rican exiles and the extensive use of airpower.

Accordingly, by mid-January 1955, Delarm flew several combat missions in this Thunderbolt, once again devoid of any markings, during which he bombed many towns close to the Nicaraguan border and provided close support to the rebels who were advancing towards San José, the Costa Rican Capital.

For many years, Delarm claimed that during one of those missions, he shot down one of the four Mustangs that the Costa Rican government had acquired during the emergency, but that was never confirmed. In Delarm's defense, it can be said that a Costa Rican fighter indeed crashed during a combat mission three days after it had been delivered. The jury is still out on this, however, and the real cause of the crash may have been the Costa Rican pilot's inexperience in such high-performance aircraft.

In the end, Somoza's clandestine operation failed miserably and late in January, the OAS intervened, forcing the invaders to withdraw back to Nicaragua. It was then when Delarm's Thunderbolt was incorporated officially into the Nicaraguan Air Force with the serial GN-71 (ex USAAF serial 44-89136.) According to the available documentation, this fighter served with the FAN until 1963, when it was purchased by Lloyd Parker Nolen of the *Confederate Air Force*, who registered it in the U.S. as N478C, and then as N47TB. It is currently disassembled but in good condition at the Cavanaugh Flight Museum in Addison, Texas.

In contrast, the fates of Somoza's Thunderbolts are sad, to say the least. Early in 1963, GN-73 crashed right after taking off from Las Mercedes, seemingly due to pilot error. As it would be expected, the accident and the maintenance nightmare the planes had become, convinced the FAN to get rid of them. Accordingly, an ad was placed in the "Trade-a-Plane" periodical and it didn't take long for William W. Martin, a Chicagoan pilot and entrepreneur, to make an offer. The details of the purchase and how the two surviving Thunderbolts were practically rebuilt to flying condition is nicely documented in the book "So I Bought An Air Force" authored by Martin himself. Suffice it to say that neither of the two fighters made it to the U.S. as both crashed during their ferry flights in 1964 and 1965. The first to go down was GN-72, which had gained the U.S. civil registration N6148U while still in Managua. This plane was abandoned on a beach in Veracruz, Mexico, after having crash-landed due to an engine problem. In the case of GN-70, U.S. civil registration N6147U, which Martin had already sold to Thomas B. Holman, it crashed near Brownsville, Texas, also due to an engine malfunction.

Regarding the PBSuccess Project, on July 12, 1954, Robertson, Brodfrost and the remaining personnel still in the Central American region were ordered to return to Opa-locka for debriefing. Wisner made this decision after confirming that Castillo Armas was feeling much more secure and the Army garrisons were under the firm control of the junta.

In contrast, project PBHistory, supported by the CIA station in Guatemala, kept producing propaganda during the following months, both locally and in the U.S. It was so effective that for many years no one was sure about what had really happened in Guatemala during the Liberation campaign, and just as Wisner had planned it, the whole affair grew into the realms of legend, despite the many inconsistencies

Funeral of Lt. Col. Carlos Castillo Armas in July 1957. (Photo credit: Life Magazine.)

that the amply publicized "official version" had.

In late August 1954, CIA operatives assigned to the spawned Guatemalan station helped Castillo Armas to become president by convincing the other members of the junta to resign. Thus, his presidency was formally inaugurated on September 1, and was reconfirmed by a plebiscite that took place on October 10. However, Castillo Armas' presidency didn't last long, because less than three years later, on July 26, 1957, he was assassinated. According to the investigation conducted by the government back then, Romeo Vásquez, a soldier assigned to the Guardia Presidencial, shot the Caudillo while he was walking along one of the National Palace's corridors. The truth is, nevertheless, that to this date the identity of the killer remains unknown and that Vásquez – who allegedly shot himself shortly after having killed Castillo Armas – was just a scapegoat.

During the following years, an alternate version of the Liberation emerged, fueled by the local left-leaning politicians and intellectuals who began questioning the official history and pointing out an U.S. involvement. The Guatemalan Army found itself in trouble too, as its officers were accused of having cowardly surrendered as soon as the Liberationists had set foot in the country.

The unrest spread quickly not only among the intellectual elites and the population, but also within the Army ranks, and to make things worse, in late 1960 it was discovered that the CIA was training a paramilitary force in the country, with aims at invading Cuba and get rid of Fidel Castro. Touched in their national pride, a handful of young officers, supported by leftist students and politicians, staged a revolt at the Matamoros Fort and at the Zacapa and Puerto Barrios garrisons, which failed within hours because the rebels weren't able to get the support of their fellow Army officers. However, this revolt established the foundations of a Marxist guerrilla movement that, months later, returned to the country and began a long and bloody civil war, supported by the Cuban regime, which by then was already backing many similar guerrilla groups that were flourishing across Latin America.

Aeschylus, the great Greek tragic dramatist, stated, "In war, truth is the first casualty", and that was precisely what happened in Latin America during the "Cold War" years. Both the U.S.-backed governments and the Communist movements set out to re-write history in a way as to validate their own political beliefs, something that resulted in a misleading portrayal of the past, which even to this date, keeps fueling the ideological confrontation, and has contributed to some extent to the rebirth of Socialism in the continent.

Perhaps the most useful lesson to be learned from this is that, even though neither the U.S. nor the Communists were altruistic in their actions, they must be taken in the tenor of the times and in the correct sociopolitical context to make any sense out of them. If we refuse to do so, we'll just be taking sides in a confrontation that should have ended many years ago.

APPENDIX I

Abbreviations and CIA Codenames

ADAM	Tactical codename for Guatemala City.
BOND	Tactical codename for the town of Puerto Barrios, Izabal, Guatemala, and the Liberation Army column assigned to attack it.
BRODFROST	Codename for Lt. Col. Malcolm H. Brodfrost, Chief of the PBSuccess Air Support Unit. (Used mostly in cables.)
CAESAR	Tactical codename for the city of Quetzaltenango, Guatemala.
CALLIGERIS	Codename for Lt. Col. Carlos Castillo Armas, Commander of the Liberation Army.
CADICK	Codename for Rip Robertson, PBSuccess Field Commander. (Used mostly in cables.)
CIA	Central Intelligence Agency.
CAT	Abbreviation for Civil Air Transport, a CIA-front airline.
DANNY	Tactical codename for the town of Esquipulas, Guatemala, and the Liberation Army column assigned to attack it.
DCI	Abbreviation for Director Central Intelligence. The Director of the CIA.
DD/A	Abbreviation for CIA Deputy Director / Administration.
DD/P	Abbreviation for CIA Deputy Director / Plans.
DDCI	Abbreviation for Deputy Director Central Intelligence.
DIR	Codename for the CIA Director (Used mostly in cables.)
DTFROGS	Codename for El Salvador.
DOC	Tactical codename for the town of Mazatenango, Guatemala.
DTROBALO	Codename for the Panama Canal Zone.
EDDIE	Tactical codename for the town of El Quiché, Guatemala.
ERRATIC	Codename for Gen. Miguel Ydígoras Fuentes.
ESCOBILLA	Codename for an unidentified PBSuccess operative in charge of collecting tactical intelligence along the combat zone.
ESCONSON	Codename for an unidentified PBSuccess operative in charge of collecting tactical intelligence from within the Guatemalan Army.
ESCROW	Codename for an unidentified PBSuccess operative in charge of collecting intelligence from within Guatemalan Communist organizations.
ESKIMOID	Codename for an unidentified PBSuccess operative in charge of collecting intelligence from within Guatemalan agrarian organizations.
ESLABON	Codename for an unidentified PBSuccess operative in charge of collecting intelligence from former members of the Caribbean Legion in Guatemala.
ESODIC-1	Codename for Col. Miguel Mendoza Azurdia. One of the Liberation Army's Field Commanders.
ESODIC-2	Codename for Col. Rodolfo Mendoza Azurdia. Chief of the Liberation Air Force.
ESOTROPE	Codename for an unidentified PBSuccess operative in charge of collecting intelligence from within women organizations in Guatemala.
ESPERANCE	Codename for an unidentified PBSuccess operative in charge of collecting intelligence from within the Partido Guatemalteco del Trabajo or PGT.
ESSENCE	Codename for an unidentified PBSuccess operative in charge of propaganda, under the direct command of PBSuccess headquarters.
FAG	Abbreviation for Fuerza Aérea Guatemalteca. Guatemalan Air Force.
FAH	Abbreviation for Fuerza Aérea Hondureña. Honduran Air Force.
FAN	Abbreviation for Fuerza Aérea Nicaragüense. Nicaraguan Air Force.
FJDEFLECT	Codename for the Civil Air Transport airline.
FJHOPEFUL	Codename for the France Air Force Base, Panama Canal Zone. Also known as "France Field."
FRANK	Tactical codename for the town of Jutiapa, Guatemala, and the Liberation Army column assigned to attack it.
GN	Abbreviation for Guardia Nacional. The Nicaraguan National Guard.
GOSS	Tactical codename for the town of Cobán, Guatemala.
HANK	Tactical codename for the town of Zacapa, Guatemala, and the Liberation Army column assigned to attack it.
HTKEEPER	Codename for Mexico City, Mexico.
HTPLUME	Codename for Panama.
IKE	Tactical codename for the town of Puerto de San José, Guatemala.
JACK	Tactical codename for the town of El Florido, Guatemala.
JMBLUG	Codename for John Peurifoy, U.S. Ambassador to Guatemala. (Used mostly in cables.)
JOHNNY	Tactical codename for the town of Chiquimula, Guatemala and the Liberation Army column assigned to attack it.
JUBATE	Codename for an unidentified PBSuccess operative in charge of collecting tactical intelligence along the Honduras – Guatemala border. Replaced JURATOR.
JUGATION	Codename for an unidentified PBSuccess operative in charge of collecting tactical intelligence along the El Salvador – Guatemala border.
K-PROGRAM	PBSuccess sub-project comprised of the KUCLUB, KUFIRE, and KUGOWN programs.
JURATOR	Codename for an unidentified PBSuccess operative in charge of collecting tactical intelligence along the Honduras – Guatemala border. Was replaced by JUBATE.
KENT	Tactical codename for the town of Casas Viejas, Honduras.
KMFLUSH	Codename for Nicaragua.
KMPAJAMA	Codename for Mexico.
KMPLEBE	Codename for Peru.
KUBARK	Codename for the Central Intelligence Agency.
KUCLUB	Codename for the PBSuccess communications program. Part of the K-PROGRAM sub-project.
KUFIRE	Codename for the PBSuccess intelligence collection program. Part of the K-PROGRAM sub-project.
KUGOWN	Codename for the PBSuccess propaganda program. Part of the K-PROGRAM sub-project.
KUHOOK	Codename for the PBSuccess paramilitary program, including the Liberation Army.
LANGEVIN	Codename for David Atlee Phillips, Chief of the clandestine radio station sub-project. (Used mostly in cables.)
LARRY	Tactical codename for the town of Entre Ríos, Guatemala.
LCFLUTTER	Codename for polygraph equipment.
LCPANGS	Codename for Costa Rica.
LINC	Abbreviation for LINCOLN.

LINCOLN	Codename for PBSuccess headquarters at Opa-locka, Florida.
MDAP	Mutual Defense Assistance Program. An U.S. military aid program.
MIKE	Tactical codename for the town of Asución Mita, Guatemala.
NICK	Tactical codename for the town of Gualán, Guatemala.
NSC	U.S. National Security Council.
OAS	Organization of American States.
ODACID	Codename for U.S. Embassy.
ODOATH	Codename for the U.S. Navy.
ODUNIT	Codename for the U.S. Air Force.
ODYOKE	Codename for the U.S. Government.
OPIM	Abbreviation for Operational Immediate. (Used mostly in cables.)
PANCHO	Alternate codename for Lt. Col. Carlos Castillo Armas, Commander of the Liberation Army.
PAR	Abbreviation for Partido de Accion Revolucionaria. A Guatemalan leftist political party.
PBCABOOSE	Codename for the PBSuccess Air Support Unit
PBPRIME	Codename for the United States.
PBRUMEN	Codename for Cuba.
PGT	Abbreviation for Partido Guatemalteco del Trabajo. A Guatemalan Communist organization.
PLAYDON	Codename for Albert Haney, PBSuccess Project Manager. (Used mostly in cables.)
QKCIGAR	Codename for Czechoslovakia.
RAP	Abbreviation for Reimbursable Air Program. An U.S. military aid program.
RRO	Abbreviation for Resident Radio Operator.
RUFUS	Alternate codename for Lt. Col. Carlos Castillo Armas, Commander of the Liberation Army.
SAHARA	Codename for the PBSuccess sub-project aimed at intruding and disrupting the Guatemalan Army radio communications network.
SALAL	Codename for the PBSuccess tactical communications center at the town of Santa Fé, Honduras.
SAMPSON	Codename for the Liberation Army's advanced command post at Chiquimula, Guatemala.
SANTA FE	Codename for the site from where Radio Liberación broadcasted, located in the town of Santa Fé, Honduras.
SARANAC	Codename for the paramilitary training site in Nicaragua.
SCRANTON	Codename for the radio operators training site in Nicaragua.
SECANT	Codename for an unidentified CIA informant within the Guatemalan Army.
SEMANTIC	Codename for an unidentified CIA informant within the Guatemalan Army.
SEQUIN	Codename for an unidentified PBSuccess operative in charge of organizing and securing intelligence networks within Guatemala.
SGUAT	Codename for the CIA station in Guatemala City. (Used mostly in cables.)
SHERWOOD	Codename for PBSuccess' Field Command Post at Managua, Nicaragua. (Used mostly in cables.)
SKILLET	Codename for Withing Willauer, U.S. Ambassador to Honduras.
SKIMMER	Codename for "The Group" that supported and financed the Liberation campaign.
SLINC	Alternate codename for LINCOLN. (Used mostly in cables.)
SOMERSET	Codename for the PBSuccess air base established at the Las Mercedes Airport, in Managua, Nicaragua.
STANDEL	Codename for Col. Jacobo Arbenz, President of Guatemala.
STANDEL-1	Codename for Col. Carlos Enrique Díaz, Chief of the Guatemalan Armed Forces.
STORAX	Codename for Anastasio Somoza García, President of Nicaragua.
SUMAC-1	Codename for Col. José Ángel Sánchez. Guatemalan Minister of Defense.
SUMAC-2	Codename for Col. Élfego Monzón, a Guatemalan Army officer assigned to the Ministry of the Interior.
SYNCARP	Codename for the Liberation Army's high command.
TGW	The identifier letters for the Guatemalan government radio station.
TOMMY	Tactical codename for the town of Morales, Izabal, Guatemala, and the Liberation Army column assigned to attack it.
TRO	Abbreviation for Tactical Radio Operator.
UFCO	Abbreviation for United Fruit Company.
UN	Abbreviation for United Nations.
USAF	Abbreviation for United States Air Force.
WASHTUB	Codename for the PBSuccess sub-project aimed at planting Soviet-made weapons in Nicaragua and Guatemala.
WHD	The CIA's Western Hemisphere Division.
WSBURNT	Codename for Guatemala.
WSHOOFS	Codename for Honduras.

APPENDIX II

Liberation Air Force Aircraft

Type	MSN	Previous ID	Comments
Cessna 180	30114	N2914A TI-224 HP-195	During the campaign was assigned the false registration HK-592. To the Guatemalan civil registry after the campaign. Fate unknown.
Cessna 140	N/A	N/A	To TG-BOH after the campaign. Fate unknown.
Douglas C-47	N/A	N/A	Leased in the Washington D.C. area. Reported in CIA declassified documents with the serial "3708." Returned to the owner after the campaign.
Douglas C-47	N/A	N/A	Leased in the Washington D.C. area. Reported in CIA declassified documents with the serial "3520." Returned to the owner after the campaign.
Douglas C-47	N/A	N/A	Purchased in the Washington D.C. area. To the Guatemalan Air Force as "0515", after the campaign. Fate unknown.
Lockheed P-38L Lightning	N/A	44-53232	To the Honduran Air Force as FAH-506 and then FAH-505, after the campaign. Currently preserved at the National Museum of the U.S. Air Force in Wright-Patterson AFB, Ohio.
Republic F-47N Thunderbolt	N/A	44-89131	To GN-73 with the Nicaraguan Air Force. Crashed at Las Mercedes due to trim problems in 1960.
Republic F-47N Thunderbolt	N/A	44-89136	To the Guatemalan Air Force as FAG-0568, then to the Nicaraguan Air Force as GN-71. Sold to Lloyd P. Nolen of the Confederate Air Force in 1963. Currently preserved at the Cavanaugh Flight Museum in Addison, Texas.
Republic F-47N Thunderbolt	N/A	44-89259	Crash-landed at Las Mercedes on June 19, 1954. Used for spares.
Republic F-47N Thunderbolt	N/A	44-89265	To the Nicaraguan Air Force as GN-72. Sold to William W. Martin in 1963. Crash-landed during ferry flight at Veracruz, Mexico, in 1964.
Republic F-47N Thunderbolt	N/A	44-89400	Crash-landed at Chiquimula, Guatemala, on June 29, 1954. Destroyed.
Republic F-47N Thunderbolt	N/A	44-89439	To the Nicaraguan Air Force as GN-70. Sold to William W. Martin in 1963. Crash-landed during ferry flight near Brownsville, Texas, in 1965.

APPENDIX III

Guatemalan Air Force Aircraft, June 1954

Type	MSN	FAG Serial	Prev. ID	Comments
North American AT-6D Texan	N/A	0682	N/A	
North American AT-6C Texan	N/A	0684	N/A	
North American AT-6D Texan	N/A	0728	44-81157	Ex FAG-50 before the 1949 re-serialing.
North American AT-6C Texan	N/A	0856	N/A	Probably crashed on June 18, 1954.
North American AT-6D Texan	N/A	0930	N/A	
North American AT-6D Texan	N/A	0940	N/A	
Boeing P-26A Peashooter	AC33-123	0672	N/A	Preserved in flying condition at the Planes of Fame Museum, Chino, California.
Boeing P-26A Peashooter	AC33-135	0816	N/A	Preserved at the National Air & Space Museum, Steven Udvar-Hazy Center, Chantilly, Virginia.
Beechcraft AT-11 Kansan	N/A	0642	42-36856	Ex B-1 before the 1949 re-serialing.
Beechcraft AT-11 Kansan	3362	0874	42-36982	Captured in Honduras on May 11, 1954, during a secret mission. To TG-O-CIV in 1957.
Beechcraft AT-11 Kansan	N/A	0792	N/A	
Douglas C-47B-DK	34406	0653	45-1136	
Douglas C-47A-DL	20046	0749	43-15580	
Beechcraft C-45	N/A	0635	N/A	
Cessna JRC-1 (UC-78) Bobcat	5286	1	43-7766 BuA 64478	To TG-CEQ-23 in December 1955
Boeing PT-17 Kaydet	N/A	0872	N/A	Assigned to the Escuela Militar de Aviación, or Military Aviation School.
Fairchild PT-19A Cornell	N/A	0678	N/A	Assigned to the Escuela Militar de Aviación, or Military Aviation School.
Fairchild PT-19A Cornell	N/A	0842	43-31513	Assigned to the Escuela Militar de Aviación, or Military Aviation School.
Fairchild PT-19A Cornell	N/A	087?	42-65542	Assigned to the Escuela Militar de Aviación, or Military Aviation School.
Fairchild PT-19A Cornell	N/A	0946	42-83611	Assigned to the Escuela Militar de Aviación, or Military Aviation School.
Ryan STM	N/A	0826	N/A	Assigned to the Escuela Militar de Aviación, or Military Aviation School.
Ryan STM	N/A	0760	N/A	Assigned to the Escuela Militar de Aviación, or Military Aviation School.
Waco VPF-7	N/A	18	N/A	Assigned to the Escuela Militar de Aviación, or Military Aviation School.

Additionally, the Guatemalan Air Force had the following aircraft in service, for which there is no conclusive information regarding their FAG serials or previous identities:

- 3 Vultee BT-15
- 10 Fairchild PT-19A
- 1 Waco VPF-7
- 3 Ryan STM

All were assigned to the Escuela Militar de Aviación (Military Aviation School), at the Los Cipresales Airbase, during the June 1954 emergency.

APPENDIX IV

PBSuccess Air Operations Phase IIIB and IV

Date	Flight No.	Take Off	Landing	Aircraft Type	Load Type	Comment
27 May	P-1	16:00	21:00	C-47	Leaflets	Leaflet drop over Guatemala City.
07 Jun	P-2	06:10	12:45	C-47	Leaflets	Leaflet drop over Guatemala City. Aborted due to bad weather.
	P-3	15:00	19:45	C-47	Leaflets	Leaflet drop over Quetzaltenango, Mazatenango, and El Quiché.
14 Jun	C-1	18:00	00:35	C-47	Weapons Ammo	Supply drop near Chiquimula.
	C-2	18:31	01:00	C-47	Weapons Ammo	Supply drop near Chiquimula.
15 Jun	C-3	02:35	08:50	C-47	Weapons Ammo	Supply drop over Zacapa – Chiquimula area. No reception team present.
	C-4	02:36	08:51	C-47	Weapons Ammo	Supply drop over Zacapa – Chiquimula area. No reception team present.
	C-5	20:00	02:05	C-47	Weapons Ammo	Supply drop over Tiquisate area. No reception team present.
	C-6	20:05	02:15	C-47	Weapons Ammo	Supply drop over Tiquisate area. No reception team present.
16 Jun	C-7	06:05	08:40	C-47	Weapons Ammo	Supply drop over Barberena area. No reception team present.
	C-8	06:10	08:40	C-47	Weapons Ammo	Supply drop over Barberena area. No reception team present.
	C-9	20:15	01:56	C-47	Weapons Ammo	Supply drop over Barberena area. No reception team present.
	C-10	20:20	01:45	C-47	Weapons Ammo	Supply drop over Barberena area. No reception team present.
17 Jun	C-11	19:30	01:20	C-47	Weapons Ammo	Supply drop over Quezaltepeque area. No reception team present.
	C-12	19:31	00:40	C-47	Weapons Ammo	Supply drop over Quezaltepeque area. No reception team present.
18 Jun	C-13	03:45	09:43	C-47	Weapons Ammo	Supply drop over Tiquisate area. No reception team present.
	C-14	04:30	10:05	C-47	Weapons Ammo	Supply drop over Tiquisate area. Aborted due to bad weather.
	C 15	21:17	02:10	C-47	Weapons Ammo Sab. Equipment	Supply drop over Palencia area. Buzzed Guatemala City.
	C-16	21:20	02:25	C-47	Weapons Ammo Sab. Equipment	Supply drop over Palencia area. Buzzed Guatemala City.

Date	Flight No.	Take Off	Landing	Aircraft Type	Load Type	Comment
19 Jun	C-17	05:00	09:45	C-47	Weapons Ammo	Supply drop over Quezaltepeque. Mandatory drop.
	C-18	05:02	09:55	C-47	Weapons Ammo	Supply drop over Quezaltepeque. Mandatory drop.
	F-1	05:31	09:40	F-47N	500 X .50 Cal MG rounds	Buzzed Guatemala City.
	F-2	05:32	09:50	F-47N	500 X .50 Cal MG rounds	Buzzed Guatemala City.
	C-19	15:55	20:13	C-47	Weapons Ammo	Supply drop over Jutiapa. No reception team present.
	C-20	15:58	20:15	C-47	Weapons Ammo	Supply drop over Jutiapa. No reception team present.
	F-3	16:20	19:30	F-47N	500 X .50 Cal MG rounds	Fighter cover for C-19 and C-20. Buzzed Jutiapa, Chiquimula and Zacapa. Crash-landed at Las Mercedes.
	F-4	16:20	19:30	F-47N	500 X .50 Cal MG rounds	Fighter cover for C-19 and C-20. Buzzed Jutiapa, Chiquimula and Zacapa.
20 Jun	C-21	11:45	17:38	C-47	Ammo Food	Supply drop over Piedra Blanca and Jutiapa areas. No reception teams present.
21 Jun	C-22	05:25	10:45	C-47	Weapons Ammo Food	Supply drop over Jocotán area. Reception team present.
	C-23	05:30	10:48	C-47	Weapons Ammo Food	Supply drop over Jocotán area. Reception team present.
21 Jun	F-5	05:50	09:45	F-47N	500 X .50 Cal MG rounds	Fighter cover for C-22 and C-23. Targets of opportunity at Zacapa. Forced light plane to land at Esquipulas.
	F-6	14:25	15:55	F-47N	2 X M105 leaflet bombs	Leaflet drop over Guatemala City. Aborted due to engine malfunction.
	C-24	17:05	21:05	C-47	Ammo Food	Supply drop over Quezaltepeque and Ipala areas. No reception team at Ipala.
22 Jun	C-25	03:50	08:55	C-47	Ammo Food	Supply drop over Champona - Entre Ríos area. No reception team present.
	F-7	05:30	08:55	F-47N	500 X .50 Cal MG rounds	Strafed El Portillo gasoline storage Tanks, buzzed Guatemala City.
	C-26	10:30	15:35	C-47	Weapons Ammo Food	Supply drops over Esquipulas and Gualán areas. No reception team at Gualán.
	F-8	11:20	14:45	F-47N	3 X M57 bombs	Armed recon flight over Zacapa area. All three bombs duds.
	C-27	15:00	19:05	C-47	Ammo Food Medical Kits	Supply drop over Champona – Entre Ríos area. Bundles captured by Army troops.
23 Jun	C-28	05:00	10:10	C-47	Ammo Food	Supply drop over Jocotán and Gualán areas. No reception team present at Gualán.
	F-9	05:40	09:15	F-47N	3 X M57 bombs	Bombing mission to Zacapa and Gualán.
	F-10	07:00	10:30	F-47N	1 X M64 bomb	Bombing mission to Chiquimula and Gualán. Pilot got lost and the flight was aborted.
	F-11	13:20	16:32	F-47N	3 X M57 bombs	Bombing mission to Chiquimula and Gualán.
	F-12	13:21	16:32	F-47N	1 X M64 bomb	Bombing mission to Chiquimula and Gualán.
24 Jun	C-29	06:15	12:05	C-47	Ammo Food	Supply drop over Chiquimula. Reception teams present.

Date	Flight No.	Take Off	Landing	Aircraft Type	Load Type	Comment
24 Jun	F-13	07:05	10:05	F-47N	1 X M64 bomb	Bombing mission to Chiquimula.
	F-14	07:05	10:05	F-47N	3 X M57 bombs	Bombing mission to Chiquimula.
	C-30	12:00	17:10	C-47	Ammo Food Medical Kits	Supply drop over Gualán. No reception team present.
25 Jun	C-31	05:20	10:30	C-47	Ammo Food	Supply drop over Chiquimula and Jalapa. Reception teams present.
	C-32	05:25	11:30	C-47	Ammo Food	Supply drop over Chiquimula and Jalapa. Reception teams present.
	F-15	06:10	09:20	F-47N	1 X M64 2 X M57 bombs	Bombing mission to Chiquimula area.
	F-16	12:10	15:40	F-47N	1 X M64 2 X M57 bombs	Bombing mission to Guatemala City. Sustained damage due to ground fire.
	F-17	12:10	15:40	F-47N	1 X M64 2 X M57 bombs	Bombing mission to Guatemala City. M57 bombs jettisoned due to malfunction.
	C-33	15:20	20:50	C-47	24 X 20lb 2 X 260lb bombs	Bombing mission to Chiquimula and Zacapa area.
	C-34	15:25	20:45	C-47	Weapons Ammo	Supply drop over Jalapa area. Reception team present.
26 Jun	C-35	05:10	10:20	C-47	Ammo Mortars Anti-tank Rifles	Supply drop over Chiquimula. Reception team present.
	F-18	06:00	10:00	F-47N	1 X M64 2 X M57 bombs	Bombing mission to Zacapa.
	C-36	08:10	13:00	C-47	Ammo Mortars Gasoline	Supply flight to Chiquimula airfield.
	F-19	08:25	10:30	P-38L	2 X M64 bombs	Bombing mission to Jalapa area. Aborted due to engine malfunction.
	F-20	08:30	12:00	F-47N	1 X M64 2 X M57 bombs	Bombing mission to Zacapa area.
	F-21	11:25	13:45	F-47N	1 X M64 2 X M57 bombs	Bombing mission to Chiquimula and Guatemala City. Mission aborted due to engine problems.
	F-22	14:00	16:40	P-38L	2 X M64 bombs	Bombing mission to Quezaltepeque and Ipala areas.
	F-23	14:10	18:10	F-47N	3 X M57 bombs	Bombing mission to Zacapa and Guatemala City.

Date	Flight No.	Take Off	Landing	Aircraft Type	Load Type	Comment
27 Jun	C-37	05:00	10:25	C-47	24 X 20lb bombs	Bombing mission to Zacapa.
	C-38	05:10	10:30	C-47	Gasoline	Supply drop over Chiquimula. Reception team present.
	C-39	05:12	09:30	C-47	Weapons Ammo Mortars	Supply drop over Chiquimula. Reception team present.
	F-24	05:15	6:00	F-47N	3 X M57 bombs	Bombing mission to Zacapa. Aborted due to engine problems.
	F-25	05:45	09:10	P-38L	2 X M64 bombs	Bombing mission to Puerto San José. Sunk the M.S. *Springfjord*. Sustained damage due to ground fire.
	F-26	06:10	09:15	F-47N	3 X M57 bombs	Bombing mission to Zacapa. Aborted due to bad weather.
	C-40	11:45	16:50	C-47	Weapons Ammo Food	Supply drop over Chiquimula. Reception team present.
28 Jun	C-41	04:10	09:10	C-47	Weapons Ammo Food	Supply drop over Chiquimula. Reception team present.
	C-42	04:15	08:15	C-47	Weapons Ammo Gasoline	Supply drop over Chiquimula. Reception team present.
	C-43	04:20	09:25	C-47	Ammo Mortars	Supply flight to Chiquimula. Picked up Rip Robertson.
	F-27	04:55	09:40	F-47N	1 X M64 2 X M57 bombs	Bombing mission to Zacapa. Intercepted USAF C-47.
	F-28	06:05	9:00	F-47N	1 X M64 2 X M57 bombs	Bombing mission to Zacapa.
	F-29	07:30	10:45	F-47N	1 X M64 2 X M57 bombs	Bombing mission to Zacapa. Aborted due to bad weather.
	C-44	12:10	17:30	C-47	Weapons Ammo Medical Kits	Supply drop over Chiquimula. Reception team present.
	C-45	13:30	18:45	C-47	Weapons Ammo	Supply drop over Chiquimula. Reception team present.
	F-30	14:50	17:10	F-47N	1 X M64 2 X M57 bombs	Bombing mission to Guatemala City.
	F-31	14:50	17:10	F-47N	1 X M64 2 X M57 bombs	Bombing mission to Guatemala City.
29 Jun	C-46	05:15	10:45	C-47	24 X 20lb 2 X 260lb bombs	Bombing mission to Zacapa.
	F-32	07:30	10:50	F-47N	3 X M57 bombs	Bombing mission to Zacapa.
	F-33	08:45	12:15	F-47N	3 X M57 bombs	Bombing mission to Zacapa. Crash landed at Chiquimula after sustaining heavy damage from ground fire.
	F-34	09:50	13:15	F-47N	3 X M57 bombs	Bombing mission to Zacapa.
	F-35	12:35	14:45	F-47N	3 X M57 bombs	Bombing mission to Zacapa. Aborted due to bad weather.

Date	Flight No.	Take Off	Landing	Aircraft Type	Load Type	Comment
30 Jun	C-47	05:15	10:15	C-47	N/A	Flight to pick up Castillo Armas at Esquipulas.
	C-48	07:10	11:46	C-47	Weapons Ammo Food	Supply drop over Champona – Entre Ríos area. No reception team present.
	C-49	12:45	N/A	C-47	N/A	Flight to El Salvador carrying Castillo Armas to the Peace Talks.

Flight number prefixes:
C = Cargo
F = Fighter
P = Psychological

NOTES

Chapter 1

1 Even though Guatemala declared its independence from Spain on September 15, 1821, with the rest of the Central American provinces and formed the Federal Republic of Central America, it wasn't until 1847, when the federation was dissolved, that Guatemala became a republic.

2 President Arévalo called these groups the "Chiquilines" or "younglings" and praised them for their "spontaneity and patriotism."

3 Gramajo Morales, *Alrededor de la Bandera* (Guatemalan National Typography Workshops, 2002), p. 225.

4 Ibid, p. 244.

Chapter 3

1 CIA declassified document DOC_0000135830.pdf, titled "Memorandum for all Staff Officers – Selection of individuals for disposal by Junta Group", dated March 31, 1954.

2 CIA declassified cable DOC_0000135930.pdf, titled "LINC 311", from PBSuccess headquarters to the CIA Director, dated January 31, 1954.

3 CIA declassified document DOC_0000928348.pdf, titled "Project PBSuccess", dated November 16, 1954, p. 80.

Chapter 4

1 CIA declassified document DOC_0000935207.pdf, titled "PBSuccess Debriefing Reports", dated September 1, 1954, p. 35.

2 CIA declassified document DOC_0000928363.pdf, titled "Operational Air Support Plan", dated March 5, 1954.

3 CIA declassified document DOC_0000914129.pdf, titled "Weekly PBSUCCESS Meeting with DD/P", dated January 19, 1954.

4 CIA declassified cable DOC_0000135978.pdf, titled "LINC 803", from PBSuccess headquarters to the Field Command Post in Managua, dated March 1, 1954.

5 CIA declassified document DOC_0000916573.pdf, titled "Memorandum for Chief of Project – Control of PBSuccess Black Flights through Panama ATC", dated April 8, 1954.

6 CIA declassified cable DOC_0000136030.pdf, titled "LINC 1260", from PBSuccess headquarters to Castillo Armas, dated March 23, 1954.

7 CIA declassified cable DOC_0000136049.pdf, titled "LINC 1414", from PBSuccess headquarters to the Air Support Unit, dated March 29, 1954.

8 CIA declassified cable DOC_0000917318.pdf, titled "LINC 1135", from PBSuccess headquarters to the Air Support Unit, dated March 18, 1954.

9 CIA declassified cable DOC_0000136868.pdf, titled "DIR 45794", from the CIA Director to PBSuccess headquarters, dated April 9, 1954.

10 CIA declassified document DOC_0000916483.pdf, titled "Memorandum for the record – Circumstances leading to the dispatch of 11 April Black Flight", date April 11, 1954.

11 CIA declassified cable DOC_0000916377.pdf, titled "[redacted] 135", from [redacted] to PBSuccess headquarters, dated April 14, 1954.

Chapter 5

1 CIA declassified document DOC_0000916210.pdf, titled "Memorandum for [redacted] – Items for inclusion in CE report", dated April 22, 1954, p. 3.

2 CIA declassified document DOC_0000916826.pdf, titled "Notes on discussion with Mr. Barnes – Present status and possible future of PBSuccess", dated May 31, 1954, p. 2.

3 CIA declassified document DOC_0000916252.pdf, titled "Memorandum for the record – Minutes of weekly PBSUCCESS meeting", dated April 21, 1954, p. 3.

4 Peer Nugent, *The Black Eagle* (Bantam Books Inc., 1972), p. 136.

5 CIA declassified document DOC_0000923784.pdf, titled "Memorandum for Director of Central Intelligence – Position Paper on PBSUCCESS", dated April 24, 1954.

6 The full report of the Guatemalan arms purchase was completed on June 23, 1954. It was circulated as CIA declassified document DOC_0000921353.pdf, titled "Guatemalan Procurement of Arms from the Soviet Orbit."

7 CIA declassified document DOC_0000916146.pdf, titled "Memorandum for the record – Notes of talk with Ambassador Willauer", dated April 26, 1954.

8 CIA declassified document DOC_0000913410.pdf, titled "General Plan of Operations", undated. For the real names of the special groups members see the CIA declassified document DOC_0000916782.pdf, titled *"Claves que acompañan el Plan General de Operaciones"*, also undated. Other members of the "Special Group A" are mentioned in the CIA declassified document DOC_0000923814.pdf, titled "ESODIC-1 and ESODIC-2 further development", dated April 1, 1954.

9 CIA declassified document DOC_0000935207.pdf, titled "PBSuccess Debriefing Reports", dated September 1, 1954, p. 26.

10 Ibid, p. 19.

Chapter 6

1 CIA declassified document DOC_0000915711.pdf, untitled and dated April 30, 1954, contains an intelligence report obtained from a Guatemalan government spy, which describes the situation surrounding the staging points in Honduras.

2 CIA declassified document DOC_0000922811.pdf, titled "Guatemalan Intelligence Activities in Honduras", dated June 2, 1954.

3 CIA declassified document DOC_0000915446.pdf, titled "Progress Report – PBSUCCESS for the period 4-10 May, 1954", dated May 11, 1954, describes the situation prevailing in Honduras at the time.

4 CIA declassified cable DOC_0000136119.pdf, titled "LINC 2525", dated May 8, 1954, from PBSuccess headquarters to Rip Robertson, orders the Field Commander to begin a contingency plan in case the Honduran government is overthrown.

5 CIA declassified document DOC_0000135031.pdf, titled "The SHERWOOD Tapes", undated, contains transcriptions of all the Radio Liberación broadcastings during the campaign.

6 Eventually, Radio Liberación used two backup transmitters. One was located in Managua, at the SHERWOOD communications center and the other was installed in a Weather Station at Key West, Florida. More information about this sub-project can be found in the CIA declassified document DOC_0000913132.pdf, titled "Selection of Site for Sherwood Program", dated March 5, 1954.

7 CIA declassified cable DOC_0000921942.pdf, titled "LINC 3821" and dated June 15, 1954, reports that a test drop over the clandestine radio station site has been successful in delivering some pre-recorded tapes. However, it seems that the practice was never implemented.

8 CIA declassified document DOC_0000922813.pdf, titled "Contact with Pancho and Manuel, 31 May" dated June 02, 1954, p. 4

9 CIA declassified document DOC_0000915450.pdf, titled "Unauthorized Landing of C-47 in Honduras", dated May 11, 1954.

10 CIA declassified document DOC_0000915750.pdf, titled "Guatemalan Matters – Air Force Capabilities", dated May 2, 1954. Also, CIA declassified document DOC_0000922555.pdf, titled "Status of Guatemalan Air Force", dated June 10, 1954.

11 Telegram No. 4220, dated May 10, 1954, from the U.S. Embassy in Tegucigalpa to the U.S. Secretary of State.

12 CIA declassified document DOC_0000915730.pdf, titled "Guatemalan Matters – Report of Czech Planes", dated May 4, 1954. Also, U.S. Department of State cable "GUAT 399" from the U.S. Embassy in Tegucigalpa to the U.S. Secretary of State.

13 CIA declassified cable DOC_0000915675.pdf, titled "LINC 2416", dated May 5, 1954, from the PBSuccess headquarters to the CIA Director.

14 CIA declassified cable DOC_0000136130.pdf, titled "LINC 2724", dated May 16, 1954, from PBSuccess headquarters for ONTRICH.

15 CIA declassified cable DOC_0000923553.pdf, titled "[redacted] 574", dated May 18, 1954, from the CIA Station in Guatemala to PBSuccess headquarters.

16 Cpt. Kirten's report on his visit to Puerto Barrios to inspect the arms shipment is contained in the CIA declassified document DOC_0000923299.pdf, titled "S.S. ALFHEM (Swedish), Arrival and activities in Puerto Barrios", dated May 20, 1954.

17 CIA declassified cable DOC_0000923469.pdf, titled "GUAT 593", dated May 19, 1954, from the CIA Station in Guatemala to PBSuccess headquarters.

18 CIA declassified cable DOC_0000136137.pdf, titled "LINC 2793", dated May 17, 1954, from the PBSuccess headquarters to ONTRICH.

19 *Prensa Libre* newspaper, news note published on May 20, 1954.

Chapter 7

1 Gramajo Morales, *Alrededor de la Bandera* (Guatemalan National Typography Workshops, 2002), p. 305.

2 The type of weapons and ammunitions brought by the M.S. Alfhem was determined until mid-June 1954 by the Agency, mostly through Castillo Armas informants. CIA declassified document DOC_0000934451.pdf, titled "Alfhem Arms Shipment", dated June 16, 1954, gives all the details.

3 Peer Nugent, *The Black Eagle* (Bantam Books Inc., 1972), p. 150.

4 CIA declassified cable DOC_0000923260.pdf, titled "LINC 3144", dated May 26, 1954, from PBSuccess headquarters to the CIA Director.

5 CIA declassified document DOC_0000923768.pdf, titled "Utilization of [redacted] owned Douglas A-20 Type Aircraft", dated May 3, 1954.

6 CIA declassified cable DOC_0000923242.pdf, titled "SHERWOOD 118", dated May 26, 1954, from PBSuccess Field Command Post to PBSuccess headquarters.

7 CIA declassified document DOC_0000923009.pdf, titled "Newspaper Clippings: Leaflet drop", dated May 30, 1954.

8 Ibid, 47, news note published on May 29, 1954.

9 "7th WING OPERATIONS HISTORY, 1952-1954", p. 12. (PDF document containing a copy of the 7th Wing Members Association's defunct website.)

10 Villagrán Kramer, *Biografía Política de Guatemala* (Facultad Latinoamericana de Ciencias Sociales – FLACSO, 1993), p. 129.

11 CIA declassified cable DOC_0000923084.pdf, titled "GUAT 699", dated May 29, 1954, from the CIA Station in Guatemala to PBSuccess headquarters.

12 CIA declassified cable DOC_0000923494.pdf, titled "LINC 3005", dated May 22, 1954, from PBSuccess headquarters to the Field Command Post and Castillo Armas.

13 CIA declassified cable DOC_0000136174.pdf, titled "LINC 3338", dated May 31, 1954, from PBSuccess headquarters to the CIA Station in Guatemala.

14 CIA declassified cable DOC_0000136190.pdf, titled "LINC 3547", dated June 6, 1954, from PBSuccess headquarters to the Field Command Post.

15 *Prensa Libre* newspaper, news note published on June 7, 1954.

16 CIA declassified document DOC_0000922536.pdf, titled "GUAT 794", dated June 9, 1954, from the CIA Station in Guatemala to PBSuccess headquarters.

Chapter 8

1 CIA declassified document DOC_0000935207.pdf, titled "PBSuccess Debriefing Reports", dated September 1, 1954, p. 46.

2 *Prensa Libre* newspaper, news note published on June 8, 1954.

3 CIA declassified document DOC_0000921394.pdf, titled "Defections of Guatemalan Air Force Pilots", dated June 22, 1954. Also, CIA declassified document DOC_0000928348, titled "Project PBSuccess", dated November 16, 1954, p. 193.

4 CIA declassified document DOC_0000921394.pdf, titled "Defections of Guatemalan Air Force Pilots", dated June 22, 1954.

5 CIA declassified document DOC_0000921957.pdf, titled "General – Operational Matters", dated June 15, 1954, p. 3.

6 CIA declassified cable DOC_0000141938.pdf, titled "LINC 3757", dated June 12, 1954, from PBSuccess headquarters to the Field Command Post.

7 CIA declassified cable DOC_0000921969.pdf, titled "SHERWOOD 233", dated June 14, 1954, from the Field Command Post to the PBSuccess headquarters.

8 CIA declassified cable DOC_0000934449.pdf, titled "DIR 05085", dated June 16, 1954, from Frank Wisner to the PBSuccess headquarters.

9 Carrozza, Anthony R., *William D. Pawley – The Extraordinary Life of the Adventurer, Entrepreneur and Diplomat Who Founded the Flying Tigers* (Potomac Books, 2012), p. 200.

10 CIA declassified document DOC_0000922536.pdf, titled "GUAT 794", dated June 9, 1954, from the CIA Station in Guatemala to PBSuccess headquarters.

11 CIA declassified cable DOC_0000136242.pdf, titled "LINC 3988", dated June 18, 1954, from PBSuccess headquarters to the CIA Director.

12 *Prensa Libre* Newspaper, news note published on June 2, 1954.

13 CIA declassified document DOC_0000921313.pdf, titled "Informal Memorandum", dated June 23, 1954, p. 8.

14 CIA declassified cable DOC_136238.pdf, titled "LINC 3970", dated June 17, 1954, from PBSuccess headquarters to the CIA Station in Guatemala, p. 2.

15 CIA declassified cable DOC_0000136228.pdf, titled "LINC 3908", dated June 16, from PBSuccess headquarters to Field Command Post.

16 CIA declassified cable DOC_0000921993.pdf, titled "DIR 04732", dated June 14, 1954, from the CIA Director to PBSuccess headquarters.

17 CIA declassified cable DOC_0000136227.pdf, titled "LINC 3904", dated June 16, 1954, from PBSuccess headquarters to the Field Command Post.

18 CIA declassified cable DOC_0000921748.pdf, titled "SHERWOOD 267", dated June 17, 1954, from the Field Command Post to PBSuccess headquarters. Also, CIA declassified cable DOC_0000921755.pdf, titled "SHERWOOD 265", dated June 17, 1954, from the Field Command Post to PBSuccess headquarters.

Chapter 9

1 CIA declassified cable DOC_0000136258.pdf, titled "LINC 4064", dated June 19, 1954, from PBSuccess headquarters to the CIA Director.

2 CIA declassified cable DOC_0000136243.pdf, titled "LINC 3993", dated June 18, 1954, from PBSuccess headquarters to the CIA Station in Guatemala. Also, CIA declassified cable DOC_0000136244, titled "LINC 3998", dated June 18, 1954, from PBSuccess headquarters to the CIA Station in Guatemala.

3 CIA declassified cable DOC_0000136236.pdf, titled "LINC 3966", dated June 17, 1954, from PBSuccess headquarters to the Field Command Post, the CIA Station in Guatemala and the CIA Director.

4 CIA declassified cable DOC 0000921723.pdf, titled "[redacted] 887", dated June 18, 1954, from the CIA Station in Guatemala to PBSuccess headquarters.

5 CIA declassified cable DOC_0000136256.pdf, titled "LINC 4057", dated June 19, 1954, from PBSuccess headquarters to the Field Command Post.

6 CIA declassified cable DOC_0000136250.pdf, titled "LINC 4036", dated June 19, 1954, from PBSuccess headquarters to the Field Command Post and the SALAL communications center.

7 CIA declassified document DOC_0000935207.pdf, titled "PBSuccess Debriefing Reports", dated September 1, 1954, p. 35.

8 CIA declassified cable DOC_0000921582.pdf, titled "GUAT 903", dated June 19, 1954, from the CIA Station in Guatemala to PBSuccess headquarters.

9 *Prensa Libre* newspaper, news note published on August 20, 1954.

10 CIA declassified document DOC_0000921316.pdf, titled "FBIS Items of Possible KUGOWN Interest", dated June 23, 1954, p. 1.

11 CIA declassified cable DOC_0000136251.pdf, titled "LINC 4039", dated June 19, 1954, from PBSuccess headquarters to the CIA Director.

12 Ibid, 63. Also, CIA declassified document DOC_0000921471.pdf, titled "GUAT 916", dated June 21, 1954, from the CIA Station in Guatemala to PBSuccess headquarters. These officers' defection is also mentioned in the U.S. Embassy telegram No. 1045, dated June 19, 1954, addressed to the PBSuccess headquarters.

13 CIA declassified document DOC_0000935207.pdf, titled "PBSuccess Debriefing Reports", dated September 1, 1954, p. 118.

14 Ibid, p. 52. Also, CIA declassified cable DOC_0000921520.pdf, titled "SHERWOOD 298", dated June 20, 1954, from the Field Command Post to PBSuccess headquarters.

15 CIA declassified document DOC_0000136282.pdf, titled "LINC 4158", dated June 22, 1954, from PBSuccess headquarters to the CIA Director.

16 Silva Girón, *La Batalla de Gualán* (Imprenta EROS, 1977), p. 43.

17 Ibid, p. 33.

18 CIA declassified document DOC_0000136267.pdf, titled "LINC 4094", dated June 20, 1954, from PBSuccess headquarters to the Field Command Post.

19 Gramajo Morales, *Alrededor de la Bandera* (Guatemalan National Typography Workshops, 2002), p. 315.

Chapter 10

1 Note 1 should be: CIA declassified document DOC_0000935207.pdf, titled "PBSuccess Debriefing Reports", dated September 1, 1954, p. 28.

2 Ibid, p. 20.

3 Ibid, p. 19.

4 Ibid, p. 50.

5 CIA declassified cable DOC_0000136291.pdf, titled "LINC 4191", dated June 22, 1954, from PBSuccess headquarters to the Field Command Post.

6 CIA declassified document DOC_0000935207.pdf, titled "PBSuccess Debriefing Reports", dated September 1, 1954, p. 20.

7 Ibid, p. 49.

8 Ibid, p. 90.

9 CIA declassified cable DOC_0000921438.pdf, titled "LINC "4194", dated June 22, 1954, from PBSuccess headquarters to the Field Command Post.

10 CIA declassified cable DOC_0000921446.pdf, titled "LINC 4172", dated June 22, 1954, from PBSuccess headquarters to the CIA Director. p. 3.

11 CIA declassified cable DOC_0000921424.pdf, titled "SHERWOOD 335", dated June 22, 1954, from the Field Command Post to PBSuccess headquarters.

12 CIA declassified cable DOC_0000920932.pdf, titled "DIR 06725", dated June 26, 1954, from the CIA Director to PBSuccess headquarters and two other undisclosed CIA stations.

13 CIA declassified cable DOC_0000136293.pdf, titled "LINC 4217", dated June 23, 1954, from PBSuccess headquarters to the Field Command Post.

14 CIA declassified cable DOC_0000934447.pdf, titled "LINC 4219", dated June 23, 1954, from PBSuccess headquarters to the Air Support Unit at France Field.

15 Ibid, p. 2.

16 CIA declassified cable DOC_0000921358.pdf, titled "SHERWOOD 352", dated June 23, 1954, from the Field Command Post to PBSuccess headquarters.

17 CIA declassified cable DOC_0000136294.pdf, titled "LINC 4223", dated June 23, 1954, from PBSuccess headquarters to the Field Command Post.

18 Silva Girón, *La Batalla de Gualán* (Imprenta EROS, 1977), p. 118.

19 CIA declassified cable DOC_0000921315.pdf, titled "SHERWOOD 360", dated June 23, 1954, from the Field Command Post to PBSuccess headquarters.

20 CIA declassified cable DOC_0000921335.pdf, titled "SHERWOOD 356", dated June 23, 1954, from the Field Command Post to PBSuccess headquarters.

21 CIA declassified cable DOC_0000921314.pdf, titled "SHERWOOD 362", dated June 23, 1954, from the Field Command Post to PBSuccess headquarters.

22 Gramajo Morales, *Alrededor de la Bandera* (Guatemalan National Typography Workshops, 2002), p. 316.

23 Ibid, p. 317.

24 Ibid, p. 318.

25 CIA declassified cable DOC_0000921310.pdf, titled "LINC 4229", dated June 23, 1954, from PBSuccess headquarters to the CIA Director.

26 Gramajo Morales, *Alrededor de la Bandera* (Guatemalan National Typography Workshops, 2002), p. 319.

27 CIA declassified cable DOC_0000136202.pdf, titled "LINC 4270", dated June 24, 1954, from PBSuccess headquarters to the Field Command Post.

28 CIA declassified cable DOC_0000921341.pdf, titled "SHERWOOD 365", dated June 23, 1954, from the Field Command Post to PBSuccess headquarters.

29 Gramajo Morales, *Alrededor de la Bandera* (Guatemalan National Typography Workshops, 2002), p. 320.30 CIA declassified cable DOC_0000136309.pdf, titled "LINC 4319", dated June 25, 1954, from PBSuccess headquarters to the CIA Director.

31 CIA declassified cable DOC_0000921143.pdf, titled "GUAT 970", dated June 26, 1954, from the CIA Station in Guatemala to PBSuccess headquarters.

32 Guatemalan Presidency, *Así Se Gestó La Liberación* (Guatemalan National Typography Workshops, 1955), p. 138.

33 CIA declassified document DOC_0000935207.pdf, titled "PBSuccess Debriefing Reports", dated September 1, 1954, p. 20.

34 Gramajo Morales, *Alrededor de la Bandera* (Guatemalan National Typography Workshops, 2002), p. 321.

35 CIA declassified cable DOC_0000921202.pdf, titled "GUAT 964", dated June 25, 1954, from the CIA Station in Guatemala to PBSuccess headquarters.

36 CIA declassified cable DOC_0000136306.pdf, titled "LINC 4296", dated June 25, 1954, from PBSuccess headquarters to the Field Command Post.

37 CIA declassified cable DOC_0000921158.pdf, titled "LINC 4305", dated June 25, 1954, from PBSuccess headquarters to the Field Command Post.

Chapter 11

1 Gramajo Morales, *Alrededor de la Bandera* (Guatemalan National Typography Workshops, 2002), p. 320.

2 Ibid, p. 320.

3 CIA declassified cable DOC_0000136970.pdf, titled "DIR 06473", dated June 25, 1954, from the CIA Director to PBSuccess headquarters.

4 CIA declassified cable DOC_0000920920.pdf, titled "SHERWOOD 400", dated June 26, 1954, from the Field Command Post to PBSuccess headquarters.

5 CIA declassified cable DOC_0000136308.pdf, titled "LINC 4318", dated June 25, 1954, from PBSuccess headquarters to the Field Command Post.

6 CIA declassified cable DOC_0000921142.pdf, titled "LINC 4311", dated June 25, 1954, from PBSuccess headquarters to the Field Command Post.

7 CIA declassified cable DOC_0000921178.pdf, titled "DIR 06474", dated June 25, 1954, from the CIA Director to PBSuccess headquarters.

8 CIA declassified cable DOC_0000136316.pdf, titled "LINC 4377", dated June 26, 1954, from PBSuccess headquarters to the CIA Director.

9 CIA declassified document DOC_0000935207.pdf, titled "PBSuccess Debriefing Reports", dated September 1, 1954, p. 20.

10 Ibid, p. 20.

11 CIA declassified cable DOC_0000921173.pdf, titled "[redacted] 068", dated June 25, 1954, from the Air Support Unit to the PBSuccess headquarters.

12 CIA declassified cable DOC_0000921213.pdf, titled "DIR 06528", dated June 25, 1954, from the CIA Director to PBSuccess headquarters.

13 CIA declassified cable DOC_0000921132.pdf, titled "LINC 4355", dated June 26, 1954, from PBSuccess headquarters to the CIA Director.

14 CIA declassified cable DOC_0000920934.pdf, titled "DIR 06723", dated June 26, 1954, from the CIA Director to PBSuccess headquarters.

15 CIA declassified cable DOC_0000920987.pdf, titled "LINC 4362", dated June 26, 1954, from PBSuccess headquarters to the Field Command Post. Also, CIA declassified cable DOC_0000920983.pdf, titled "LINC 4419", dated June 27, 1954, from PBSuccess headquarters to the Field Command Post.

16 CIA declassified cable DOC_0000920973.pdf, titled "LINC 4440", dated June 27, 1954, from PBSuccess headquarters to the CIA Director, p. 2.

17 Gramajo Morales, *Alrededor de la Bandera* (Guatemalan National Typography Workshops, 2002), p. 324.

18 CIA declassified document DOC_0000935207.pdf, titled "PBSuccess Debriefing Reports", dated September 1, 1954, p. 21.

19 CIA declassified cable DOC_0000920973.pdf, titled "LINC 4440", dated June 27, 1954, from PBSuccess headquarters to the CIA Director, p. 3.

20 CIA declassified cable DOC_0000920978.pdf, titled "SHERWOO 430", dated June 27, 1954, from the Field Command Post to PBSuccess headquarters.

21 CIA declassified cable DOC_0000920977.pdf, titled "SHERWOOD 427", dated June 27, 1954, from the Field Command Post to PBSuccess headquarters.

22 CIA declassified cable DOC_0000921131.pdf, titled "LINC 4371", dated June 26, 1954, from PBSuccess headquarters to the Field Command Post.

23 Schlesinger and Kinzer, *Bitter Fruit - The Story of the American Coup in Guatemala* (The Harvard University, David Rockefeller Center for Latin American Studies, 2005), p. 193.

24 CIA declassified cable DOC_0000921130.pdf, with the title redacted, dated June 26, 1954, from [redacted] (possibly the CIA Station in Mexico) to PBSuccess headquarters and the Field Command Post.

25 CIA declassified cable DOC_0000934430.pdf, titled "SHERWOOD 446", dated June 28, 1954, from the Field Command Post to PBSuccess headquarters.

26 CIA declassified cable DOC_0000920955.pdf, titled "LINC 4398", dated June 27, 1954, from PBSuccess headquarters to the CIA Director.

27 Ibid, p. 2.

28 Ibid, 162.

29 Ibid, 162. Also, CIA declassified document DOC_0000921030.pdf, untitled, dated June 28, 1954, from [redacted] (possibly the CIA Station in Mexico) to the CIA Director.

30 CIA declassified document DOC_0000921076.pdf, titled "SHERWOOD 443", dated June 28, 1954, from the Field Command Post to PBSuccess headquarters.

31 CIA declassified document DOC_0000921027.pdf, titled "LINC 4472", dated June 28, 1954, from PBSuccess headquarters to the CIA Director, p. 3.

32 Frank Wisner cabled all PBSuccess stations that day, ordering the personnel to "Comply with directives from this HQS in spirit as well as letter and not be guided by local talk or sources." (CIA declassified cable DOC_0000921114, titled "LINCOLN 4514", dated June 29, 1954.)

33 CIA declassified cable DOC_0000136331.pdf, titled "LINC 4477", dated June 28, 1954, from PBSuccess headquarters to the CIA Director.

34 CIA declassified cable DOC_0000921050.pdf, titled "NR 12", dated June 28, 1954, from Castillo Armas to the Field Command Post.

35 CIA declassified cable DOC_0000921014.pdf, titled "[redacted 986], dated June 28, 1954, from the CIA Station in Guatemala to the CIA Director.

Chapter 12

1 Schlesinger and Kinzer, *Bitter Fruit - The Story of the American Coup in Guatemala* (The Harvard University, David Rockefeller Center for Latin American Studies, 2005), p. 206.

2 Villagrán Kramer, *Biografía Política de Guatemala* (Facultad Latinoamericana de Ciencias Sociales - FLACSO, 1993), p. 170.

3 CIA declassified cable DOC_0000921099.pdf, titled "SHERWOOD 463", dated June 29, 1954, from the Field Command Post to PBSuccess headquarters.

4 CIA declassified cable DOC_0000920938.pdf, titled "DIR 06724", dated June 26, 1954, from the CIA Director to PBSuccess headquarters.

5 Schlesinger and Kinzer, Bitter Fruit - *The Story of the American Coup in Guatemala* (The Harvard University, David Rockefeller Center for Latin American Studies, 2005), p. 209.

6 CIA declassified cable DOC_0000921008.pdf, titled "GUAT 990", dated June 28, 1954, from the CIA Station in Guatemala to PBSuccess headquarters.

7 CIA declassified cable DOC_0000136334.pdf, titled "LINC 4494", dated June 28, 1954, from PBSuccess headquarters to the Air Support Unit.

8 CIA declassified cable DOC_0000920766.pdf, titled "[redacted] 002", dated June 30, 1954, from the CIA Station in Guatemala to PBSuccess headquarters.

9 Putzeys Rojas, *Así se Hizo La Liberación* (Guatemalan National Typography Workshops, 1976), p. 291.

10 Ibid, p. 292.

11 CIA declassified document DOC_0000920767.pdf, titled "LINC 4510", dated June 29, 1954, from PBSuccess headquarters to the Field Command Post.

12 CIA declassified document DOC_0000920781.pdf, titled "SHERWOOD 495", dated June 30, 1954, from the Field Command Post to PBSuccess headquarters.

13 CIA declassified document DOC_0000136345.pdf, titled "LINC 4538", dated June 30, 1954, from PBSuccess headquarters to the CIA Director.

14 CIA declassified document DOC_0000921124.pdf, titled "FLASH FROM PERA", dated June 29, 1954, from Castillo Armas to the Field Command Post.

15 Putzeys Rojas, *Así se Hizo La Liberación* (Guatemalan National Typography Workshops, 1976), p. 296.16 CIA declassified document DOC_0000920756.pdf, titled "NR 5", dated June 30, 1954, from the Field Command Post to Castillo Armas.

17 CIA declassified document DOC_0000920757.pdf, titled "FLASH FROM PERA", dated June 30, 1954, from Castillo Armas to the Field Command Post.

18 Putzeys Rojas, *Así se Hizo La Liberación* (Guatemalan National Typography Workshops, 1976), p. 309.

19 Ibid, p. 312.

20 CIA declassified document DOC_0000920771.pdf, titled "SHERWOOD 502", dated June 30, 1954, from the Field Command Post to PBSuccess headquarters.

21 CIA declassified document DOC_0000920833.pdf, titled "SHERWOOD 506", dated July 1, 1954, from the Field Command Post to PBSuccess headquarters.

Chapter 13

1 CIA declassified document DOC_0000136347.pdf, titled "LINC 4543", dated June 30, 1954, from PBSuccess headquarters to the Field Command Post.

2 A partial description of PBHistory activities is detailed in CIA declassified document DOC_0000920205, titled "Report Activity", dated July 28, 1954.

3 CIA declassified document DOC_0000920799.pdf, titled "LINC 4543", dated June 30, 1954, from PBSuccess headquarters to the Field Command Post.

4 CIA declassified document DOC_0000920831.pdf, titled "LINC 4565", dated June 30, 1954, from PBSuccess headquarters to the CIA Director.

5 CIA declassified document DOC_0000136354.pdf, titled "LINC 4585", dated July 1, 1954, from PBSuccess headquarters to the CIA Director.

6 CIA declassified document DOC_0000137000.pdf, titled "DIR 08329", dated July 9, 1954, from the CIA Director to PBSuccess headquarters.

7 CIA declassified document DOC_0000924687.pdf, titled "GUAT 116", dated August 3, 1954, from the CIA Station in Guatemala to the CIA Director. Also, Wer, En Guatemala los Héroes Tienen Quince Años (ARMAR Editores, 2003), p. 127.

8 *Prensa Libre* newspaper, news note published on August 7, 1954.

9 CIA Intelligence Bulletin No. 49, dated December 24, 1954, p. 7.

BIBLIOGRAPHY

Declassified documents of the Central Intelligence Agency, retrieved from the FOIA – CIA website at www.foia.cia.gov from 1997 to 2014.
Aircraft maintenance and accident records obtained from the Maintenance Echelon of the Guatemalan Air Force, between the years 2005 and 2009.
News notes published by the Guatemalan newspapers *Prensa Libre* and *El Imparcial* between May and August 1954, retrieved from the Hemeroteca Nacional, at Guatemala City, from 1999 to 2014.

Books

100 Años de Zacapa y sus Antecedentes Históricos by Alvaro Enrique Palma Sandoval. Published by the "José de Pineda Ibarra" Press, Guatemalan Ministry of Education, 1973.
Alrededor de la Bandera by General (Ret.) Héctor Alejandro Gramajo Morales. Published by the Guatemalan National Typography Workshops, 2002. ISBN 99922-2-096-1.
Así se Gestó la Liberación
Official publication of the Divulgation, Culture and Tourism Secretariat, Guatemalan Presidency. Published by the Guatemalan National Typography Workshops, 1955.
Así se Hizo la Liberación by Guillermo Putzeys Rojas. Published by the Guatemalan National Typography Workshops, 1976.
Biografía Política de Guatemala. by Francisco Villagrán Kramer. Published by the Facultad Latinoamericana de Ciencias Sociales – FLACSO, 1993.
Bitter Fruit – The Story of the American Coup in Guatemala 2nd Edition by Stephen Schlesinger and Stephen Kinzer. Published by the Harvard University, David Rockefeller Center for Latin American Studies, 2005. ISBN 0-674-01930-X
Central American and Caribbean Air Forces By Daniel by P. Hagedorn. Published by Air-Britain, 1993. ISBN 0-85130-210-6
Central American and the Caribbean Civil Aircraft Registers by Ian P. Burnett (Editor.) Published by Air Britain, 1978. ISBN 0-85130-059-6
Democracies and Tyrannies of the Caribbean by William Krehn. Published by Lawrence Hill & Co., 1984. ISBN 0-88208-169-1
Despacho Presidencial by Juan José Arévalo. Published by Editorial Oscar De León Palacios, 1988.
Doing Business With Dictators – A Political History of the United Fruit in Guatemala, 1899-1944 By Paul J. Dosal. Published by SR Books, 1993. ISBN 0-8420-2475-1
Dos Yanquis Más Contra Guatemala – Réplica a la Fruta Amarga by Carlos Manuel Pellecer. Published by EDINTER, 1986.
En Guatemala los Héroes Tienen Quince Años by Carlos Enrique Wer. Published by ARMAR Editores, 2003. ISBN 999-22-41-05-9
Guatemala, La Historia Silenciada – Tomo I – Revolución y Liberación by Carlos Sabino. Published by the Fondo de Cultura Económica de Guatemala, S.A., 2009. ISBN 978-99922-48-52-2
Honduras – State for Sale by Richard Lapper and James Painter. Published by Russell Press, 1985. ISBN 0-906156-23-8
Killing Hope – U.S. Military and CIA Interventions Since World War II by William Blum. Published by Common Courage Press, 1986. ISBN 1-56751-053-1
La Batalla de Gualán by Col. (Ret.) César Augusto Silva Girón. Published by Imprenta EROS, 1977.
Legacy of Ashes – The History of the CIA by Tim Weiner. Published by Anchor Books, 2007. ISBN 978-0-307-45562-8 (Electronic edition.)
Memorias – Tomo II – 1st Edition by Gen. (Ret.) Guillermo Flores Avendaño. Published by the Editorial del Ejército (Guatemalan Army Press), 1974.
Mexican and Central American Armor by Julio Montes. Published by Darling Productions, 2001. ISBN 1-892848-08-2
My War with Communism as told to Mario Rosenthal by Miguel Ydígoras Fuentes. Published by Prentice Hall, 1963. Library of Congress Catalog Card Number 63-14483
Observing Our Hermanos de Armas – U.S. Military Attachés in Guatemala, Cuba and Bolivia, 1950-1964 by Robert O. Kirkland. Published by Routledge, 2003. ISBN 0-203-57789-2 (Electronic edition.)
Paz Tejada: Militar y Revolucionario by Carlos Figueroa Ibarra. Published by the Instituto de Ciencias Sociales y Humanidades, Benemérita Universidad Autónoma de Puebla, 2004. ISBN 99922-61-31-5
Republic P-47 – The Final Chapter by Dan Hagedorn. Published by Phalanx Publishing Co. ISBN 0-9625860-1-3
Secret History – The CIA's Classified Account of its Operations in Guatemala, 1952 – 1954 by Nick Cullather. Published by the Stanford University Press, 1999. ISBN 0-8047-3311-2
Shattered Hope: The Guatemalan Revolution and the United States 1944-1954 by Piero Gleijes. Published by Princeton University Press, 1992. ISBN 0-691-07817-3
So I Bought An Air Force by William W. Martin. Published by Two Harbors Press, 2013. ISBN 978-1-938690-36-5
The Banana Men – American Mercenaries and Entrepreneurs in Central America, 1880-1930 by Lester D. Langley. Published by University Press of Kentucky. ISBN 0-8131-1891-3
The Black Eagle by John Peer Nugent. Published by Bantam Books Inc., 1972.
The Very Best Men – Four Who Dared: The Early Years of the CIA by Evan Thomas. Published by Simon & Schuster, 1995. ISBN 0-684-81025-5 (Electronic edition.)
William D. Pawley – The Extraordinary Life of the Adventurer, Entrepreneur and Diplomat Who Founded the Flying Tigers by Anthony R. Carrozza. Published by Potomac Books, 2012. ISBN 978-1-59797-719-7 (Electronic edition.)
Working in Remote Countries: CAT in New Zealand, Thailand-Burma, French Indochina, Guatemala and Indonesia by Joe F. Leeker. Published by the University of Texas at Dallas, 2013. (Electronic edition.)

News Article: **"Pasarán a la Historia las Hazañas del Sulfato, participante decisivo en el éxito de las fuerzas libertadoras"** by Ángel Monasterio. Published in the Guatemalan periodical "La Hora Dominical" on July 11, 1954.
News Article: **"Revolution by Air"** by Lt. Col. Theodore J. McAdam. Published in Volume 7, Number 10, of the periodical "Air Intelligence Digest" of the USAF's Directorate of Intelligence, in October 1954.

ABOUT THE AUTHORS

Mario Overall – Co-founder of the Latin American Aviation Historical Society, he studied Systems Engineering at the Mariano Galvez University of Guatemala. He served in the Guatemalan Air Force as a Computer Specialist and then in the same capacity with the Narcotics Affairs Section of the U.S. Embassy to Guatemala. He has authored more than 15 articles related to the history of military aviation in Central America, which have been published in renowned magazines in the U.S., Spain, Brazil, Mexico, England, France and Poland. He also collaborated with several authors in their research work about Latin American Aviation History.

Dan Hagedorn – Curator and Director of Collections at The Museum of Flight at historic Boeing Field in Seattle, Washington. He is a graduate of Villa Maria College, the State University of New York, and the Command and General Staff College (U.S. Army, post-graduate). He was previously Adjunct Curator and Research Team Leader at the National Air and Space Museum, Smithsonian Institution, Washington, DC for 19 years. Prior to that, he served in the U.S. Armed Forces for 27 years in leadership and intelligence positions worldwide and has, to date, authored 21 monographs or books detailing various aspects of aviation and aerospace history. In conjunction with the 150th Anniversary of the Smithsonian Institution, he was named an Unsung Hero of the Smithsonian Institution and was awarded the Orden Merito Santos-Dumont by the Brazilian Government for services to Latin American aviation history, in which he specializes.

ACKNOWLEDGMENTS

Far from being just a book, what you now have in your hands is the result of a journey that began more than 15 years ago. A journey that couldn't have been possible without the constant support of an excellent group of individuals who, right from the start, volunteered their invaluable help to our research work.

Hence, our infinite gratitude goes to Tulio Soto, who made available to us his extensive library about aviation history and Guatemalan politics; Tulio also took upon himself the tedious task of revising and correcting the book's manuscript, besides contributing several great anecdotal episodes about the events that occurred in Guatemala in 1954.

We must thank also John Davis, a good friend and excellent aero-historian who, despite being very busy with a myriad of projects, always took the time to respond our queries about aircraft identities and their final fates. Our gratitude goes also to Gary Kuhn, our mentor and long-time friend, who contributed bits and pieces of aviation and political history, besides pointing the way during certain times in which we were dealing with difficult topics.

Lt. Col. (USAF Ret.) Luis Fuentes, editor of the *Air & Space Power Journal En Español* magazine, also deserves a mention here, since he became our eyes at the USAF University Library at Maxwell AFB, Alabama, where he retrieved important documentation for our research. In Honduras, Amado Aguiluz, another great aero-historian, had our back and contributed important information about the previously undocumented involvement of that country's air force during PBSuccess.

In Guatemala, Herbert Erdmenger contributed with interesting anecdotal pieces, shared with us his most valued photos of the infamous "Sulfatos", and lent us hard-to-find books about the events of 1954. Also, in Guatemala, Rodolfo Mendoza, son of Col. Rodolfo "Fito" Mendoza, opened his family's vault and allowed us to explore invaluable documents as well as excerpts of his unpublished book about "La Liberación."

Last but not least, our work couldn't have been completed without "on the field" research; and for this Carlos Overall volunteered to be our guide along impassable roads, deep ravines and steep hills lost somewhere between Zacapa and Chiquimula. There, we got a grasp of the terrain picked for the Liberation's offensive and the difficulties it posed, especially during Guatemala's long rainy season.

To all of them, a big thank you!